KENTUCKY/TENNESSEE
TRAVEL+SMART™ TRIP PLANNER

KENTUCKY TENNESSEE

TRAVEL◆SMART™ TRIP PLANNER

Susan Williams Knowles

John Muir Publications
Santa Fe, New Mexico

Acknowledgments
The author wishes to thank Lynne Bachleda, Robert Cheatham, Roby Cogswell, Mark Fraley, Dan Holton, Patty Bladon Lawrence, Andrew Saftel, Donna Tauscher, and Jane Harris Woodside for their invaluable assistance.

This book is dedicated to my mother, Margaret Anderson Williams, who grew up on the border of Kentucky and Tennessee and gave me an appreciation for both nature and culture.

John Muir Publications, P.O. Box 613, Santa Fe, New Mexico 87504

Printed in the United States of America.
First edition. First printing September 1996.

ISSN 1087-8335
ISBN 1-56261-297-2

Cover photo: Unicorn Stock Photos/Jean Higgins
Back cover photos: *top*—Mary Entrekin
          bottom—Peggy Schaefer
Maps: American Custom Maps — Albuquerque, NM USA
Editors: Dianna Delling, Peggy Schaefer, Chris Hayhurst, Tama Montgomery
Design: Janine Lehmann and Linda Braun
Typesetting: Golden Graphics
Production: Marie Vigil, Nikki Rooker
Graphics Coordinator: Tom Gaukel
Printing: Publishers Press

Distributed to the book trade by
Publishers Group West
Emeryville, California

HOW TO USE THIS BOOK

The *Kentucky/Tennessee Travel+Smart Trip Planner* is organized into 14 destination chapters, each covering the best sites and activities, restaurants, and lodging available in a specific destination. The author has thoroughly researched the numerous choices in each destination to bring you only the best options, saving you time and money in your travels.

Each chapter contains:

• User-friendly maps of the area, showing all recommended sights, restaurants, and accommodations.
• "A Perfect Day" description—how the author would spend her time if she had just one day in that destination.
• Sightseeing highlights, each rated by degree of importance: ✯✯✯ Don't miss; ✯✯ Try hard to see; ✯ See if you have time; and No stars—Worth knowing about.
• Selected restaurant, lodging, and camping recommendations to suit a variety of budgets.
• Helpful hints, fitness and recreation ideas, insights, and random tidbits of information to enhance your trip.

The Importance of Planning. Developing an itinerary is the best way to get the most satisfaction from your travels, and this guidebook makes it easy. First, read through the book and choose the places you'd most like to visit. Then, study the color map on the inside cover flap and the mileage chart (page 12) to determine which ones you can realistically see in the time you have available and at the travel pace you prefer. Using the Planning Map (pages 10–11), map out your route. Finally, use the lodging recommendations to select your accommodations.

Some Suggested Itineraries. To get you started, six itineraries of varying lengths and based on specific interests follow. Mix and match according to your interests and time contraints or follow a given itinerary from start to finish. The possibilities are endless. *Happy travels!*

SUGGESTED ITINERARIES

With the *Kentucky/Tennessee Travel•Smart Trip Planner* you can plan a trip of any length—a 1-day excursion, a getaway weekend, or a 3-week vacation—around any special interest. To get you started, the following pages contain six suggested itineraries geared toward a variety of interests. For more information, refer to the chapters listed—chapter names are bolded and chapter numbers appear inside black bullets. You can follow a suggested itinerary in its entirety, or shorten, lengthen, or combine parts of each, depending on your starting and ending points.

Discuss alternative routes and schedules with your travel companions—it's a great way to have fun, even before you leave home. And remember: don't hesitate to change your itinerary once you're on the road. Careful study and planning ahead of time will help you make informed decisions as you go, but spontaneity is the extra ingredient that will make your trip memorable.

Best of the Region Tour

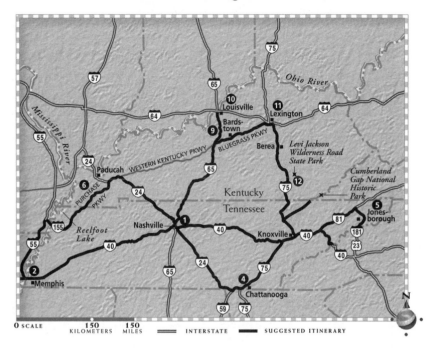

This "greatest hits" tour includes the Cumberland Gap, once the gateway to the western territories; Reelfoot Lake, created by an earthquake in 1811; and one of Kentucky's Shaker communities, whose large stone community buildings were erected when most people were still living in log cabins.

❶ Nashville (Music City, U.S.A.)

❷ Memphis

❹ Chattanooga

❺ Northeast Tennessee (Jonesborough—Tennessee's oldest town)

❻ Western Waterlands, Reelfoot Lake, And Paducah

❾ Bardstown and Historic Central Kentucky ("My Old Kentucky Home," whiskey distilleries, Shaker Village at Pleasant Hill, Fort Harrod—Kentucky's first settlement)

❿ Louisville

⓫ Lexington

⓬ Cumberland Gap, Wilderness Road, and Berea

Time needed: 1½ to 2 weeks

Nature Lover's Tour

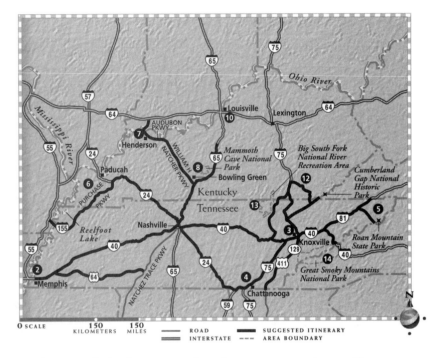

On this tour, which takes you west from the eastern mountains, you'll experience terrain and vegetation roughly equivalent to those found as far north as Canada, as far west as Missouri, and as far south as Louisiana.

② **Memphis** (Scenic Route 64: Natchez Trace National Parkway)

③ **Knoxville** (Scenic Route 411: Cherokee National Forest)

④ **Chattanooga** (South Cumberland State Recreation Area)

⑤ **Northeast Tennessee** (Roan Mountain State Park)

⑥ **Western Waterlands, Reelfoot Lake, and Paducah**

⑦ **Henderson** (John J. Audubon Park and Museum)

⑧ **Bowling Green and Mammoth Cave** (Mammoth Cave National Park)

⑩ **Louisville** (Falls of the Ohio Interpretive Center)

⑫ **Cumberland Gap, Wilderness Road, and Berea**

⑬ **Rugby and the Big South Fork** (Big South Fork National Recreation Area, Daniel Boone National Forest, and Obed Wild and Scenic River)

⑭ **Great Smoky Mountains National Park**

Time needed: 3 weeks

Family Fun Tour

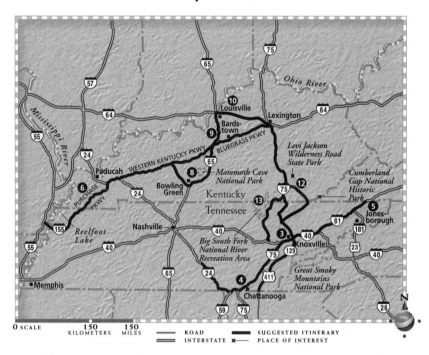

```
O SCALE      150        150       ROAD              SUGGESTED ITINERARY
          KILOMETERS   MILES      INTERSTATE  ✕——   PLACE OF INTEREST
```

These are the old stomping grounds of Daniel Boone, Lewis and Clark, and Davy Crockett. Experience the beauties of nature and the rugged wilderness that the early Indians found here with challenges of your own.

❸ Knoxville (Museum of Appalachia, scenic Tennessee "Overhill")

❹ Chattanooga (Tennessee Aquarium, Creative Discovery Museum, Ocoee river rafting and Scenic Route I-24: Tennessee Backroads)

❺ Northeast Tennessee (Jonesborough Storytelling Festival, Nolichucky river rafting, *The Wataugans* outdoor drama)

❻ Western Waterlands, Reelfoot Lake, and Paducah

❽ Bowling Green and Mammoth Cave (Mammoth Cave, Shaker Museum)

❾ Bardstown and Historic Central Kentucky (Fort Harrod, Shaker Village)

❿ Louisville (Kentucky Derby Museum, Science Center, Belle of Louisville)

⓬ Cumberland Gap, Wilderness Road, and Berea

⓭ Rugby and the Big South Fork (Big South Fork Nat'l Recreation Area)

Time needed: 2½ weeks

Music and Art Tour

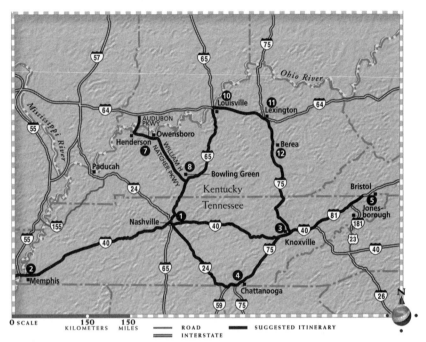

You'll find outstanding dance, theater, and music in big-city venues, and a variety of bluegrass and country music events in cities and towns throughout Kentucky and Tennessee. This tour will take you to some of the best.

❶ **Nashville** (Grand Ole Opry, theater, dance, art museums)

❷ **Memphis** (Memphis Arts Festival, Opera Memphis, and much more)

❸ **Knoxville** (Knoxville Museum of Art, Knoxville Ballet)

❹ **Chattanooga** (Hunter Museum, Tivoli Theater, Bessie Smith Music Hall)

❺ **Northeast Tennessee** (Bristol: Birth of Country Music Alliance Music Series; Jonesborough: National Storytelling Festival)

❼ **Henderson and Owensboro** (W.C. Handy Blues Fest, International Bluegrass Festival)

❽ **Bowling Green and Mammoth Cave** (Horse Cave Theater Series)

❿ **Louisville** (Humana Theater Festival, Waterside Art and Music Festival, Actor's Playhouse, Louisville Symphony, ballet, art museums)

⓫ **Lexington** (Singletary Center, University of Kentucky art museum)

⓬ **Cumberland Gap, Wilderness Road, and Berea** (Berea Crafts Festival, Traditional Music Festival)

Time needed: 2 weeks

Traditional Arts and Folk Culture Tour

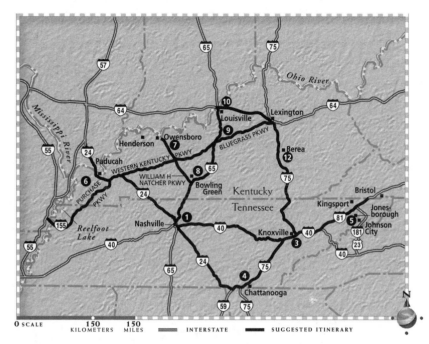

In the midst of the high-tech revolution, what is becoming of the old ways—of making things by hand and using methods learned by patient imitation? You'll find the answer in the repositories of folk heritage listed here.

❶ **Nashville** (Country Music Hall of Fame, Ellington Agricultural Museum)

❸ **Knoxville** (Jubilee Community Arts, Museum of Appalachia, Community Craft Co-op in Norris)

❹ **Chattanooga** (folk art, crafts, traditional music, Tennessee Backroads)

❺ **Northeast Tennessee** (National Storytelling Headquarters, Carroll Reese Museum, Archives of Appalachia, Down Home Music Club, Bays Mountain Heritage Farmstead Museum, Birthplace of Country Music Alliance)

❻ **Western Waterlands, Reelfoot Lake, and Paducah**

❼ **Henderson and Owensboro** (BBQ and Bluegrass Festivals)

❽ **Bowling Green and Mammoth Cave** (Shaker Museum at South Union)

❾ **Bardstown and Historic Central Kentucky** (Shaker Village, music)

❿ **Louisville** (folk art, crafts, storytelling, local history)

⓬ **Cumberland Gap, Wilderness Road, and Berea** (Appalachian heritage, crafts, music)

Time needed: 2 weeks

History and Prehistory Tour

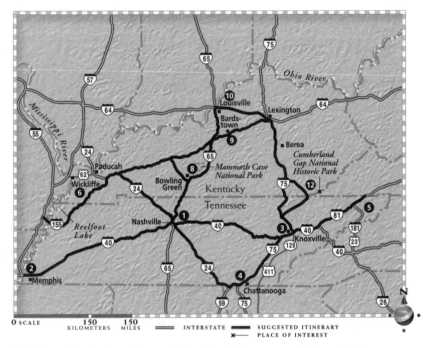

Visit these destinations for a cohesive historical tour — and throw in the geological history of the Cumberland Mountains for good measure.

❶ **Nashville** (The Hermitage, Tennessee State Museum)

❷ **Memphis** (Chucalissa, Slavehaven, National Civil Rights Museum, Highway 64 Scenic Route: Pinson Mounds, Shiloh Civil War Battlefield)

❸ **Knoxville** (Museum of East Tennessee History, University of Tennessee McClung Museum, Hwy 411 Scenic Route: Tennessee "Overhill")

❹ **Chattanooga** (African-American History Museum, Civil War Battlefields, I-24 Scenic Route: Old Stone Fort)

❺ **Northeast Tennessee** (Jonesborough, Washington Co. History Museum)

❻ **Western Waterlands, Reelfoot Lake, and Paducah** (Wickliffe Mounds)

❽ **Bowling Green and Mammoth Cave** (Mammoth Cave, Shaker Museum)

❾ **Bardstown and Historic Central Kentucky** (Fort Harrod, Shaker Village at Pleasant Hill, Perryville Civil War Battlefield)

❿ **Louisville** (Falls of the Ohio, historical museums)

⓬ **Cumberland Gap, Wilderness Road, and Berea**

Time needed: 2 to 3 weeks

USING THE PLANNING MAP

A major aspect of itinerary planning is determining your mode of transportation and the route you will follow as you travel from destination to destination. The Planning Map on the following pages will enable you to do just that.

First, read through the destination chapters carefully and note the sites that intrigue you. Then, photocopy the Planning Map so you can try out several different routes that will take you to these destinations. (The mileage chart that follows will help you to calculate your travel distances.) Decide where you will be starting your tour of Kentucky and Tennessee. Will you fly into Nashville, Louisville, or Knoxville, or will you start from somewhere in between? Will you be driving from place to place or flying into major transportation hubs and renting a car for day trips? The answers to these questions will form the basis for your travel route design.

Once you have a firm idea of where your travels will take you, copy your route onto one of the additional Planning Maps in the Appendix. You won't have to worry about where your map is, and the information you need on each destination will always be close at hand.

Mary Entrekin

Planning Map: Kentucky/Tennessee

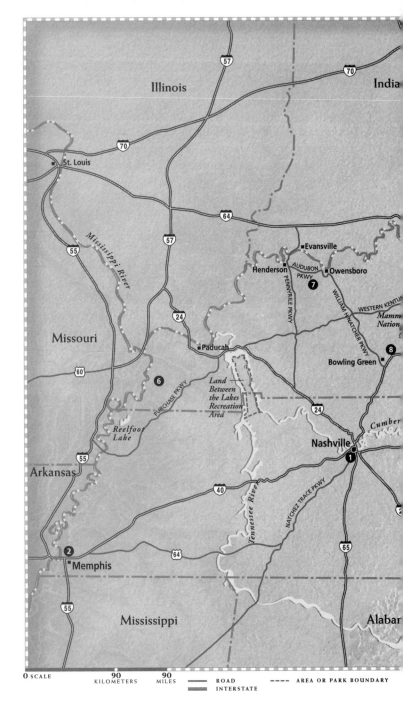

O SCALE   90 KILOMETERS   90 MILES   ROAD   AREA OR PARK BOUNDARY   INTERSTATE

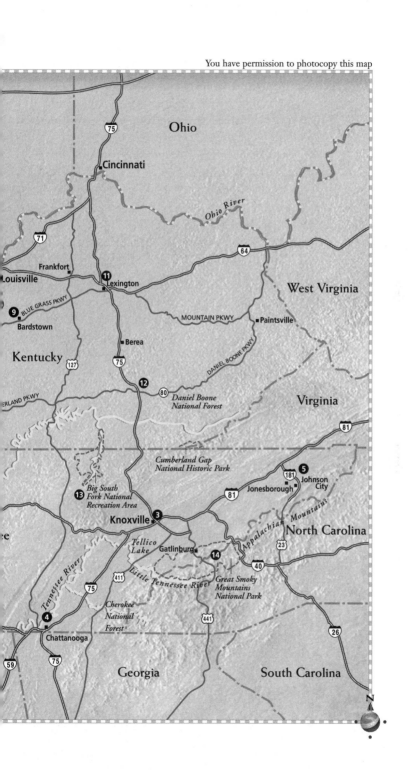

KENTUCKY/TENNESSEE MILEAGE CHART

	Memphis, TN	Nashville, TN	Knoxville, TN	Chattanooga, TN	Jonesborough, TN	Paducah, KY	Henderson, KY	Owensboro, KY	Bowling Green, KY	Bardstown, KY	Louisville, KY	Frankfort, KY	Lexington, KY	Berea, KY	Cumberland Gap, TN	Rugby, TN
Nashville, TN	208															
Knoxville, TN	385	177														
Chattanooga, TN	315	140	107													
Jonesborough, TN	477	269	92	199												
Paducah, KY	168	136	313	276	455											
Henderson, KY	279	156	333	296	475	100										
Owensboro, KY	287	125	302	265	444	131	31									
Bowling Green, KY	267	59	236	199	378	151	97	66								
Bardstown, KY	359	151	209	291	274	210	147	116	92							
Louisville, KY	381	180	241	320	317	230	121	108	114	43						
Frankfort, KY	420	212	192	299	257	264	171	158	153	61	50					
Lexington, KY	414	206	170	277	235	266	202	171	147	56	71	22				
Berea, KY	450	242	130	237	195	289	226	195	183	79	122	62	40			
Cumberland Gap, TN	440	232	55	162	97	358	304	273	207	177	220	160	138	98		
Rugby, TN	391	183	71	119	163	293	239	208	142	207	250	190	168	128	84	
Gatlinburg, TN	425	217	40	147	94	353	373	342	276	249	292	232	210	170	90	111

WHY VISIT KENTUCKY AND TENNESSEE?

Kentucky and Tennessee, located virtually in the middle of the United States, are as much a part of the early history of this country as they are of our contemporary culture. They may seem in a way familiar—even to those who have never set foot here. Perhaps your relatives came through on their way west or south, perhaps you raise horses, or have taken up quilting, or are a connoisseur of fine whiskey or pipe tobacco. Perhaps you own antique furniture, baskets, or pottery made by Tennessee or Kentucky artisans. Perhaps you have followed the paths of Daniel Boone, Sequoyah, Davy Crockett, Lewis and Clark, Abraham Lincoln, Ida B. Wells, or Alex Haley in your mind's eye so that their surroundings became visible to you long before you had the opportunity to see them for yourself. Coming to these lands in person will add richness to your understanding of our country's history and provide insights into the character of its early peoples. Seeing Mark Twain's *Huckleberry Finn* performed by the nationally prominent cast at Louisville's Actor's Playhouse just a few blocks from the Ohio River pulled me all the more deeply into the story and its contemporary relevance. Mark Twain, whose parents came from Tennessee, was incredibly clever at lambasting racial injustice, the pomposity and foolishness of political and religious leaders, the fallacy of the conventional wisdom, all the while promoting the value of plain common sense.

Aside from fascinating history and rich culture, you'll also find incredible natural beauty here. From the mountainous eastern regions, to the grasslands and rolling hills at the heart of each state, to the western flatlands of the Mississippi River, both states reveal a surprising diversity of outdoor environment. One of the best things about exploring this wonderland of nature is that one can, at times, feel like a pioneer or one of the first Indians to inhabit this land—looking down into a vast mountain valley or carefully picking one's way along a scarcely trodden forest path. Like a protective net, state and national park facilities crisscross these states, providing technical resources, interpretive displays, guided activities, and a wide assortment of lodging.

Denizens of both states display not only a reverence for history but also a passion for tradition. Following the leads in this book, you'll encounter authentic customs and folkways that have been passed down from generation to generation—concerning everything from farming to folk art to food. Inquiries about all three will be answered with pride and, more often than not, downright friendliness. Driving the scenic routes, stopping at small out-of-the-way towns and historic homes, standing where our ancestors stood, tasting the local cuisine at every opportunity, and spending the night in places that remind you of where you are the minute you awaken, will grant you the fullest experience of Kentucky and Tennessee. To the aware visitor, many of the region's strongest traditions can also be found reflected in the larger cities—in the architectural details, in the street names and commemorative sites, in the old institutions and neighborhoods, in the regional specialities on many menus—once you know what you're looking for.

HISTORY AND PREHISTORY

The geologic history of the region spans a wide chronology. Fossil remains from the Devonian period, 400 million years ago when the whole region was covered by tropical seas, can be found today along the Ohio river at Louisville, near its historically unnavigable shoals. The formation of the river valley during the last two glacial epochs scraped the land back to the level of the formerly undersea fossils. The presence, in both Kentucky and Tennessee, of mammoths and mastodons and the prehistoric humans who hunted them 10,000 years ago is scientific fact. Strata of minerals, veins of igneous stone, and deposits of sedimentary rock have been exposed in jutting rocky hillsides and deep gorges and can be read like a book to reveal the story of this land.

The first peoples to inhabit the area spread through the region following the wide network of navigable waterways. The Archaic Indians and their Woodland period successors inhabited caves, left traces of their ceremonies, and blazed hunting trails through both states. Before the arrival of the first white settlers, Mississippian Indians had established a few large cities and a number of ceremonial sites along the Tennessee and Mississippi rivers. In a few instances, the Cherokee (in the east) and the Chickasaw (in the west) took over the sites. At Mammoth Cave, at Pinson Mounds, at Chucalissa, at Wickliffe Mounds, and in farmer's fields in both states, plenty of traces of these peoples remain. Their history is still being written. Artifacts that now reside in many local and state museum collections are parts of a puzzle that is only very slowly being fitted together. It is clear that trade with Gulf Coast tribes, and possibly with the pre-Columbian peoples of Mexico, had been established by the most ancient Indians. Ceremonial ball games somewhat similar to those of the ancient Maya were still being played by the East Tennessee Cherokee when Louis Philippe made his visit to the United States in 1797. Many fascinating found and excavated objects have never been fully studied. Sadly, some of the critical evidence needed for this research may have been destroyed in the aftermath of the Indian Removal of 1838 or by the Tennessee Valley Authority's re-engineering of the land and water of East Tennessee, which contained important Cherokee homelands.

In the second half of the eighteenth century, pioneer settlers (mostly English, Scottish, and Scots-Irish—Irish who settled in Scotland for a period before making the journey across the Atlantic) came down from Virginia into Tennessee. After the treaty of Sycamore Shoals in 1775, many continued on through the Cumberland Gap into Kentucky, following the trail created by Daniel Boone and a group of 30 men working for Richard Henderson's Transylvania Land Company. Both in eastern Tennessee and along the Wilderness Road in Kentucky, you can find frontier life interpreted at museums such as the Bays Mountain Farmstead Museum and the Museum of Appalachia, at "living history" historic homes such as Rocky Mount and White Hall, at reconstructed fortified settlements such as Fort Boonesborough and Fort Harrod, and in homesteads that have remained almost fully preserved such as Hensley settlement at Cumberland Gap and Cades Cove in the Great Smoky Mountains National Park.

Since both states were formed in the 20-year period following the American Revolution, many of the original landowners, the founders of cities and towns, and the first public officials in Kentucky and Tennessee were Revolutionary War heroes. Clarksville, Indiana (just across the river from Louisville), and Clarksville, Tennessee, were named for Louisville's founder George Rogers Clark. His younger brother William founded Paducah, Kentucky, after his return from his famous expedition with Meriwether Lewis, on a piece of land granted to George Rogers Clark. Knoxville was named after George Washington's Secretary of War. The names of the region's major rivers—Kentucky, Tennessee, Ohio, and Mississippi—all derive from American Indian designations—and the states were named accordingly. Many other place names reflect the heritage of the English settlers who arrived before statehood, such as Cumberland, Kingsport, Lexington, Richmond, Bristol, and Elizabethton.

The architectural history of this country is well illustrated in buildings that have been carefully preserved or lovingly restored throughout both states. While the homes of prosperous eighteenth-century Tennesseans tended toward the rustic (they were, after all, built by frontiersmen, hunters, and farmers), the earliest fine homes in Kentucky belonged to the very wealthy. In the Kentucky capital of Frankfort, palatial Federal-style brick homes, built in the late 1790s for some of the state's first legislators, stand just as they did then in a quiet neighborhood right next to the river. Visitors will find the commanding "centre houses" of two early nineteenth-century Shaker settlements convincing proof of the superiority of shared economy during the early years of this country, when most Tennesseans and many Kentuckians were living in little more than log cabins. The prosperity in both states before and after the Civil War ensures that almost every one of the popular architectural styles of the nineteenth and early twentieth centuries are well represented. Louisville, Nashville, and smaller towns like Henderson, Paducah, and Clarksville were thriving river and railroad towns with large brick warehouses for the safe storage of goods and multi-storied Victorian homes for prosperous merchants. Many towns in East Tennessee grew up along the railroad lines built to connect Richmond to Knoxville and Atlanta.

On the eve of the Civil War, Knoxville was poised to become a major industrial center, with a network of train tracks serving the mining and timbering operations of the Cumberland Mountains and freight links to the south and east. Memphis was the gateway marketplace for the cotton plantations of the Delta, and Nashville and Chattanooga were vital transportation centers for the movement of goods around the South. Kentucky, with its important trade ports at strategic points along the Ohio and Mississippi Rivers and the huge land holdings of gentlemen farmers and horsemen in its fertile center, formed the northern border of the slave states. Both Kentucky and Tennessee were split by divided loyalties during the Civil War, and their historic battlefields—Chickamauga, Shiloh, and Perryville—are saturated by the blood of native sons. This most painful period of our history seems very close at hand when one passes a Confederate monument in either state.

There is a lot to be learned about this country's economic development simply by observing physical reminders of the historical demography of these two states. Early transportation and trade routes into a scarcely populated land; the confusing settlement patterns and allegiances of British, French, American Indians, and American frontiersmen during the Revolutionary War era; the brash arrogance of homesteaders plunging into what they supposed were uninhabited territories; the blind cruelty of many early leaders towards anything and anyone who stood in their way; the wholesale export and exploitation of natural resources; the spread of shipping and railroad commerce; the growth of a major agricultural infrastructure; the rise of manufacturing after the Civil War; the impact of freed African Americans and women on the work force; the rise of organized labor; and finally, the post-industrial aftermath—all have left instructive marks here. Across both states there can be found memorial markers for the Trail of Tears, monuments to the region's first entrepreneurs, lands wasted by mining and manufacturing, well-built railroad depots, riverside shipping warehouses and factories (most no longer in use), and nostalgic reminders of a once-dominant agricultural system.

TRADITIONAL ARTS AND FOLK CULTURE

We can learn a great deal about the character of those who settled these lands by studying cultural expressions such as language, handicrafts, and customs. In many pockets of rural society, and in preserved historical colonies such as Kentucky's two Shaker villages, one can experience folkways that date back to the late eighteenth and early nineteenth centuries. The fact is that traditional ways of doing things, like farming, quilting, woodcarving, and cooking, can be found in full practice around both states. Folk tradition is not only emulated, but also respectfully reinterpreted by contemporary craftspersons. This is one of the country's most active craft-producing areas. The physical environment—the mountains, grasslands, rivers, and general patterns of nature—serves as inspiration for folk artists working in isolated areas, as well as for ever-increasing numbers of urban and rural craft artists. Craft fairs, storytelling festivals, and traditional music celebrations are an important part of community life in both states. The Tennessee Crafts Fair, held in early May in Nashville, and similar fairs in Bell Buckle, Monteagle, Gatlinburg, and Memphis show off Tennessee's wealth of craft production. The Kentucky Art and Craft Foundation maintains permanent exhibit spaces around the state to keep the works of Kentucky artisans before the public at all times. Berea, Kentucky, home to a dense population of craft shops, holds several traditional craft and music events yearly.

Bluegrass music, whose locus of development forms a triangle around eastern Tennessee, eastern Kentucky, and southwest Virginia, is widely performed all around the region. Summer bluegrass festivals and fiddling contests are annual events in cities like Owensboro and Henderson, Kentucky, and in Clarksville, Smithville, and Murfreesboro, Tennessee. Many take place in more rural locations like Renfro Valley and Rough River Dam, Kentucky, and Cosby, Bolivar, Woodbury, and Nine Mile, Tennessee. A brochure put out by the Folk Arts Program of the Tennessee Arts Commission a few years back listed over 30 annual fiddling contests in Tennessee. Held in farmer's barns, local schools, or community centers, these events often last several days, while fans sit around the campfire trying out new licks, RVs are pulled into a circle like covered wagons, and outdoor country kitchens dispense beans, barbecue, and cornbread.

While strains of the musical heritage of the British Isles can be heard within the bluegrass idiom, there are also many practitioners of traditional Irish, English, and Scottish music and dance throughout the Appalachian region. English contra dancing is popular in Berea, Kentucky, and at several venues around Knoxville and Nashville, Tennessee, and you can find both mountain and hammered dulcimers being played during Pineville, Kentucky's annual dulcimer contest. Small music clubs from Cincinnati to Knoxville, Whitesburg to Bowling Green, and Johnson City to Nashville feature acoustic musicians on guitar, dulcimer, fiddle, and pennywhistle playing the sprightly jigs and mournful ballads of their forefathers who settled this area.

Celebrations of culture—like the revival of the street game "dainty" in Louisville's Germantown; the annual "Roley Hole Marble" tournament at Tennessee's Standing Stone State Park; the National Storytelling Festival in Jonesborough, Tennessee; the Corn Island Storytelling Festival in Louisville; and folk medicine festivals at Red Boiling Springs, Tennessee, and Wickliffe Mounds, Kentucky—can be found here in abundance. Harvest festivals for tobacco, pumpkins, cotton, apples, and peaches are widely held in both states. Wildflower walks begin as early as April, and strawberries are honored during the month of May in numerous locations, but the most unusual springtime offering is probably the Ramp (a cousin of the onion) Festival, whose queen is crowned in Cosby, Tennessee. As you make your way across the rural landscape, hand-lettered signs on the backroads will point you to the workshops of birdhouse, basket, and willow furniture makers, while Kentucky parkway and interstate highway signs list antique shops and historic districts alongside food, gas, and lodging.

FINE ARTS

Contemporary classical musicians, visual artists, and creative writers are, as anywhere in the United States, to be found clustered around the major universities' music, art, and literature departments. Both Tennessee and Kentucky have several large state universities and a number of fine private universities and colleges that attract top artists to teaching positions. In both states, however, it is primarily in the major cities—Louisville, Memphis, Nashville, Lexington, Knoxville, and Chattanooga—that one finds the symphonies, opera companies, art museums, commercial galleries and nonprofit art spaces, and the literary events. An exception to this rule is Kentucky's strong network of professional theater companies, which are headquartered not only in Louisville and Lexington, but also in Bowling Green, Horse Cave, and Paducah. Some smaller cities in both states have symphony orchestras, such as those in Kingsport and Oak Ridge in Tennessee and Owensboro, Kentucky. Artists following the national trend of moving away from the omnipotent artistic centers are also arriving here to swell the ranks of painters and sculptors in Louisville, Memphis, and Nashville. The rapid growth of Nashville's music industry is attracting untold numbers of musicians, music producers, screenwriters, and design and film professionals. And every year at Nashville's Southern Festival of Books, there are more and more "locals" among the nationally recognized coterie of writers.

CUISINE

Southern cooking is made up of a variety of types and styles of food. Just like the language of southern speakers, it has been formed not only from the traditional culinary vocabulary of England, Ireland, and Scotland, but also has been drawn from the African vernacular recipes, with its basic syntax coming from American Indian food preparation, and its idiomatic expressions from the many pockets of ethnic German, Swiss, Italian, and Greek immigrants who settled in the region. Of course, any cuisine is dependent upon the availability of ingredients, and regional innovations often arise out of substitutions made from necessity.

Kentucky and Tennessee are as bountiful in foodstuffs as the other southern states. The growing season is long and summertime harvests yield a wide variety of vegetables and fruits. Sweet corn, perfectly ripe red tomatoes, cucumbers, strawberries, blackberries, blueberries, beans, squash, and okra are commonly found on menus in both the humblest of plate lunch diners and the fanciest of restaurants during the summer months. When you drive out into the countryside, you'll see long, low chicken houses and muddy pig yards on rural farms, fields full of grazing cattle, and occasionally, sheep and goats. The cold mountain streams harbor trout, and catfish are plentiful in rivers and lakes. Apples, nuts, and berries grow in the wild, but their widespread cultivation ensures their availability for apple and pecan pies, strawberry jam, and blueberry pancakes.

Wherever you find down-home food, at lunch counters and small local restaurants, you'll find seasonal specialties like fried green tomatoes (after the first frost), fresh mustard greens, sliced tomatoes, blackberry cobbler, cucumbers, and onions. Winter menus in these same sorts of inexpensive restaurants rely on soup beans (dried beans cooked slowly in water with ham hock), chow-chow pickle relishes, stewed fruits and vegetables, grits, hominy, potatoes, and cornbread. Bacon, pork chops, and barbecued pork shoulder are likely to be on the menu, as are fried catfish and fried chicken. Establishments such as these reflect local culinary custom, availability of food in the community, and sometimes the origin of the community founders. Okra, yams, and stewed greens, all staples of the African diet, grow well in southern soil. Their presence on southern tables indicates the influence of African slaves who moved from one wealthy landowner's kitchen to another, spreading cooking lore and practice from one generation of cooks to the next. Corn, dried beans, potatoes, tomatoes, squash, and other native fruits, nuts, and vegetables have been cultivated by American Indians since the agricultural Woodland peoples.

Soul food restaurants offer all of the above, but usually with the addition of what were once the cheapest meats—gizzards, livers, hearts, brains, intestines (chitlins)—often fried or in unusual preparations that many have grown to enjoy. Other regional favorites may also have arisen out of the same sort of "make do" spirit, such as dishes that combine game with vegetables and other meats, like Kentucky Burgoo and Virginia Brunswick Stew. These may have had their origins with the early settlers who were trying to mask the taste of poorly dressed meats. Barbecuing, a method of smoking meat with or without sauce, can also be used to disguise the taste of meats often thought to be inedible, like mutton or groundhog. A standard southern cooking method with numerous variants, barbecue (sometimes spelled bar-b-q) is thought to have its origins either in the Mexican *barbacoa* (pit cooking) or the

French method of roasting a whole pig *barbe a queue* (from beard to tail).* Barbecuing is something of an institution in southern cooking—there is an extensive literature on it, everyone has their own opinion about what is "real" barbecue, and at least two cities in Tennessee and Kentucky claim to be the barbecue capital of the world. If you are interested in the folklore of food, barbecue makes for an endless topic of conversation and there is no limit to the hours one can spend in field research. I frequently turn off the road on just a whiff from a smoking barbecue pit. With the exception of Memphis, where you're as likely to find crusty barbecued spareribs in thick, sweet sauce as a chopped pork sandwich, and northern Kentucky, where mutton is cooked in a spicy tomato sauce, most of the barbecue places in both states serve pit-cooked, pulled pork or half chickens with a vinegar, tomato, and hot pepper sauce.

An Old South Sunday dinner at home or a meal at one of the many fine regional restaurants will feature traditional dishes calling for once highly prized ingredients such as thinly sliced aged salt-cured ham, breast meat of chicken or turkey, white flour, aged cheese, chocolate, refined sugar, choice fruits, and nuts. These recipes originated at the bountiful tables of Kentucky and Tennessee's privileged citizens. Country ham and beaten biscuits are still considered something special and can be found on silver trays at cocktail parties and occasionally on restaurant menus. The famous Kentucky Derby Pie is a rich concoction that features pecans, chocolate, butter, sugar, and lots of eggs. Bourbon candy, a dark chocolate coating over a cream filling containing bourbon and pecans, was invented in Frankfort during Prohibition. The delicious Kentucky Hot Brown, which had its origins as a luncheon specialty at Louisville's Brown Hotel, is composed of sliced roast turkey, sometimes with the addition of country ham, a bechamel sauce, sliced tomato, aged white cheddar, and a strip of bacon baked on top of toast points. Chicken salad, made with white meat only, often includes pecans, grapes, raisins, almonds, or other delicacies in addition to the usual mayonnaise and celery. Iced tea, a variation on the customary British beverage that was, doubtless, invented to suit the warm southern summer weather, is consumed year-round, with a sprig of fresh mint added in summer. Traditional British fare such as roasts of beef, pork, and lamb with accompanying jellies and condiments are usually served with some

* John Egerton, *Southern Food*, p. 49; N.Y.: Alfred A. Knopf, 1987.

sort of potatoes and have always been found on the tables of prosperous southerners. Fried chicken and fresh-caught fish are frequent additions and have been known to appear on southern plates as early as breakfast time.

While Italian and Greek restaurants, and the occasional authentic Jewish deli, can be found relatively intact in locations where they were established decades ago in both states, the cuisine of newer immigrant groups like Mexicans, Middle Easterners, and Thai peoples has only recently become readily available here. There are many excellent family-owned restaurants in small and large cities alike where you will find both the specialties and the prices a pleasant surprise. Because of the strong presence of Japanese industry in the region, there are also a number of fine sushi restaurants—some with specialties of the house written only in Japanese.

FLORA AND FAUNA

The diverse terrain of Kentucky and Tennessee, from mountainous regions and high plateaus to riverbanks, acres of flat or rolling farmland, and swampy wetlands, is home to a variety of plants and animals. Extreme variations of geography in one location, such as the South Cumberland wilderness area of Tennessee, can encompass as wide a variety of plant life as is found in certain parts of Canada. The same can be said of bird populations, which vary not only according to terrain but also according to altitude. The Great Smoky Mountains National Park, whose highest peaks rise to over 6,500 feet and whose lowest valleys sink to under 2,500 feet, attracts three distinct categories of birds. Many of those in the highlands, above 4,000 feet, are Canadian species. Waterfowl are abundant in both states because of the vast network of rivers and streams in the east and the wetlands areas and large lakes in the west.

The park naturalists at Mammoth Cave, Kentucky, have published a checklist of some 250 birds that have been sighted in the park in recent years. This list could be used as a bird watching guide for the middle territories of both states, far away from both the mountains and the low-lying waterlands.

The streams, rivers, and lakes of both states offer a wide variety of freshwater fish—from the cold water mountain, brown, and rainbow trout and smallmouth and redeye bass, to lake fish such as largemouth bass, brim, crappie, and catfish. Crawfish, turtles, and mussels are also found in the rivers. Mussel fishing was once a thriving industry along the Tennessee river in West Tennessee, for mussel shell buttons were much in demand until plastic buttons began to be manufactured in the first quarter of the twentieth century.

Domesticated animals—cattle, horse, hogs, sheep, goats, chickens, and even a few emus—are visible in fenced fields throughout both states. Chipmunks, squirrels, groundhogs, and rabbits are as commonly spotted in neighborhood yards as they are in the rural areas, along with the occasional raccoon or opossum. Out in the country, you'll come upon wildlife out in the open, especially near lakes and rivers. White-tailed deer, wild turkeys, ducks, geese, quail, and pheasants are often seen. Visitors to both states who venture away from the busy roads and city centers to camp in the wild are likely to hear bobcats, raccoons, possums, and skunks prowling about under cover of darkness. Coyotes can sometimes be heard yelping in the distance, especially where there are livestock farms nearby.

In the Great Smoky Mountains, where black bears and red wolves are protected species, visitors are asked to keep food locked away and to make sure that even the charred remains of meats cooked on outdoor grills do not find their way into the wild animal food chain. Bears like densely wooded areas and open thickets where they can easily find the wild nuts and berries that are their primary sources of food. In recent years, park naturalists have begun a program of relocating bears and wolves to prior native habitats, such as the Big South Fork, in order to restore the normal balance of animal life.

Human interference in the natural order of things, especially the wholesale logging of the past and the voracious trapping and hunting that took place in the early years of this country, has taken its toll on the native animal population. Certain species of birds have all but vanished, and the change in air quality has affected many types of plants. The industrial pollution of air and water in this century has created some problems in Tennessee that are only now being recognized and addressed. Reforestation has been taking place for some years now and some previously endangered species are beginning to be restored. Non-native animals, such as the wild boar and the rainbow trout, are being systematically hunted and fished out in the Great Smoky Mountains.

Visitors should be aware that poisonous flora and fauna, which could put a damper on any vacation, are present in these parts, if only in a few forms. As avid hikers know, in the woods and lowlands of this area there are a wide variety of snakes. Copperheads and timber rattlesnakes in fields and forests as well as water moccasins and cotton-mouth near the edges of rivers and lakes are the poisonous ones. Most snakes will scurry for cover long before you see them, but sunny days will find them basking in the sun on rocks or logs—so look before you step. Yellow jackets and other forms of wasp can give a nasty sting to which many people are highly allergic. Standing water and stilled breezes make good breeding grounds for mosquitoes, especially in late summer. In recent years, ticks have become more of a problem, especially the almost invisible seed ticks. When walking in high grass or dense forest during the summer months, it is advisable to wear socks covered with some sort of insect repellent. Those who are susceptible to poison ivy will find it growing here in abundance, so stay away from three-leaved vines climbing on tree trunks.

In the eastern parts of both states, a wide variety of wildflowers and wild flowering trees and shrubs, such as azalea, mountain laurel, rhododendron, dogwood, and redbud make the spring and summer months particularly beautiful. Because of the range of elevations in the region, you can find the same plant blooming in different locales from April to July. Deep in the woods and in shady spots on park hillsides grow the most delicate wildflowers. Over seven varieties of trillium—a three-leaved relative of the lily that has a central white, pink, or yellow flower—grow in the higher elevations. Varieties of the wild orchid, with descriptive names like Lady's Slipper and Jack in the Pulpit, will delight a child's imagination. And the wild versions of garden flowers, such as the tiny Dutch iris, Lily of the Valley, and the primrose, can be found alongside Pipsissewa, May Apple, and Indian Pipe. Many woodland plants were used by the Indians and early settlers for medicinal purposes. Some, like the bark and root of ginseng, are thought to have aphrodisiac powers and still bring a good price on today's market.

Many parts of both states remain heavily wooded, and deciduous trees mixed with evergreens create a spectacular fall display. Fall colors—the yellows of poplars, beeches, and birch trees, and the reds of maple, sweet gum, and red oak—appear first in the higher elevations, sometimes as early as the beginning of October near the Cumberland Gap, Roan Mountain, and the Smokies. You can still find a few areas of virgin forest deep in the protected areas of both states, and, in addition to the extensive state park lands, there are thousands of acres of privately owned timberland. But in the 1930s, the Civilian Conservation Corps replanted many acres of logged timberland with evergreens, so that in many locations today's visitor will encounter luxuriant stands of pine where there once stood hardwood forests.

GEOGRAPHY

The high ridges of the Appalachian chain run north-south through the eastern portion of both states, with their western watershed draining into both Tennessee and Kentucky. The Clinch, Holston, Nolichucky, Tellico, and Hiwassee Rivers all join ultimately at the Tennessee River. Kentucky's Cumberland, Red, and Kentucky Rivers feed into the Ohio. The Tennessee and the Ohio are two of the major source rivers of the massive Mississippi River, while numerous other tributaries run through both states. The Great Smoky Mountains includes the two highest peaks in the eastern U.S.: Mt. Mitchell, North Carolina, which is 6,684 feet above sea level and Mt. LeConte, Tennessee, which stands at 6,643 feet. Kentucky's mountainous east is less lofty. Its highest point is Black Mountain, 4,145 feet above sea level, located near the Virginia border between Harlan and Whitesburg.

The descent from the Appalachian mountain range takes place in stages, from foothills to plateau, then down into great wide valleys punctuated by occasional clusters of hills and bowl-like lakes. The Cumberland Plateau, which stretches from Kentucky down through Tennessee, into northern Alabama and the northeastern tip of Mississippi, is the last vestige of the Appalachian chain. The plateau's geography includes jagged limestone outcroppings, dramatic rock gorges, deep riverbeds, and spreading finger lakes as it levels off into the rolling hills and open grasslands of central Kentucky and Tennessee. The eastern edge of the Appalachian Mountains is much more dramatic, with abrupt peaks and drops. The long Sequatchie Valley, which traverses Tennessee from north to south, was once a single rock ridge that split apart into a relatively narrow "rift" valley with 800-foot walls on either side.

The Kentucky Bluegrass and the Cumberland Basin of Tennessee contain some of the richest farmland in the country. Fields are planted with tobacco, corn, soybeans, and wheat, while cattle and horses peacefully graze in rich pastures. Around the edges of the basin, where the land begins to rise toward the plateau, sheep and goats straddle limestone boulders as they crop the grass. In Kentucky the western portion of this area is pockmarked with lakes and underground caves. Seams of coal and other minerals, once heavily mined here, are still a source of income for many Kentuckians. As it rolls west, the land grows flatter and begins gradually to descend toward the Mississippi. Crossing the wide Tennessee River or gazing out at the Ohio as it passes by Henderson and Owensboro seems somehow to take you back in time, to an age when everything depended on the river in one way or another. Riverboats still ply these waters and barges carry coal, lumber, and manufactured goods from the heartlands of these two states to outside markets.

The western portions of both states contain flat, open fields good for high yield farming and lots of rich river bottom land. Southwest Kentucky and northwest Tennessee are joined by the Land Between the Lakes, a recreation area located at the confluence of the Tennessee and Cumberland Rivers, which were dammed by the Tennessee Valley Authority to create Kentucky Lake and Lake Barkley. In southwestern Tennessee, where the fields must be irrigated and the sun beats down relentlessly in the summer, cotton was, and still is, the primary crop. The mighty Mississippi River flows along the western edge of both states, from whence Kentuckians and Tennesseans of the past could either follow a fast-moving route to New Orleans—for many years the center of southern commerce and culture—or cross over into the rough-edged civilization of the western frontier states of Missouri, Arkansas, and Texas.

OUTDOOR RECREATION

Nearly every type of outdoor sport can be undertaken in Kentucky and Tennessee. In fact, the only thing lacking is the ocean— scuba divers are forced to qualify for certification in lakes formed within abandoned rock quarries! While one can walk the portion of the Appalachian Trail that passes through northeast Tennessee in a few days, and the Sheltowee Trace in several weeks' time, the mountainous areas of both states provide so many hiking routes that it is not possible to take all of them on in one lifetime. The serious rock climber will find challenging locales throughout the Appalachian chain, including Kentucky's Red River Gorge, the Wild and Scenic Obed River, the escarpment of the Cumberland Plateau, and Lookout Mountain, Tennessee. White-water lovers will enjoy the rapids of Big South Fork, Nolichucky Gorge, and the Ocoee River, site of the 1996 Olympic white-water events.

These two states are a fisherman's (or woman's) paradise—whether you wade into small cold streams using a fly or spin rod, troll from a bass boat, or go in for sport fishing in the deep lakes and swift rivers. In most cases, either a Tennessee or Kentucky fishing license is required and a trout stamp is necessary. For Kentucky fishing information and a list of licensed fishing guides, call (502) 564-4336. Check the listings in Tennessee's vacation guide for optimum seasons and locations. It's free; call (800) TENN-200. The many recreational lakes created by the Tennessee Valley Authority (TVA) are perfect for water sports like swimming, boating, and water-skiing, while canoeists and kayakers will find both quiet meanders and rushing waters on the many rivers.

Biking and running are popular activities in both states, as much of the land is gently rolling and the climate is temperate. The Tennessee Department of Transportation has mapped five bicycle routes; phone (615) 741-5310. Kentucky Bike Tour features six statewide routes that can be obtained by writing to them at P.O. Box 2011, Frankfort, KY 40602. The Tennessee State Park System has sponsored a series of Saturday running events called the Annual Running Tour. The races take place during the fall and winter months at different parks around the state and vary in length from 5 to 13 miles. Many cities have running clubs that offer weekly or monthly group events. Check with outdoor outfitters for details.

Southeastern Tennessee calls itself the hang-gliding capital of the East. Chattanooga's Lookout Mountain is the home of several training facilities, and the lower Sequatchie Valley town of Dunlap is the site of regular club activities and nationally recognized hang-gliding events.

PRACTICAL TIPS

HOW MUCH WILL IT COST?

If you are prepared to spend $125–$150 per day while traveling through these two states, and follow many of the suggestions in this book, you can enjoy lovely and unusual accommodations, visit memorable destinations, and taste the best local cuisine, with some luxury touches and a few splurges thrown in. A true bargain hunter who is not given to indulging costly whims in food, lodging, or mementos, could do this trip for as little as $85 a day; campers might manage on about $20 less. My advice is to avoid summertime and special event rates in Nashville, Memphis, Louisville, and Lexington; be wary of autumn "leaf season," when the mountains are heavily touristed; and call ahead for cabin reservations at the state parks, for they are moderately priced and a stay in a rustic setting will add immeasurably to your visit.

Accommodations located on the major east-west and north-south interstate routes remain pretty consistent in price with the major hotel rates across the country, often making them more expensive than one might expect for an isolated location. While I have included them in the reference materials for some destinations, I choose these only out of necessity, either when arriving late at night, when everything else is booked, or when your B&B host answers the door looking like Count Dracula.

Generally speaking, you should allow an average of $60–$70 per hotel room night. Many bed and breakfasts will cost a bit more, but keep in mind that they are often including breakfast for two in the total price. Some small family-owned motels charge as little as $35 for a double room, but you'll make up for it by paying $90–$120 per night in Louisville, Lexington, Nashville, Chattanooga, or Memphis. Of course, sharing a room with your traveling companion will reduce your costs considerably, and if you don't mind carrying gear, an occasional camp-out will save you money as well. There are many clean and well-maintained camping spots in state and national parks where a campsite goes for under $10, and sleeping under the stars may provide just the right change of pace from a hectic touring schedule.

A simple breakfast should cost somewhere from $6–$8. I often manage for half that by carrying my own fruit and picking up a bagel or muffin and coffee at the best coffee place in town. Lunches can also be toted, for wherever you go, you'll find roadside picnic tables or scenic spots for alfresco eating beside rivers and streams or at high mountain overlooks. Lunches at local diners will generally cost you no more than $5 for a "meat and three," or a vegetable plate with biscuits or cornbread. A BBQ sandwich heaped with coleslaw will tide me over any day—maximum cost $4. For a seated lunch in a nice restaurant, expect to pay anywhere from $8–$15 including tip. Dinners range in price depending upon whether you like wine or beer with your meal and the extent to which you have decided to indulge yourself. It would be easy to spend $100 or more for two people eating out at one of the better restaurants in Louisville, Nashville, Memphis, Lexington, Chattanooga, or Knoxville. But a nice meal with a glass of wine or a beer can be found in all of these cities for $25 or less per person and a no-frills but delicious and healthful dinner for as little as $10.

Incidental costs, such as gasoline, admission prices, film, bottled water, and snacks, can be held to around $25 a day if you are vigilant. As a tourist, my weaknesses are books, unusual food items, and anything handmade. Kentucky and Tennessee crafts are not cheap, but this is the place to purchase them, for their markets in the rest of the country will price them higher than at home and you might be passing up the chance to see the artist at work. My advice is to set aside several traveler's checks early in the trip just in case you find the handmade Shaker-style rocker you've always wanted in Berea, Kentucky, or Jonesborough, Tennessee.

WHEN TO GO

April–May and September–October are the nicest months. Spring flowers and autumn colors are both spectacular, the days are warm and dry, and the nights are fresh and cool. June can be very pleasant, and, though sometimes hot, it is almost always sunny and usually drier than July and August, which are guaranteed to be hot and humid.

Horse racing season begins as early as April in Kentucky, so secure a room in or around Lexington ahead of time if you plan to go, and, of course, staying in a Louisville or Lexington hotel during the Kentucky Derby festivities of early May would put a strain on anyone's wallet.

Summer is tourist season everywhere, but especially in Nashville, when hotel prices are at peak level and country music fans crowd into the Music Row souvenir shop/museums of Barbara Mandrell, Randy Travis, and Hank Williams Jr. and stand, sweating, in long lines for lunch at the new Hard Rock Café. Memphis is just plain sweltering in July and August and, unless you are a native of New Orleans or Houston, you too will find it unpleasant.

In the fall, college football weekends in Nashville, Knoxville, and Memphis can make it difficult to find a reasonably priced room. University of Kentucky basketball in Lexington draws huge crowds that fill most of the downtown hotels near the arena. The Great Smoky Mountains National Park, Big South Fork, Daniel Boone National Park, and the state parks in the eastern portion of both states are crowded during peak leaf season (mid-October, usually) and the small motels, bed and breakfasts, and country inns on their periphery often increase their prices accordingly.

I find traveling in off-season quite rewarding. You don't have to keep to a schedule of hotel reservations, and you get a glimpse of the routines of "real-life" people in the region. Like a kid out of school, I have always taken pleasure in being off when everyone else was at work. One word of warning, avoid traveling in January when many historic sites are closed, and you are likely to encounter the heaviest snows of the season.

CLIMATE

Spring and fall temperatures stay in the 60- to 80-degree range, with nights dropping into the 40s and 50s with relatively low humidity. Summer months can be quite humid and hot, with temperatures remaining in the 90s for weeks at a time in July and August. You'll find flowers blooming in sunny spots as early as mid-February, and the months of March through May offer both wildflowers and garden flowers galore. Summers are sunny. The days are long, and with ample rainfall the flowers, fruits, and vegetables generally thrive. Many gardeners plant a second crop of lettuce and garden peas in the fall, hoping that frost will not come until after Halloween. On rare occasions, a Tennessee Thanksgiving table will feature sliced tomatoes just off the vine.

December is likely to be cold and wet, with snow most likely in January, accumulating a yearly average of 1–1½ feet. As in the old adage, March comes in like a lion—often with howling winds and driving rains—but April is more likely to be sunny than showery, with temperatures ranging from the 60s into the 80s.

TIME ZONES

The eastern portion of both states, which includes the cities of Lexington, Knoxville, and Chattanooga, is in the Eastern Time Zone—the dividing line running roughly just outside the easternmost ridge of the Cumberland Mountains. Louisville, Nashville, and Memphis are on the leading edge of the Central Time Zone, which includes most of the Midwest and Texas. In the summertime, this means that daylight stretches past 9 p.m. in the eastern region, making it easy for travelers to set up camp late in the day or to take a scenic drive after supper.

TRANSPORTATION

This region is served by a number of airports, cross-country buses pass through its major cities, and major north-south and east-west interstate highways crisscross both states. Kentucky and Tennessee are centrally located, and driving from home may not be as prohibitive in time or mileage as you might think—one full day of driving from Nashville will get you as far as Washington, D.C.; Dallas, Texas; New Orleans, Louisiana; Kansas City, Missouri; or Chicago, Illinois. Railroad passenger service is all but nonexistent here now, although the freight lines are still active. Memphis is served by an Amtrak north-south route connecting it to New Orleans and Chicago; and both Cincinnati and Atlanta also have Amtrak passenger service. Amtrak has a toll-free reservation and information phone line: (800) 872-7245.

If you plan on flying to the area, Nashville International Airport has the best airline connections, with nonstop flights to many cities on American, Delta, Southwest, U.S. Air, United, TWA, Continental, AmericaWest, and others. Louisville, Memphis, and Knoxville are also served by many of the major airlines. Lexington and Chattanooga have good airports that support both nonstop and commuter flights. Cincinnati's airport is actually located in northern Kentucky, and the huge Atlanta airport is just two hours south of Chattanooga.

Car rentals are available at all of the airports. It is best to reserve ahead and look for discounts (AAA, airline frequent flyer, travel promotion) because most travelers through the region are business people and prices tend to remain high and availability low for week day rentals. Besides Avis, Hertz, National, Budget, Alamo, Thrifty, and Dollar—all of which can be reached toll-free and are generally located in the major airports—Sears and Enterprise are national companies that serve many cities without airports, often with lower rates.

All of the destinations, itineraries, and scenic routes in this book can be reached by a regular passenger vehicle, except on rare winter occasions when even the major highways become impassable for a day or so in the higher elevations. For the adventuresome traveler, a bicycle trip across these two states could be plotted with information from the Tennessee Department of Transportation and the Tennessee State Parks, and the Kentucky Bike Tour organization. There are a number of outdoor outfitters in the region who not only sell but also rent camping equipment, and a bike could be bought here and sold at the end of the trip, as is often done for European bike trips.

CAMPING, LODGING, AND DINING

If you intend to camp your way across Kentucky and Tennessee, I suggest you begin by getting information from both state park systems right away. Both provide a wide selection of cheap, clean, well-maintained campgrounds that are open year round. When you arrive, check in at one of the local outdoor outfitters to purchase useful items you might have forgotten and to inquire about other good camping spots, white-water outfitters, bike routes, out-of-the-way hiking trails, rock climbing venues, or other points of local interest. Often the folks who work at these shops are devoted sportsmen and women who are both friendly and knowledgeable.

I've included bed and breakfasts among my recommended lodgings for three reasons: first, a B&B, likely to be housed in a historic home, is often the nicest place to stay in a small town; second, you might learn something about the town's culture from your hosts; and third, a home-cooked breakfast is a nice way to start a day of touring—it gets you up and out. I have tried to include small locally owned hotels whenever possible, for in my experience they are often in a safer, more attractive location; better maintained; and at least as cheap as their national counterparts, which tend to be placed alongside the exits of interstate highways or near large shopping centers. Some campgrounds and motel courts include small, separate cabins. Usually without television or telephone, these are often considered "budget" accommodations, but I prefer them for their privacy and rustic charm.

In the moderately priced category, I recommend the wonderful old cabins in the state parks, most of which rent for $50–$60. This includes linens, a small kitchen, one or two bedrooms, and a fireplace or screened porch. The modern state park lodges offer rooms in the same price range if you prefer more standard accommodations. Most bed and breakfasts fall into this same price range if you add $10–$20 for the price of breakfast for two. For the same cost you should be able to find a room at the nicest motel in any small town, some of the old historic hotels, or any national chain motel located in a rural area or along a major highway.

The outstanding historic inns and luxury B&B destinations charge upwards of $80 for a double room. The contemporary resort cabins at the state parks also fall into this price range, and so do most downtown hotels in large cities. The most expensive hotel rooms you'll find in the region are historic hotels that have been restored to their former glory in the major cities, and new luxury resort inns, where a room for two without breakfast can cost anywhere from $110–$150. Many of these hotels offer weekend packages, state and federal employee rates, and all manner of discounts when their occupancy falls below a certain percentile. Don't be afraid to bargain with them as evening draws near, for a night of pampered slumber is good for the soul.

I love to eat. I love the taste of fresh foods in season, and I love learning the culinary customs of places and people. I believe that one of the best ways to get to know a locale is to experience its characteristic cuisine. Accordingly, this guidebook recommends many simple eateries that visitors might not even consider at first glance. The budget category (usually well under $10) includes local diners, old-fashioned soda fountains, storefront ethnic restaurants, the new wave of upscale coffee-houses that serve a limited but often very good menu, and places that serve regional specialties, some for carry-out only. My moderately priced ($10–$25) recommendations include health food restaurants, restaurants located at historic sites, and restaurants that serve regional specialities in an aesthetic environment with good service. The only chain restaurants you'll find in this book are the brew pubs, because they make interesting local beers and ales at the different locations. In the fine restaurant (that is, expensive) category, I have tried to point out the one-of-a-kind historic sites—places that can function as a kind of touchstone for the traditional cuisine of a region. Once some para-meters have been established, you can begin to judge the creative chefs and young innovators for yourself as you visit the popular restaurants in Louisville, Lexington, Knoxville, Memphis, Chattanooga, and

Nashville, and move into their spheres of influence in Atlanta, Cincinnati, Richmond, Charlotte, and Birmingham. Such gourmet moments will make a dent in your travel budget, but southern hospitality is most fully experienced at the dining table, so I hope you will make several fine restaurant outings a priority no matter what your itinerary. While some of the newest immigrants to the area are just starting out with budget-level dining rooms, you will also find excellent and authentic French, Italian, and Mediterranean restaurants in these cities. I have not listed those here, for although many are quite good, they also tend to be expensive. Instead, I have tried to point out those restaurants that feature an interesting local ambiance or interpret the local cuisine, in hopes that visitors will come away with a lasting sense of where they have been.

RECOMMENDED READING

This region wears its stereotypes like burrs on a dog's coat—impossible to get rid of and so numerous that, in the aggregate, no particular one seems to be more harmful than any other. To better understand their sources, read about them in the words of some of the finest writers to depict the people and places of Tennessee and Kentucky. Robert Penn Warren, Peter Taylor, and Caroline Gordon hailed from the northern Tennessee and south central Kentucky area near Nashville; Bobbie Ann Mason and Wendell Berry are still writing from central Kentucky; and Mary Lee Settle and James Still, from Kentucky's Appalachian region. James Agee and Cormac McCarthy wrote with tragic humor and empathy about Knoxville and the mountains of East Tennessee, and Nikki Giovanni's humor and toughness reflect her Knoxville upbringing. Wilma Dykeman, noted author of many books about the East Tennessee region, hosts a radio program in conjunction with Knoxville symphony performances on WUOT, 91.9.

Independent filmmaker Ross Spears has produced excellent documentaries on James Agee and the TVA. Especially insightful is his *Long Shadows*, a study of the aftermath of the Civil War. Films like *Coal Miner's Daughter* and *Nashville* will give viewers a caustic glance back at the now-powerful country music establishment, and more recently, *The Firm*, by John Grisham, presents an accurate portrait of Memphis and a cynical view of the contemporary South. Appalshop, a nonprofit creative workshop in Whitesburg, Kentucky, has produced documentary films, art exhibits, books, and records reflecting the rich culture of

Appalachia. They also produce an excellent Kentucky public radio program entitled "Go Tell It on the Mountain," which features interviews, cultural news, and regional music. For a publications list or for more information, you can call them at (606) 633-0108. Similarly, the Center for Southern Folklore, located on Beale Street in Memphis, collects regional cultural expressions on documentary film, in sound recording, and in a series of publications. They can be reached at (901) 525-3655. It used to be that a traveler could scan the local daily newspaper to take the pulse of the next town on his or her itinerary. In these days of national newspaper syndicates and sensationalist front page stories, this is, unfortunately, no longer true. However, many cities have thriving alternative papers that come out weekly, biweekly, or even monthly that will prove more helpful to visitors seeking to put a finger on the cultural scene. These papers are usually free, and popular budget breakfast places, coffee houses, and music venues will normally have dispenser racks out front. By the same token, public radio stations, many of which are run by the state universities in Kentucky and Tennessee, have assumed the role of community bulletin boards for cultural happenings, so tune to the low end of the FM dial as you approach any sizable city in either state. Louisville, Lexington, Richmond, and Bowling Green in Kentucky and Johnson City, Knoxville, Chattanooga, Nashville, and Memphis in Tennessee have National, American, or International Public Radio affiliate stations.

For general travel information, a calendar listing of special events and festivals, and a free state map, you can request a vacation guide booklet from Tennessee by calling (800) TENN-200 (1996 is Tennessee's Bicentennial) and from Kentucky by calling (800) 225-TRIP.

There are several bed and breakfast associations that might be able to send you advance literature on member B&Bs. Others merely serve as reservation services. The Kentucky Bed and Breakfast Association publishes an extensive map/guide brochure; call (800) 292-2632 to have them send you one. Kentucky Homes will give you information about Louisville B&Bs, (502) 635-7341. There are two Lexington area membership groups: Bluegrass B&B, (606) 873-3208, and B&B of Lexington, (800) 526-9801 or (606) 252-3601. There is a 24-hour room reservation service in Tennessee that serves not only hotels and motels but also B&Bs and country inns, (800) ENJOY TN. The Tennessee B&B Innkeepers Association lists only B&Bs in historic houses, (800) 820-8144, and the Natchez Trace B&B Reservation Service has ten Tennessee inns in their registry,

(800) 377-2770. In Nashville, B&B Clearinghouse serves the whole state, (800) 458-2421 or (615) 331-5244. The Memphis B&B Clearinghouse can be reached by calling (901) 726-5920. Explore B&B listings on the Internet at www.bbonline.com.

The following references provide especially good support materials for several areas of interest that have been suggested in the destination chapters of this book:

Miles, Jim. *Piercing the Heartland: A History and Tour Guide of the Fort Donelson, Shiloh, and Perryville Campaigns.* Nashville: Rutledge Hill Press, 1991. This book is a wonderful driving guide to the areas around these battlefields and contains fascinating battle narratives by a Civil War buff.

Rozema, Vicki. *Footsteps of the Cherokees: A Guide to the Eastern Homelands of the Cherokee Nation.* Winston-Salem, N.C.: John F. Blair, 1995. This paperback book, which offers a summary of historical events leading to the 1838 removal of the Cherokee, is a guidebook to 19 geographic areas, about half of which are in Tennessee and North Carolina and the rest in Georgia and Alabama.

Sehlinger, Bob. *Canoeing and Kayaking Guide to the Streams of Kentucky.* Birmingham: Menasha Ridge Publications, 1994. Published in paperback, this book is based on a year and a half of field research by the author.

Thornborough, Laura. *The Great Smoky Mountains.* New York: Thomas Crowell, 1937. This charming volume was written during the first years of the national park's formation. Although now long out of print, the book is valuable not only for its historical perspective but also for the author's well-expressed environmental stance.

1
NASHVILLE

Nashville, located in the gently rolling hills of north central Tennessee, has a metropolitan area population count nearing 1 million and is rapidly becoming the state's largest city. Three interstate highways cross here—which partly accounts for the popularity of country music among truck drivers. Nashville's greatest fame rests upon the booming business of country music. Although widely known as the country music capital of the world, musicians of all stripes can be heard in Nashville's music venues, from its smoky barrooms to its balconied concert halls.

The historic buildings of downtown Nashville are undergoing tremendous renovation and restoration. The Ryman Auditorium, home to the original Grand Ole Opry (which moved to a contemporary auditorium in the Opryland theme-park complex in the 1970s) has been restored to its former glory. The honky-tonks of lower Broadway, considered eyesores until just a few years ago, managed to escape the wrecking ball and are finally receiving their due from music-oriented visitors and historians of early country music. Just down the street, the 4-story, 1-block deep brick structures of the riverfront warehouse district and the late nineteenth-century limestone Customs House (½-mile up Broadway, the main east-west artery of Nashville) bear witness to Nashville's early history as a center of river trade. ◼

NASHVILLE

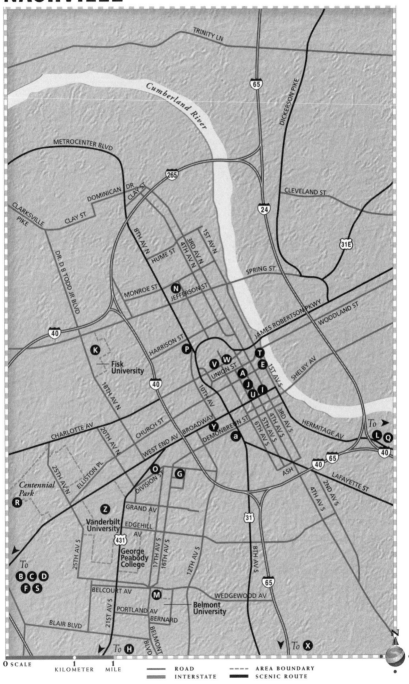

Cumberland River

TRINITY LN

METROCENTER BLVD

DOMINICAN DR

CLARKSVILLE PIKE

CLAY ST

DR. D B TODD JR BLVD

CLEVELAND ST

DICKERSON PIKE

HUME ST

MONROE ST

JEFFERSON ST

SPRING ST

8TH AV N

3RD AV N
4TH AV N

1ST AV N

JAMES ROBERTSON PKWY

WOODLAND ST

HARRISON ST

Fisk University

18TH AV N

UNION ST

SHELBY AV

1ST AV S

CHARLOTTE AV

CHURCH ST

WEST END AV

BROADWAY

DEMONBREUN ST

10TH AV

20TH AV N

HERMITAGE AV

6TH AV S
5TH AV S
4TH AV S
3RD AV S

To

ASH

LAFAYETTE ST

25TH AV N

ELLISTON PL

DIVISION ST

2ND AV S

4TH AV S

Centennial Park

GRAND AV

Vanderbilt University

EDGEHILL AV

George Peabody College

25TH AV S

17TH AV S
16TH AV S

12TH AV S

8TH AV S

BELCOURT AV

To

Belmont University

WEDGEWOOD AV

BLAIR BLVD

21ST AV S

PORTLAND AV

BERNARD

BELMONT BLVD

To

To

N

SCALE

KILOMETER   MILE

ROAD
INTERSTATE

AREA BOUNDARY
SCENIC ROUTE

Sights

A The Arcade

B Belle Meade

C Belle Meade Plantation

D Cheekwood

E City Walk

F Collector's Gallery

G Country Music Hall of Fame and Museum

H Cumberland Gallery

I Hatch Show Print

J Downtown Presbyterian Church

K Fisk University

L The Hermitage

M Historic Belmont

N In The Gallery

A Life and Casualty Tower

O Local Color Gallery

P Museum of Tobacco Art and History

Q Opryland U.S.A

R Parthenon

S Percy Warner Park

T Riverfront

U Ryman Auditorium and Lower Broadway

V State Capitol

W Tennessee Performing Arts Center (TPAC)

W Tennessee State Museum

X Travellers Rest

Y Union Station

Z Vanderbilt University and George Peabody College

a Zeitgeist Gallery

Note: Items with the same letter are located in the same place.

A PERFECT DAY IN MUSIC CITY

Nashville's temperate climate almost always permits outdoor exercise early in the morning. Jog around Centennial Park, or for a surprisingly "north woods" experience, hike one of the loop trails at Radnor Lake. After coffee and a healthful fruit and nut muffin at Slice of Life, visit the Country Music Hall of Fame up the street, whose exhibits are unfailingly good, and Hatch Show Print, still a going business on lower Broadway, where you can see who is having a traditional block print poster done for their next Nashville appearance. Peek inside the Parthenon at the gigantic statue of Athena and walk across Centennial Park to Hog Heaven, a great barbecue stand that even serves a smoked turkey sandwich. Spend the rest of the afternoon at Elder's (used) Books on Elliston Place and at White Way Antique Mall. Nashville music events can get crowded quickly, so call ahead for reservations. Have a nightcap at Merchant's Restaurant on lower Broadway; you'll hear music-making until well after midnight in many of the honky tonks down the street.

MORE NASHVILLE FACTS

Nashville, Tennessee's capital, was founded in 1779 by James Robertson and John Donelson, whose Fort Nashborough has been reconstructed on the west bank of the Cumberland River, now First Avenue. During the War Between the States, Nashville, a city of Confederate sympathies, was occupied by Federal troops because of its strategic location. Nashville is still a crossroads of the upper South and a current center of economic growth, as recent downtown skyscrapers attest. While it is home to Truckstops of America and Peterbilt, Nashville has also traditionally been a printing and publishing center, and in recent years it has become a mecca for the rapid rise of private hospital care companies, such as Columbia/HCA and Healthtrust. Nashville prides itself on its nickname "the Athens of the South," and it is a matter of debate whether that name has its origin in that fact that Nashville is home to so many universities or that Centennial Park contains a full-scale replica of the Parthenon.

SIGHTSEEING HIGHLIGHTS

★★★ **City Walk**—This is the Metro Historical Commission's marked walking trail through downtown, and it's a great way to get a feel for the early history of Nashville. Look for the teal blue stripe on the sidewalk and historical markers bearing silhouetted figures. The walk begins on First Avenue at Fort Nashborough. Admission to the fort is free. Phone: (615) 862-7970. (1 hour)

★★★ **Country Music Hall of Fame and Museum**—The Hall of Fame on "Music Row" is a terrific museum of country music history that traces its roots from traditional Scotch-Irish to blues to bluegrass. The Hall of Fame is run by the **Country Music Foundation**, which houses a fine library and archives, has the best gift shop on Music Row, and runs historic Studio B. By the way, Music Row is 16th and 17th Avenues and Demonbruen Street, where you'll find record label headquarters, music studios, talent agencies, and souvenir shop/museums of various country singers. Admission is $8.95 per adult, $3.95 per child. Address: 16th Avenue South, approximately 10 blocks west of downtown. Phone: (615) 256-1639. (1½ hours)

★★★ **Downtown Presbyterian Church**—This historic church building is one of Nashville's architectural wonders. Designed around 1830 by William Strickland, architect of the state capitol, this rare example of Egyptian revival architecture has stained glass windows featuring papyrus motifs and interior trompe l'oeil paintings of a columned courtyard. Address: Church Street and Fifth Avenue. Phone: (615)254-7584. (¼ hour)

★★★ **The Hermitage**—One of the best interpreted and restored historic sites in the country. The Hermitage, which was the home of Andrew Jackson, actually began as a 2-story log cabin. The house was built in 1821 with a Greek revival facade added after a fire in 1836. There is also an interpretive center. Admission is $7.50 per adult, $4 for children ages 6–12. Address: 4580 Rachel's Lane, Hermitage. Phone: (615) 889-2941.

★★★ **The Parthenon**—Built originally in 1897 as the Art Building for the Tennessee Centennial Exposition, the Parthenon was rebuilt in 1931. It now houses a permanent art collection, a 42-foot sculpture of Athena Parthenos by Tennessee sculptor Alan LeQuire, and reproductions of the Elgin marble friezes from the Athenian original. Admission is $2.50 per adult, $1.25 per child. Closed on Monday. Address: West End Avenue, in Centennial Park. Phone: (615) 862-8431. (1 hour)

★★★ **Riverfront**—First and Second Avenues from Broadway to the County Courthouse consist of a row of deep brick warehouses into which goods were loaded from the Cumberland River in the early days of the city. Even today, this is still a lively commercial area of the city. Check out **Butler's Run**, a new covered passageway between the two streets; **Market Street Brewery**, Nashville's own brewpub; and the old **Acme Feed and Seed**, still located at the corner of First and Broadway, where you can find everything from spring plant starts to free dog dips on Saturdays. Address: First and Second Avenues, downtown.

★★★ **Ryman Auditorium and Lower Broadway**—Don't miss the high temple of country music, at Fifth Avenue between Broadway and Commerce (615-889-6611). The beautifully remodeled Ryman hosts a variety of country, gospel, bluegrass, pop, and rock events and occasional musical theater. Call for tickets. Admission is $4 per adult, $2 per child. (1 hour) After the show, walk through the alley to the back door of **Tootsie's Orchid Lounge**, where legendary Opry performers came to grab a quick one between shows. Stroll down Broadway to Gruhn Guitars, the famous music store with museum quality instruments for sale and a widely knowledgeable staff. **Hatch Show Print**, 1 block further, between Third and Fourth Avenues, is a historic show poster shop where you can see woodblock printing still being done (615-256-2805). Pawn shops, honky-tonks, and record stores are all still in business and remain much as they were when the Opry was still downtown.

★★ **Cheekwood**—Leslie Cheek, a wealthy wholesale grocery broker, built this English manor house on the eve of the Great Depression. The Georgian-style house sits on 55 acres and is now a fine and decorative arts museum. The grounds include botanical gardens and greenhouses, changing exhibits, seasonal botanic events, and educational programs. An admission fee is charged. Address: 1200 Forrest Park Drive. Phone: (615) 356-8000. (2 hours)

★★ **Collector's Gallery, Cumberland Gallery, In the Gallery, Local Color Gallery,** and **Zeitgeist Gallery**—Spend a morning or afternoon checking out Nashville's visual arts scene at these commercial galleries who represent local and regional artists. You can pick up a Nashville Association of Art Dealers guide at any one of them or find a

Nashville Scene for current exhibit listings. The **Nashville Arts Gallery**, run by the Greater Nashville Arts Foundation, and The **Tennessee Arts Commission Gallery** (both downtown nonprofit galleries) offer top quality local and regional art exhibits as well. The **Nashville International Airport** has an innovative program of live music and changing art exhibits.

✯✯ **Fisk University**—This historic campus, built in 1866 and named after Union General Clinton B. Fisk, was one of the first historically black colleges. Park and walk around the campus. The most striking building is the Victorian, towered **Jubilee Hall**, now a dormitory, where you can view the portrait of the famed Jubilee Singers, whose performances of negro spirituals helped raise money for the University and took them to the court of Queen Victoria. Across campus, the **University Library** houses important works of art, manuscript and archival collections related to the Harlem Renaissance. In the campus center, the Administration Building contains wall murals by Harlem Renaissance artist Aaron Douglas. The **Carl Van Vechten Gallery of Fine Art** houses a collection of American modern art donated by Alfred Stieglitz and Georgia O'Keeffe as well as important works by African-American artists of the first half of the twentieth century. Admission to the gallery is free, although a donation is requested. Closed Monday. Address: D.B. Todd Boulevard and 17th Avenue. Phone: (615) 329-8453. (1½ hours)

✯✯ **State Capitol**—This elegant and stately building was designed by William Strickland around 1825. His drawings and a model are on display at the Tennessee State Museum. The grounds contain monuments to historical Tennesseans and Capitol Hill affords a nice view west and north of the city. Guided tours are available. Address: Charlotte Avenue at Seventh Avenue. Phone: (615) 741-2692. (¾ hour)

✯✯ **Tennessee State Museum**—Located on the lower floors of the Tennessee Performing Arts Center, the museum offers beautiful historical exhibits and changing art exhibits. Admission is free. Address: Fifth Avenue and Deaderick Street. Phone: (615) 741-2692. (1 hour)

✯✯ **Travellers Rest**—This is my favorite historic house in Tennessee because it is off the main tourist routes and looks very much as it might have 200 years ago. The home of Judge John

Overton (founder of Memphis), it was built in 1799 and is beautifully maintained and interpreted, with a number of Overton's possessions still in place in rooms throughout the house. Overton, Andrew Jackson's law partner, named his house after Jackson's favorite horse, Traveller. Admission is $5 per adult, $2 for children ages 6–12. Address: 636 Farrell Parkway. Phone: (615) 832-2962.

☆ **The Arcade**—This collection of shops is one of the oldest enclosed shopping arcades in the country. Visit the **P-Nut Shop** (you'll smell the roasting nuts as soon as you enter) and walk around the upstairs balcony where the frosted glass door offices look like Humphrey Bogart's in *The Maltese Falcon*. Address: Between Fourth and Fifth Avenues.

☆ **Belle Meade Plantation**—This historic house and its grounds were once the home of William Gates Harding, whose stables were famous in the early years of Tennessee statehood when Andrew Jackson rode mounts from Belle Meade. Admission is $6 per adult, $2 for children ages 6–12. Phone: (615) 356-0501. (1 hour)

☆ **Historic Belmont**—This antebellum mansion was built by Nashville's wealthiest woman, Adelicia Hayes Acklen, in 1850. Now located on the campus of Belmont University, it is worth a stroll through grounds still defined by a Palladian villa landscape plan and iron garden statuary. The house itself is filled with the high Victorian furniture and European decorative art collected by its mistress. Admission is $4 per adult, $1 for children ages 6–12. Phone: (615) 269-9537.

☆ **Life and Casualty Tower**—Nashville's first skyscraper, this late 1940s art deco building is a reminder of the city's historical prominence as an insurance center. L&C and National Life and Accident (now combined as American General) started in Nashville, as did American Express. Until the Bell South Tower was built several years ago, no Nashville building had been allowed to exceed its 27-story height. Inquire about the observation deck for a great view of the city. Address: Fourth Avenue and Church Street.

☆ **Museum of Tobacco Art and History**—This museum to one of Tennessee's major cash crops is operated by U.S. Tobacco Company, whose snuff is still made next door. As tobacco farming fades from our landscape, this fascinating museum offers a glimpse into its distinguished past. It includes a good gift shop. Admission is free. Address: Eighth Avenue North and Harrison. Phone: (615) 271-2349.

✯ **Opryland U.S.A.**—The theme park, country music museum, and the Grand Ole Opry auditorium are all included in the Opryland complex. Tickets to the Opry, which is held on Friday and Saturday nights, cost $14–$16 and can be obtained by calling (615) 889-3060. During the summer months, there are matinee performances Tuesday and Thursday. The Opryland complex, owned by Gaylord Entertainment, also features a convention hotel, interpretive exhibits, the Roy Acuff Theatre for individual performances, and a year-round schedule of music-related activities. It is surrounded by a plethora of souvenir shops, restaurants, motels, and campgrounds that cater to country music fans. The Opryland theme park, which includes the museums, several live music shows, and amusement park rides, closes in October and reopens in March. A day pass for adults costs $26.95 and $16.95 for children ages 4–11.

✯ **Union Station**—Nashville's Romanesque Revival–style train station is now a hotel. The train shed behind, in dire need of restoration, is on

Country Music Hall of Fame

the National Register of Historic Places as one of the largest metal structures in the country. Address: Broadway.

✯ **Vanderbilt University** and **George Peabody College**—These two campuses are now part of the same university system. Stroll the tree-lined Vanderbilt University campus, whose oldest buildings date from 1873—the trees are labeled for an educational recreational experience. Stop in at the **Fine Arts Gallery**, located in the Victorian gymnasium; the modern **Sarratt Student Center**; and the main library **Special Collections** room to see current exhibits. Check the desk at the Sarratt Student Center for film, concert, and Great Performances series events. Address: West End and 21st Avenues South. Phone: (615) 322-2471. (1½ hours)

Belle Meade—Located where West End Avenue extends to become Harding Road, this is one of Nashville's wealthier neighborhoods. Belle Meade Boulevard is a favorite walking, jogging, and biking path for many. It ends in **Percy Warner Park**, a public park full of wooded hiking paths and paved drives through rolling Middle Tennessee hills.

Tennessee Performing Arts Center (TPAC)—This site is worth seeing only if the schedule of events is enticing. There are three theaters where you can find Broadway Shows and major musical performances in all genres, including the fine **Nashville Symphony**, **Nashville Ballet**, and **Nashville Opera**. Look for performances by the outstanding **American Negro Playwright Theater**, **Tennessee Dance Theatre**, and **Tennessee Repertory Theatre** groups. **Humanities Outreach Tennessee** offers special daytime performances for Tennessee schoolchildren throughout the year, so if you are traveling with kids, you might want to check it out. Address: 505 Deaderick Street. Phone: (615) 741-7975.

FITNESS AND RECREATION

Nashville has lots of parks for walking, jogging, and biking. The centrally located **Centennial Park** adjoins the **Centennial Sportsplex**, which features an indoor pool, outdoor tennis courts, and an ice rink. A nominal fee is charged for admission to the Sportsplex. For more information call (615) 862-8400. **Edwin and Percy Warner Parks**, located in west Nashville about 10 miles from downtown, are open year-round for hiking, running, and biking. **Edwin Warner Nature Center** offers educational programs and guided hikes for children, call (615) 352-6299. **Radnor Lake Natural Area**, on Otter Creek Road between Franklin and Hillsboro Roads, was a gift from the L&N Railroad to the state of Tennessee. It offers extensive hiking trails and a scenic drive by the lake and is open from dawn to dusk. Contact the visitor's center for information, (615) 373-3467. There is a large network of **YMCAs** in Nashville, and the downtown YMCA features a rooftop pool. The **Vanderbilt University Track** is open to the public. Check with Cumberland Transit, (615) 327-4093, and Bike Pedlar, (615) 329-2453, both on West End Avenue near Vanderbilt University, for information on local biking, rock-climbing, and water sports in the area as well as indoor recreation venues that might be open for public use.

Nashville is also a center for such recreational healing arts as therapeutic massage and yoga; check the *Nashville Scene* for listings. **Yoga Source**, at Cummins Station, (615) 254-9642, offers a full range of massage instruction, and the **Yoga Room** is a long-time Nashville favorite, (615) 383-6197. **West Side Athletic Club** offers evening yoga classes on a pay-as-you-come basis, (615) 352-8500.

FOOD

There are lots of options for interesting, moderately priced food in Nashville. The luxury restaurants can be easily duplicated or surpassed in other cities, so I would recommend saving your money for a nicer place to stay in the right part of town. One exception is the newly reopened **Capitol Grille** in the Hermitage Hotel (231 Sixth Avenue North). A cozy and elegant dining room located downstairs in this beautiful Beaux Arts building, the Grille has a new chef who is serving new American cuisine with a southern touch (dinner entrees $15–$25, also open for lunch, call 615-244-3121).

The most famous breakfast in town is at the **Loveless Motel and Café**, about 15 miles out in the country on Highway 100. The Loveless, which now has mail-order country hams and preserves, specializes in hot biscuits, redeye gravy, country ham, homemade peach and blackberry preserves, and fried chicken. Call for reservations, (615) 646-9700. Also open for lunch and dinner. Nearer at hand are: the **Pancake Pantry**, Hillsboro Village near Vanderbilt University, (615) 383-9333; **Slice of Life**, Division Street near Music Row, (615) 329-

NASHVILLE

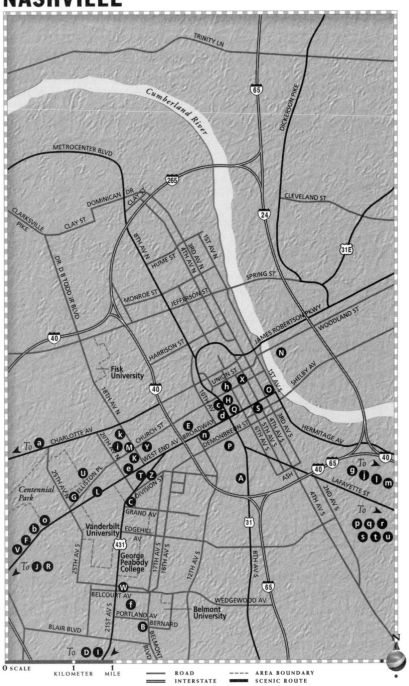

TRINITY LN

Cumberland River

65

DICKERSON PIKE

METROCENTER BLVD

CLEVELAND ST

265

DOMINICAN DR
CLAY ST

24

CLARKSVILLE PIKE

CLAY ST

CLAY ST

31E

DR. D B TODD JR BLVD

8TH AV N

HUME ST

MONROE ST

3RD AV N
4TH AV N

1ST AV N

SPRING ST

JEFFERSON ST

40

HARRISON ST

JAMES ROBERTSON PKWY

WOODLAND ST

Fisk University

18TH AV N

40

UNION ST

N

SHELBY AV

1ST AV S

10TH AV

h **x**

C **H** **O**
d **Q** **S**

3RD AV S
4TH AV S

HERMITAGE AV

To **a**

CHARLOTTE AV

20TH AV

k
i **M** **Y**
M **K**
e
T **Z**

CHURCH ST

WEST END AV

E
n

BROADWAY

DEMONBREUN ST

5TH AV S
6TH AV S

P

40

65

To **g** **j** **l** **m**

To **p** **q** **r**
s **t** **u**

25TH AV

U

GILLETON PL

G **L**

DIVISION ST

C

GRAND AV

A

ASH

40

2ND AV S

LAFAYETTE ST

Centennial Park

G **b**
o

V **F**

To **J** **R**

Vanderbilt University

EDGEHILL AV

31

4TH AV S

8TH AV S

25TH AV S

17TH AV S
16TH AV S

12TH AV S

65

George Peabody College

431

W

BELCOURT AV

f

PORTLAND AV

Belmont University

WEDGEWOOD AV

BLAIR BLVD

21ST AV S

BERNARD

B

BELMONT BLVD

To **D** **I**

N

O SCALE

| 1 | 1 |
KILOMETER   MILE

ROAD ———— AREA BOUNDARY

INTERSTATE ■■■■ SCENIC ROUTE

Food

- Ⓐ Arnold's
- Ⓑ Bongo Java
- Ⓒ The Boundry
- Ⓓ Bread & Company
- Ⓔ Café 123
- Ⓕ Cakewalk Café
- Ⓖ Calypso Café
- Ⓗ Capitol Grille
- Ⓘ Clayton-Blackmon
- Ⓙ Corner Market
- Ⓚ DaVinci's Pizza
- Ⓛ Elliston Place Soda Shop
- Ⓜ Garden Allegro
- Ⓝ Gerst Haus
- Ⓞ Ichiban
- Ⓟ Jules Bar Car
- Ⓠ Koto
- Ⓡ Loveless Motel and Café
- Ⓢ Merchant's
- Ⓣ Midtown Café
- Ⓤ Mosko's Muncheonette
- Ⓥ Nashville Bagel
- Ⓦ Pancake Pantry
- Ⓦ Provence
- Ⓖ Rotier's
- Ⓧ Satsuma
- Ⓨ Sitar
- Ⓩ Slice of Life
- Ⓦ Sunset Grille
- ⓐ Sylvan Park
- ⓑ Vandyland
- ⓒ Varallo's

Lodging

- ⓓ Clubhouse Inn
- Ⓦ Commodore Inn & Guest House
- ⓔ Days Inn West End
- Ⓧ Doubletree
- ⓔ Hampton Inn
- Ⓗ The Hermitage Hotel
- Ⓕ Hillsboro House
- ⓖ Holiday Inn
- ⓗ Holiday Inn Crowne Plaza
- Ⓘ Loew's Vanderbilt Plaza
- Ⓙ Marriott
- ⓚ Med Center Inn
- Ⓛ Opryland Hotel
- Ⓗ Renaissance
- ⓜ Sheraton
- ⓝ The Union Station
- Ⓞ Vanderbilt Holiday Inn

Camping

- ⓟ Anderson Road Campground
- ⓠ Cook Campground
- ⓡ Holiday Nashville Travel Park
- ⓢ Opryland USA KOA
- ⓣ Poole Knobs Campground
- ⓤ Seven Points Campground

Note: Items with the same letter are located in the same area.

2525, mostly health food and delicious, also open for lunch and dinner (great for people-watching); **Nashville Bagel**, 3009 West End Avenue, (615) 329-9599, they bake their own bagels for sit down or take out; and **Bongo Java**, 2007 Belmont Boulevard, a funky coffeehouse with an innovative menu and carry-out baked goods, open 7 a.m.–midnight (615) 385-5282. The newly opened **Provence** on 21st Avenue South in Hillsboro Village has great coffee and french pastries and breads (615-386-0363).

Lunch options range from "meat and three" plate lunches, to gourmet carry-out, to elegant power lunch restaurants. In the inexpensive category try: **Varallo's**, downtown on Church Street; **Arnold's**, at 605 Eighth Avenue South; or **Sylvan Park**, at 4502 Murphy Road, for an authentic down-home experience. You'll rub shoulders with some interesting folks and taste some real Southern cooking.

A Nashville original is **Gerst Haus**, 228 Woodland Street, (615) 256-9760, the former tasting room restaurant for Nashville's Gerst Brewery. Worth it for the atmosphere, and some of the food is quite good. Although it is no longer brewed in Nashville, you can get the tasty reddish Gerst beer on tap. Open for dinner; Sunday nights feature polka dancing.

Three great old lunch counters near Vanderbilt University are **Elliston Place Soda Shop**, 2111 Elliston Place, (615) 327-1090; **Rotier's**, 2413 Elliston Place, (615) 327-9892; and **Vandyland**, 2916 West End Avenue, (615) 327-3868. Vegetarians will like **Garden Allegro** on 1805 Church Street. Moderate prices accompany a trip for exceptional carryout sandwiches and more from **Mosko's Muncheonette** at 2204 Elliston Place, (615) 327-3562; **Clayton-Blackmon** at 4117 Hillsboro Road in Green Hills (615-297-7855); **Bread & Company** at 4105 Hillsboro in Green Hills and at 106 Page Road in Belle Meade; and the **Corner Market** at Westgate Shopping Center in Belle Meade. If you are in the mood, treat yourself to a civilized lunch at **Satsuma**, a downtown "tearoom" that serves delicious comfort food, including the best yeast rolls I've ever tasted (417 Union Street, 615-256-0760). Open only for lunch, it is usually crowded, so go early or late. **Koto**, 137 Seventh Avenue North, (615) 255-8122, and **Ichiban**, 109 Second Avenue North, (615) 254-7185, are downtown Sushi restaurants, both exceptional and both open for dinner. **Midtown Café** (102 19th Avenue, 615-320-7176), **Cakewalk Café** (3001 West End, 615-320-7778), and the **Sunset Grille** (2001 Belcourt Avenue, 615-386-3663), all in the Music Row and Vanderbilt University area, serve some of Nashville's best lunches to Nashville's best-known customers. Prices are moderately expensive but worth it. All are open for dinner. Other wonderful dinner options in this price range would include **Café 123**, 123 12th Avenue North, and **The Boundry**, 911 20th Avenue South, (615) 321-3043. Less expensive and less formal, but still great dinner choices would include: **Sitar** (Punjabi) at 21st and West End Avenues (615-321-8889); **DaVinci's Gourmet Pizza**, on 1812 Hayes Street, which has many innovative vegetarian selections (615-329-8098) and **Calypso Café** (Americanized Caribbean) at 2424 Elliston Place, (615) 321-3878.

At the end of the day, or after an evening of music, try **Jules Bar Car** at Cummins Station for a sunset cocktail or a nightcap. Featuring pool tables and a view out over the railroad tracks, Jules restaurant serves a late night menu on weekends. **Merchant's**, located in an historic lower Broadway drug store, 401 Broadway, used to be one of my favorites, but it is now pricey and inconsistent. Their ground-floor bar, however, still has a nice ambiance and features live jazz on weekend nights.

LODGING

The area around Vanderbilt University and Music Row is the most desirable location for lodgings away from the tourist attractions, as Nashville is a city of neighborhoods. Neighborhood hotels are all but nonexistent in Nashville now. There are two bed and breakfast reservation services in Nashville at (615) 331-5244 and (615) 383-6611. There are also two statewide services with toll-free numbers: (800) 947-7404 and (800) 458-2421. Two B&Bs in convenient locations near Hillsboro Village are **Commodore Inn and Guest House**, (615) 269-3850, and **Hillsboro House**, (615) 292-5501. There are a number of acceptable, larger hotels in this area including **Loew's Vanderbilt Plaza** (inquire about corporate rates and weekend specials, for this is primarily a business establishment, 615-320-1700). Other good choices include the **Vanderbilt Holiday Inn**, (615) 327-4707; **Hampton Inn**, (615) 329-1144; **Med Center Inn**, (615) 329-1000; and **Days Inn West End**, (615) 327-0922. Downtown choices include the exceptional ambiance of the **Union Station**, (615) 726-1001, and the **Hermitage**, (615) 244-3121, both in historic buildings (again, inquire about weekend specials). The **Holiday Inn Crowne Plaza**, (615) 259-2000; **Doubletree**, (615) 244-8200; and the **Renaissance**, (615) 255-8400, all in the center of downtown, are fine modern hotels.

The **Clubhouse Inn**, Ninth Avenue and Broadway, is a remodeled Sheraton, (615) 244-0150. Near the airport, a group of similar hotels includes **Marriott**, (615) 889-9300; **Sheraton**, (615) 885-2200; and **Holiday Inn**, (615) 834-0620. **Opryland Hotel**, (615) 883-2111, is a colossal convention hotel. Avoid the cheap motels on Murfreesboro Road, Nolensville Road, and Eighth Avenue South, and exercise caution at any of the inexpensive motels just off the interstate highways.

CAMPING

There are several campgrounds near Opryland, off Briley Parkway, where your neighbors are likely to be country music aficionados. Try **Holiday Nashville Travel Park**, (615) 889-4225, or **Opryland U.S.A. KOA**, (615) 889-0282. Both are open year-round and feature lots of sites and hookups. Another, more pleasant-sounding, option would be to stay near Percy Priest Lake, although these sites may be crowded in summer. Some options in that area include: **Anderson Road Campground**, (615) 361-1980, no hookups; **Cook Campground**, (615) 889-1096; **Poole Knobs Campground**, (615) 459-6948, no hookups (all of these are open May–September); and **Seven Points Campground**, (615) 889-5198, hookups, open April–November.

NIGHTLIFE

For music in Music City, the first thing you should do on arrival is check club listings in *The Tennessean*, *The Banner*, and the *Nashville Scene*. If you don't see any names you know, just go anyway; you'll be glad you did. Try the **Station Inn** at 402 12th Avenue South (bluegrass and traditional music, 255-3307) for some of the best picking around; **Bluebird Café** (4104 Hillsboro, 383-1461), **Douglas Corner Café** (2106 Eighth Avenue South, 298-1688), or **The Sutler** (1608 Franklin Road, 297-9195) for singer-songwriters and small bands. Try **328 Performance Hall** (328 Fouth Avenue South, 259-3288), **12th and Porter Playroom** (Exit/In, 2208 Elliston Place, 321-4400), or **Ace of Clubs** (114 Second Avenue South, 254-ACES), for major acts in club venues. A new Nashville hangout is a small joint outside of town in Leiper's Fork named **Green's Grocery**. It's the former Ernie's Smokehouse, where local musicians and their often famous friends from out of town go to pick for each other. Call (615) 790-0117 and see if they will tell you who might be stopping in.

Tickets to the **Grand Ole Opry** can be obtained at Opryland (615) 889-6611 and are sometimes difficult to find in tourist season. Also check the schedule at the **Ryman Auditorium** (615) 889-6611 before you make a final decision about the Opry, which can be more of an event than a musical experience. The Ryman's fine acoustics and almost sacred past make any performance there something special.

The **Tennessee Performing Arts Center (TPAC)** hosts the very fine Nashville Symphony season, along with the Nashville Opera, Nashville Ballet, and Tennessee Repertory Theatre. Broadway shows and other traveling companies can also be found at TPAC. Call Ticketmaster at (615) 737-4849 for details.

Multiplex theaters in and around Nashville show first-run Hollywood offerings. **Belcourt Theater** in Hillsboro Village, (615) 742-8123, and **Sarratt Cinema** at Vanderbilt University, (615) 322-2471, show first-run foreign films along with "avant-garde" American films. **Franklin Cinema**, on Main Street in Franklin, (615) 790-7122, does the same and serves beer. Nashville is also home to the **Sinking Creek Independent Film Festival**, which premieres new independent films each November. Call (615) 322-3485 for special events at other times of the year.

Sports options include **Vanderbilt University's** basketball teams (both men's and women's can be counted on year in and year out), (615) 322-3544, and the **Nashville Sounds** offers fine minor league baseball action, (615) 242-4371. The **Nashville Knights** (ice hockey) will soon face off in the new 10,000-seat arena downtown, and there are serious rumblings about bringing major-league football to Nashville, so stay tuned for other sporting events. (615) 255-7825.

HELPFUL HINTS

Nashville has two public radio stations that do a fine job advertising public events and local cultural happenings—**WPLN** at 90.3; and **WMOT**, a primarily jazz-oriented station from Middle Tennessee State University in Murfreesboro, at 89.5. The *Nashville Scene* (www.nashscene.com) is a fine weekly alternative paper that can be found free all over town—check it out for music, film, and art gallery listings. I also recommend the new *Nashville Life*, a bimonthly magazine with a lively informative tone that covers the cultural life of the city.

For a great souvenir of Nashville, pick up a six pack of **GooGoo Clusters**—chocolate covered mounds of caramel, marshmallow, and peanuts. The debate rages on over whether the acronym for this candy invented in 1912 actually stands for Grand Ole Opry, and **Standard Candy Company** isn't talking. Standard Candy also makes old-fashioned straight peppermint sticks that come packed in their famous blue metal King Leo can. You can call them at (800) 226-4340 to place an order.

Nashville, a major publishing center, has a number of good bookstores. **Davis-Kidd Booksellers** (4007 Hillsboro Road, 292-1404), with several stores in other Tennessee cities, started here. Check out **Elder's** (2115 Elliston Place, 327-1867) and **Dad's Old Books** (4004 Hillsboro Road, 298-5880) if you are in the market for antique books. The **Southern Festival of Books** and its companion, Antiquarian Book Fair, sponsored by the Tennessee Humanities Council, take place in early October on Legislative Plaza downtown. If you can plan your trip to include this wonderful free event—which brings authors and audiences together in intimate settings and promotes the love of reading for all ages—do it. For more information about the festival, call (615) 320-7001.

Scenic Route: Antebellum Home Tour of Franklin and Columbia

A drive out Franklin Road (Hwy 31) or Hillsboro Road (Hwy 431) will take you through Tennessee horse country. **Franklin**, 20 miles southwest of Nashville, was founded in 1799 and is one of the best-preserved and restored historic towns in the region. **Carter House**, an 1830 antebellum home, was the site of the November 1864 Battle of Franklin. **Historic Carnton Plantation**, an 1826 plantation house located just outside the city, served as a hospital after the battle. Pick up the newly published "Tennessee Antebellum Trail" brochure at one of these houses; it will direct you to others in the region, or call (800) 381-1865. Admission to Carter House is $5 per adult, $1.50 per student. Phone: (615) 791-1861. Admission to the Carnton Plantation is $5 per adult, $1.50 per student. Phone: (615) 791-0903.

There are many good antique shops in and around Franklin, and several galleries and craft shops on and around Main Street. A pleasant morning or afternoon could easily be passed here.

ANTEBELLUM HOME TOUR OF FRANKLIN AND COLUMBIA

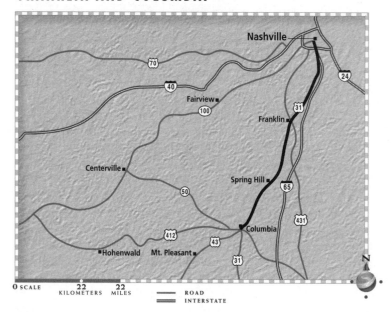

Choices Restaurant, at 108 Fourth Avenue South, is excellent for a lunch or dinner splurge. Behind Choices is **Merridee's Bread Basket**, which makes great sandwiches on whole-grain breads. Set aside two to three hours for browsing around Main Street.

Continue south on Hwy 31 to **Spring Hill**, where you can pick up a driving tour of the area at the public library at Main and Depot Streets. Before the Civil War, the gently rolling farmlands of Maury County were one of the wealthiest parts of the state. Today, Spring Hill houses the GM Saturn car plant, which stands surrounded and virtually hidden by the vast acreage purchased from many of the old families in the area. Many of the grand brick homes for which this section is known once stood on large plantations and bear such poetic names as *Rippa Villa* and *Walnut Grove*. In 1850, Columbia, which has a well-preserved downtown historic district, was the third largest city in Tennessee, after Memphis and Nashville. The presence of many plantations means that slave labor was a major factor in the prosperity of the region.

The **Mount Lebanon** area of downtown Columbia was the site of the first Baptist Church (1843) for free blacks in Tennessee. The Canaan community, located out Mt. Pleasant Pike, was settled by freed slaves after the War ended. **The Canaan School for Blacks**, which was founded in 1917, educated many local citizens until after World War II. **Rippa Villa**, just outside of Spring Hill, is open as a visitor's center and museum for the surrounding area. You can pick up the APTA (Association for the Preservation of Tennessee Antiquities) guide to the area there. Driving around, you'll see lots APTA markers designating sites that are not necessarily open to the public, testaments to the dense architectural wealth of this community. You can visit the **Atheneaum** (1835) and the boyhood home of James K. Polk (1816) in downtown Columbia. You can also pass by the private **Clifton Place** (1838), home of Gideon Pillow; **Hamilton Place** (1831), home of Lucius Polk; and **Bethel Place** (1830s), another Polk family home, on your way to **Rattle and Snap** (circa 1850), the home of George Washington Polk. Admission to *Rattle and Snap* is $7.50 per adult, $5 per senior, $2.50 for children ages 6–12. Address: 6 miles south of Columbia on Hwy 243. Phone: (615) 379-5861. (2–3 hours) ◼

2
MEMPHIS

High on the bluffs overlooking the Mississippi River stands the city of Memphis. Once a mid-fifteenth-century Mississippian Indian site known as Chucalissa, it is now a town of about 1 million inhabitants. Memphis calls itself the home of the blues and the birthplace of rock 'n' roll. The city can back both claims—W.C. Handy wrote "Memphis Blues" here in 1909 as a campaign song for E.H. "Boss" Crump, and Sun Recording Studios nurtured the mid-1950s boogie-woogie blues style that Elvis Presley promoted with "Hound Dog" and "Don't Be Cruel" into a worldwide music mania.

Once a gathering place for former slaves after the Civil War, Memphis seems destined to have played a major part in the twentieth-century drama of American race relations. Today the Lorraine Motel, where Martin Luther King was shot in 1968, has been preserved as part of the National Civil Rights Museum, located within a few blocks of W.C. Handy's famous Beale Street neighborhood. Several blocks away, Front Street faces the river and is still "Cotton Row," a site of active commerce as bales of cotton arrive from points south in late summer, just as they have for generations. The famous downtown Peabody Hotel, where visitors can marvel at the opulence that cotton money built, has been restored to its former splendor, as has the Orpheum Theater, where one can hear Opera Memphis just a stone's throw from the all-night music on restored Beale Street. ◼

MEMPHIS

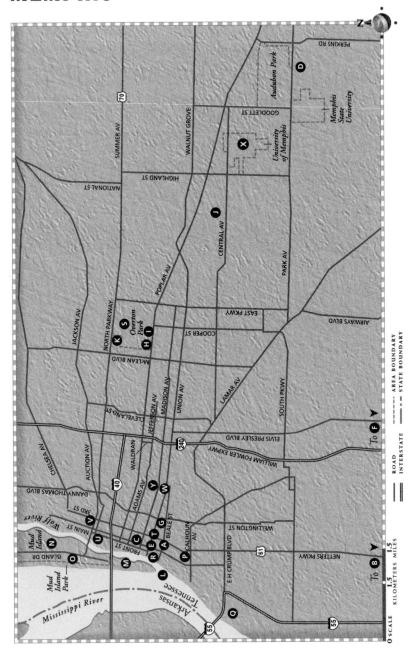

Sights

- **A** Beale Street
- **B** Chucalissa
- **C** Cotton Row and Main Street Trolley
- **D** Dixon Gallery and Gardens
- **E** Fire Museum of Memphis
- **F** Graceland
- **G** Hunt-Phelan House
- **H** Memphis Brooks Museum of Art
- **I** Memphis College of Art
- **J** Memphis Pink Palace Museum and Planetarium
- **K** Memphis Zoo
- **L** Mississippi Riverfront
- **M** Mississippi River Museum
- **N** Mud Island
- **O** Mud Island Museum Park
- **P** National Civil Rights Museum
- **Q** National Ornamental Metal Museum
- **R** Orpheum Theater
- **S** Overton Park

- **T** Peabody Hotel
- **U** The Pyramid
- **V** Slavehaven, the Burkle Estate
- **W** Sun Studio
- **X** University of Memphis Art Museum
- **Y** Victorian Village

A PERFECT DAY IN MEMPHIS

Overton Park is a great place for an early morning walk or jog, especially before the heat of a summer's day arrives. After coffee at Otherlands Coffee Bar on Cooper, get over to Sun Studios for a tour, and stop in at Delta-Axis Gallery around the corner in the Marshall Arts artist's studio co-op. Visit the back-to-back Memphis Brooks Museum of Art and Memphis College of Art and have lunch at the Brooks' Brushmark Restaurant whose patio seating overlooks the park. Head downtown for a tour of the National Civil Rights Museum then continue south down historic Main Street to the National Ornamental Metals Museum. Located on a high bluff, the west-facing gardens offer a nice sunset view overlooking the Mississippi. Stop for drinks in the cocktail lounge of the Peabody Hotel for great people watching and a glimpse of the famous ducks who live on the roof. Dine across the street at Automatic Slim's Tonga Club, and ask at the bar where to go for Memphis nightlife.

MORE MEMPHIS HISTORY

Before the Europeans arrived in the person of Hernando DeSoto in 1541, Mississipian period Indians dwelt near the modern city on the shores of the powerful wide brown river, called by the Chickasaw "Father of the Waters". The restored fifteenth-century village of Chucalissa, a Choctaw word meaning "abandoned house," is located just south of the city and can be visited today. The French founded Fort Assumption on the high bluffs overlooking the river in 1739, the same location as the modern city. Modern Memphis was founded by Andrew Jackson's close friend Judge John Overton of Nashville in 1819, after the Chickasaw Indian treaty of 1818 ceded control of West Tennessee to the United States. Overton named it for the ancient Egyptian city whose name meant "place of good abode." River trade made Memphis prosperous, and the city's capture was a boon to the Federal Forces in 1862.

SIGHTSEEING HIGHLIGHTS

If you want to get a feel for the breadth of Memphis, take Poplar Avenue, one of the city's main east-west arteries, into town from the I-240 loop. Poplar, which dead-ends at the river, runs from suburban neighborhoods and prosperous shopping centers to less-affluent commercial areas, past mid-town's Overton Park and its historic neighborhoods, and through the industrialized no-man's land of downtown right into the River City.

★★★ **Beale Street**—Ike Turner once said you could once find "anything you were looking for" on Beale Street. This famous street is close to downtown Memphis and within walking distance of the Peabody Hotel. There are lots of touristy music clubs and restaurants on Beale now, including one owned by the reigning godfather of the blues, Mr. B.B. King. You can also visit the **Daisy Theater**, which is now the **Beale Street Blues Museum**, and see performances at the **New Daisy Theater** to get a sense of the old ambiance of Beale. **W.C. Handy's Home**, at Beale and Fourth, has been made into a museum that charges a modest admission fee of $2 per adult, $1 per student. Phone: (901) 522-1556. **The Center for Southern Folklore**, a nonprofit institution dedicated to the preservation of Southern folk culture and expression, has a storefront at 130 Beale, where you can watch their excellent *All Day and All Night* documentary about historic Beale Street and pick up a printed walking tour. Phone: (901) 525-3655. (1–2 hours)

★★★ **Chucalissa**—A restored fifteenth-century Choctaw Indian village, this site includes mounds and a plaza, as well as exhibits on southeastern Indians. It is managed by the Department of Anthropology at University of Memphis, which has also included a working excavation trench display. Call ahead to make sure they are open. Admission is $3 per adult, $2 per child. Address: Take Third Street south to Winchester Road, and turn right on Mitchell. Phone: (901) 785-3160. (1 hour)

★★★ **Graceland**—Walking through the faded decor of Elvis' "mansion" with a freshly combed young tour guide, spending time in the gaudy "trophy room" of Elvis excess, standing at the memorial garden and reading the sentiments on floral arrangements that arrive in quantity on a daily basis, and finally being deposited at the huge commercial operation across the street is enough to make one weep for the failure of innocence and the corruption of the American Dream. The 20-minute film that begins your visit is quite good. Using lots of old footage, it chronicles the incredible appeal of the young Elvis. Entrance to the visitor's center and gift shop is free, if you just want to pick up souvenirs. There are separate charges for all other parts of the complex, which includes the airplane, automobile, and memorabilia museums in addition to the house itself. Parking costs $2. The basic mansion tour is $9 per adult, $4.75 for children 12 and under. An all-inclusive ticket is $17 per adult, $11 for children 12 and under. Phone: (800) 238-2000 or (901) 332-3322. (1–3 hours)

★★★ **Memphis Brooks Museum of Art**—Housed here are collections ranging from classical to contemporary art and a portion of the Kress collection of Italian Renaissance masterpieces. This excellent museum mounts important temporary exhibitions in their extensive changing exhibit galleries. There is a continuous schedule of films, lectures, and family workshops throughout the year. And the Brushmark Café serves consistently good food at moderate prices. Admission to the museum is free, except for special exhibits. The museum stays open late on Thursday evenings. Phone: (901) 722-3500. (1½ hours)

Mary Entrekin

★★★ **Memphis Zoo**—This popular attraction was founded in 1906 and has a distinctive Egyptian-style pillared gateway. Admission is $6 per adult, $4 per child. The zoo is open year-round, with seasonal hour changes. Phone: (901) 276-WILD. (2 hours)

★★★ **National Civil Rights Museum**—The architects designed this building to incorporate the Lorraine Motel, where Dr. Martin Luther King was assassinated in 1968, into the museum itself. The museum features interactive exhibits that make visitors feel as if they are experiencing these dramatic moments in our country's history for themselves. Admission is $5 per adult, $4 per student, and $3 for children 12 and under. Hours: Open until 6 p.m. in summer; closed Tuesday. Phone: (901) 521-9699. (1½ hours)

★★★ **National Ornamental Metal Museum**—Located on a bluff overlooking the Mississippi River at the south end of town, this is my favorite undiscovered museum in Tennessee. Not only does it feature a permanent collection of decorative and utilitarian objects made of metal, but it has a regular schedule of changing exhibits that includes some of the finest contemporary work in metal being done today. The facilities include a gift shop with unusual handmade items and an outdoor working blacksmith shop—the last time I was there they were restoring a huge statue of Elvis. Admission is $2 per adult, $1 per student. The museum is closed Monday. Phone: (901) 774-6380. (1½ hours)

★★ **Memphis Pink Palace Museum and Planetarium**—A hybrid history and natural history museum, the Pink Palace is located in a palatial pinkish stone home that once belonged to the owner of Piggly Wiggly grocery stores. The museum is now home to an eclectic range of permanent exhibits, changing exhibits, and a new IMAX theater whose inaugural presentation is "Ring of Fire." Phone (901) 320-6362 for IMAX reservations. Call for admission prices. Open daily. Address: 3050 Central. Phone: (901) 320-6320. (1½ hours)

★★ **Orpheum Theater**—A beautifully restored 1928 vaudeville playhouse, the theater is essentially the intersection of Main and Beale. The schedule at the Orpheum includes both music and musical theater productions. Check to see if **Opera Memphis** is performing here while you are in town; they have been creating excellent original productions (some based on William Faulkner stories) for the past several years. Call for the schedule of performances and to inquire about tours of the building. Address: 203 S. Main. Phone: (901) 525-7800 or (901) 525-3000.

★★ Peabody Hotel—Memphis' historically elegant hotel features an ornate, gilded interior architecture that sparkles and lends an air of excitement to just sitting in the lobby bar, watching the well-heeled clientele. Promptly at 11 a.m. and 5 p.m., a small cadre of ducks are paraded off of an elevator and around the lobby before being returned to their rooftop home. Children will be delighted by this freebie, whose Boston counterpart was chronicled in Robert J. McCloskey's children's classic *Make Way for Ducklings*. Address: Second and Union Streets. Phone: (901) 529-4000. (½ hour)

★★ Sun Studio—Still an active recording studio, this is the spot where musicians can feel the vibes of their famous predecessors like Elvis, Carl Perkins, Johnny Cash, Roy Orbison, and Jerry Lee Lewis. Admission is $7.50 per adult, free for children under 12. Hours: Open daily for tours, from 9:30 a.m. to 6:30 p.m.; gallery/gift shop and café are open 9 a.m. to 7 p.m. Address: 706 Union. Phone: (901) 521-0664. (1½ hours)

★ Cotton Row and Main Street Trolley—Take in Front Street's Cotton Row and hop on the restored **Main Street Trolley** line to get a feel for old Memphis for only 50 cents. The trolley operates until midnight every day except Sunday. Phone: (901) 577-2640.

★ Dixon Gallery and Gardens—Housing a noted collection of Impressionist art, this museum is located in the Dixon Mansion and surrounded by seasonally landscaped gardens. The museum has nice galleries in an adjacent wing for changing exhibits of fine and decorative arts and is open every day but Monday. The gardens are open Mondays for half the regular admission price of $5 per adult, $3 per student, $1 per child. Address: 4339 Park Avenue. Phone: (901) 761-5250. (1½ hours)

★ Fire Museum of Memphis—Currently under construction, the museum is located in the Fire Engine House #1, which dates from 1910. It will offer a complete history of firefighting as well as a reference library. Phone: (901) 452-9973.

☆ **Mississippi Riverfront**—The Mississippi Riverfront area has recaptured the imagination of local officials and is currently being redeveloped. The face-lifting originally began in 1982 with a monument to the river: **Mud Island Museum Park**. Marking the northern boundary of downtown's riverfront footage is **The Pyramid**, a new 32-story glass indoor sports arena. Stroll or walk the riverfront area, taking the monorail to **Mud Island (☆☆)** to see an interpretive outdoor scale model of the river and visit the **Mississippi River Museum**. Admission to the grounds only is $2 per person, while admission to all attractions it is $6 per adult, $1 for children under 12. Phone: (800) 507-6507. (1–2 hours)

☆ **Overton Park**—Located in midtown, this scenic park includes not only a public golf course, but also the city's zoo and art museum. Also located amidst the winding walking paths and driving lanes of this lovely park is the **Memphis College of Art**, which has a fine academic art program, a gallery open to the public, and an active children's art program. Phone: (901)726-4085.

☆ **Slavehaven, the Burkle Estate**—Slavehaven, built by German immigrant Jacob Burkle in 1849, served as a way station on the Underground Railroad. A tour of the house reveals secret tunnels and trap doors. On display are artifacts that tell the story of the slave era. Admission is $5 per adult, $3 per student. Advance reservations are required. Address: 826 N. Second Street. Phone: (901) 527-3427. (1 hour)

☆ **University of Memphis Art Museum**—Housing permanent collections of Egyptian and West African art, the museum also features an outstanding yearly schedule of contemporary exhibits. Admission is free. Phone: (901) 678-2224. (1 hour)

☆ **Victorian Village**—Several of the homes in an area along Adams Avenue have been restored to period splendor and are now open to the public. The **Woodruff-Fontaine House**, at 680 Adams, is an 1870 French-style dwelling that features changing exhibits of textiles, clothing, and antique furniture. Admission is: $5 per adult, $2 per student. Phone: (901) 526-1469. The **Mallory-Neely House**, at 652 Adams, dates from circa 1850 but was remodeled in 1890. It is closed Monday and during January and February. Admission is $4 per adult, $3 per student. Phone: (901) 523-1484. The tiny clapboard **Magevney House**, 198 Adams, was built in the 1830s and is furnished in the period. Admission is free, and Magevney House is also closed January and February. Phone: (901) 526-4464.

Hunt-Phelan House—This home, along with **Slavehaven**, was an active site during the Civil War and has recently been opened to public view. The staunchly Old South residents at the **Hunt-Phelan House** vacated their home when the city was occupied by Union forces in June 1862. It became Grant's headquarters for some months and was later used as a sort of Federal Red Cross hostel, where some of the first teachers who came south under the auspices of the Freedmen's Bureau were boarded. The house was returned to the family, who brought back a lot of the original furnishings and spent a number of years repairing and restoring the house. The Freedmen's Bureau school on the grounds is being restored. Admission is $10 per adult, $9 per student, $6 for children ages 5–12. Hours: Open daily in summer, weekends in winter. Address: 553 Beale. Phone: (901) 344-3166. (1 hour)

Memphis also has a number of fine contemporary art galleries, both nonprofit and commercial. A partial listing would include: **Rhodes College Clough Hanson Gallery**, (901) 726-3000; **Delta Axis Gallery** (cutting-edge nonprofit space), (901) 522-9946; **Kurts Bingham Gallery** (national and regional artists), (901) 683-6200; **Albers Fine Art** (fine craft emphasis), (901) 683-2256; and **Ledbetter Lusk** (new this year, regional emphasis), (901) 767-3800.

FITNESS AND RECREATION

In Memphis you need places to cool off in the summer. There is a YMCA downtown with an old indoor pool, and most of the downtown hotels (including the Peabody) have indoor fitness facilities with pools. The suburban hotels and the Union Street Holiday Inn have outdoor pools. There is also a pool at Mud Island, and access is included in the general admission fee. The Memphis Park Commission has a number of public swimming pools and tennis courts around town call (901) 325-5759 for locations.

On cool mornings or evenings going to a park is popular with Memphians. **Overton Park**, in midtown, makes a great place to bike, walk, or run. There is also a public golf course in the park. Phone:

(901) 725-9905. The **Lichterman Nature Center**, 5992 Quince
Road, has a 3-mile trail and a 10-acre lake. It is primarily an environmental education center and wildlife sanctuary set in the midst of 65
acres. Admission is $2 per adult, $1 for students and seniors. The
center is closed Monday. Phone: (901) 767-7322.

There are two state parks in the Memphis area, both of which
offer recreational facilities. **Meeman-Shelby**, 15 miles north of the
city, has swimming, boating, horseback riding, and hiking. It is open
daily until 10 p.m. and admission is free. Phone: (901) 876-5215.
T.O. Fuller State Park, which includes the **Chucalissa
Archeological Museum** within its boundaries, has an 18-hole golf
course and a swimming pool. Phone: (901) 543-7581.

FOOD

Memphis calls itself the pork barbecue capital of the world, but it may
be *the* barbecue capital of the world, with nearly 100 BBQ restaurants.
The Memphis in May World Championship Cooking Contest and the
Mid-South Fair every fall feature competitive barbecue pits. Chopped
pork and slabs of ribs, served with a sweet, thick sauce, are what I think
of as Memphis BBQ. Recommendations for Memphis' best are a tough
call, for everyone you ask has a different favorite, and there are many
neighborhood eateries that see few outside customers. The best recom-
mendation is the site of a smoking pit out back.

All over town you will find **TOPS**. The atmosphere is nothing
special, and the pork sandwiches are on the greasy side, but it's the real
thing—barbecue cooked in an on-the-premises pit. **Corky's BBQ** has
several locations, including 5259 Poplar, and they ship around the
country (901-685-9744). Their crusty pork sandwiches and lightly
charred, very tender ribs are good. **John Will's,** at 5101 Sanderlin,
winner of the Mid-South Fair BBQ Cook-off, comes highly recommended. One of the top local favorites is the 1950s-style hangout
called the **Pig 'n' Whistle**, with two locations (2740 Bartlett and 7144
Winchester). Made famous in a John Hiatt song, the **Rendezvous**,
downtown at 52 S. Second near the Peabody Hotel and Beale Street,
serves an unusual, dry slab of ribs. This large restaurant has a nonetheless cozy atmosphere, but it does a substantial tourist business, so you
might want to call ahead (901-523-2746). If you want to sample what
many experts across the state consider the ultimate pork barbecue,
make the journey 40 miles east on Hwy 70 to Mason, Tennessee,

MEMPHIS

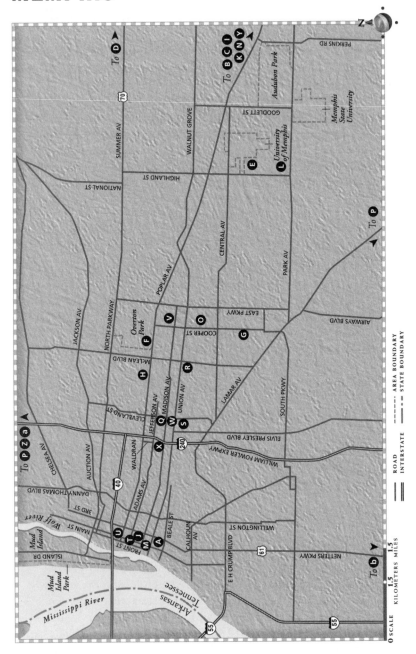

Food

- Ⓐ Automatic Slim's Tonga Club
- Ⓑ Belmont Bar and Grille
- Ⓒ Bosco's
- Ⓓ Bozo's Pit Bar-B-Q
- Ⓔ Brother Juniper's College Inn
- Ⓕ The Brushmark Restaurant
- Ⓐ Café Espresso
- Ⓖ Café Ole
- Ⓗ Café Society
- Ⓘ Corky's BBQ
- Ⓙ Cupboard Too
- Ⓚ John Will's
- Ⓛ La Montagne
- Ⓜ Little Tea Shop
- Ⓝ Lulu Grille
- Ⓖ Marena's
- Ⓞ Otherlands Coffee Bar
- Ⓟ Pig 'n' Whistle
- Ⓐ Rendezvous
- Ⓠ Saigon Le
- Ⓡ Squash Blossom
- Ⓢ TOPS

Lodging

- Ⓣ Comfort Inn Downtown
- Ⓤ Crowne Plaza
- Ⓥ French Quarter Suites
- Ⓦ Hampton Inn
- Ⓡ Holiday Inn Union
- Ⓧ Lowenstein-Long House
- Ⓐ Peabody Hotel
- Ⓨ Ridgeway Inn

Camping

- Ⓩ Fort Pillow
- ⓐ Meeman-Shelby State Park
- ⓑ T.O. Fuller

Note: Items with the same letter are located in the same area.

where **Bozo's Pit Bar-B-Q** has been in operation since 1923. It is now owned by the daughter of its founder, Thomas J. "Bozo" Williams.

For breakfast try **Brother Juniper's College Inn**, near the University of Memphis, at 3519 Walker, (901) 324-0144, or grab a fresh-baked scone at **Otherlands Coffee Bar**, 641 S. Cooper (open 8–8 daily).

Lunch suggestions include **Café Ole** in the Cooper-Young area at 959 S. Cooper. It's friendly and inexpensive and serves imaginative neo-Mexican dishes, (901) 274-1504. The **Little Tea Shop**, at 71 Monroe, was established in 1910 and is Memphis' oldest restaurant. It's open Monday–Friday and serves Southern-style plate lunches, (901) 525-6000. The **Cupboard Too**, at 149 Madison, was voted the #1 restaurant for home-cooked food by *Memphis* magazine, (901) 527-9111. **Café Espresso**, at the Peabody Hotel downtown and at the Ridgeway Hotel on 5679 Poplar, along with **The Brushmark Restaurant** at Memphis Brooks Museum, (901) 722-3555, are all fine

Unicorn/Ron Holt

upscale lunch spots. The **Squash Blossom**, now on Union Avenue and also at 5101 Sanderlin, is a locally popular health food store with a lunch counter. **Automatic Slim's Tonga Club**, 83 S. Second in downtown, serves fresh, lively cuisine at moderate prices for lunch or dinner, (901) 525-7948. **Bosco's**, which claims to be Tennessee's first brewpub, is located at 7615 W. Farmington, (901) 756-7310.

A local favorite for dinner is **Marena's**, 948 S. Cooper, which serves lively continental and Mediterranean cuisine in an old house and is worth a splurge. Call for reservations, (901) 725-1009. **La Montagne**, 3550 Park, serves gourmet vegetarian specialties in a cozy atmosphere, (901) 458-1060. **Café Society**, 212 N. Evergreen, is a charming and friendly midtown spot that serves delicious nouvelle cuisine. The fine **Lulu Grille**, at 565 Erin Drive, and the **Belmont Bar and Grille**, at 4970 Poplar, whose specialty is the steak sandwich, are neighborhood restaurants with faithful followings, as is **Saigon Le**, 51 N. Cleveland, a wonderful, inexpensive Vietnamese restaurant near Memphis College of Art.

LODGING

Famous beyond reason but quite nice, the **Peabody Hotel** is Memphis' only historic luxury hotel, (800) PEABODY. Other downtown hotels include the **Crowne Plaza** at 250 N. Main on the riverfront, one of the first luxury Holiday Inns in the country since that company started in Memphis, (800) 2-CROWNE. The **Comfort Inn Downtown**, 100 N. Front, has double rooms with a river view for $85, (800) 228-5150. Near the medical center area are some reasonably priced national chain hotels such as **Hampton Inn**, 1180 Union. In midtown, the **Holiday Inn Union**, 1837 Union, is convenient and quiet, and the **French Quarter Suites**, at 2144 Madison, are also convenient but cater to executives and charge high rates—ask about weekend specials. At I-240 and Poplar are a number of hotels, including the very nice **Ridgeway Inn** at 5679 Poplar, whose restaurant Café Espresso is good and moderately priced. Phone: (800) 822-3360.

Bed and breakfast accommodations in Memphis can be obtained through a local clearinghouse service, Bed and Breakfast in Memphis, Box 41621, Memphis, TN 38174-1621, call (901) 726-5920 for information or, for reservations only, call (800) 336-2087. **Lowenstein-Long House**, 217 N. Waldran Blvd., is convenient to both downtown and midtown and is an interesting historic house. It is furnished with antiques, and perfectly adequate but not fancy. It has hostel accommodations on the premises, and breakfast is a self-service affair, good rates, phone: (901) 527-7174.

CAMPING

Memphis is a big, spread-out city. It would not occur to me to want to camp there. For the more dedicated camper, however, there are two state parks (call 800-421-6683) with facilities relatively nearby: **T.O. Fuller** (near Chucalissa Village) has camping and **Meeman-Shelby State Park**, 15 miles north, has cabins. **Fort Pillow**, 50 miles north, also has campsites.

NIGHTLIFE

Check the *Memphis Flyer* alternative weekly paper or the *Memphis Commercial Appeal* for listings. If you are a dyed-in-the-wool blues fan, listen to local radio station WEVL, located in the low 80s on the FM band to find out what is happening on the blues scene, as it is not always found in the local media. This radio station, the most grassroots flavored one I've ever heard, is run by volunteers. Listening in will help anyone understand why Memphis is the blues capital of the world.

Memphis nightlife runs the gamut from so-smoky-you-can't-stand-it blues bars, to fine local theater, to opera. The nightclubs on Beale are now sanitized and popularized versions of the real thing, for the most part. Not to be ignored, however, is **B. B. King's Blues Club**, which features a stellar lineup nearly every night. The "King of Beale Street" stops in every now and again (901-524-KING). To find others, you'll have to inquire in the right places, for they are mostly in neighborhoods around town. Theater performances are regularly scheduled at **Playhouse on the Square**, at Overton Square, 51 S. Cooper, (901) 726-4656, and the **Circuit Playhouse**, at 1705 Poplar, (901) 726-4656. **Opera Memphis**, a fine local opera theater group, performs at the **Orpheum Theater**, 197 S. Main, and also puts on Broadway-type shows and classical and popular music. The Orpheum can be reached at (901) 525-3000. The **University of Memphis** has both an excellent theater and fine music program. Call to see what is playing during your visit.

Poetry readings and local roots-oriented theater can be found in conjunction with the **Blues City Cultural Center**. The **New Daisy**, on Beale, also mounts a variety of local blues and rock performance events, (901) 525-8979. Lest you think Memphians groove only on blues and jazz, check out the variety of **Newby's** bill, (901) 452-8408, or the large, high-energy dance club **Six One Six**, at 616 Marshall, which features rave nights, disco nights, and national rock music acts (closed Monday, 902-526-6552). There is a lively alternative rock scene in Memphis, home to ARDENT studios, so look for local heroes like Mudboy and the Neutrons among the club listings.

Memphis is also a sports-oriented town, and the shiny new **Pyramid** hosts University of Memphis basketball games, professional hockey, and other sports. For information call (901) 678-2331.

Scenic Route: Hwy 64, Memphis to Savannah

State highway 64 runs across the southern part of Tennessee, roughly paralleling the border, from Memphis to Monteagle. Because this is truly the road less traveled, much of it is far from any interstate highway. There are many small, very Southern-seeming towns along the way that have remained much as they were in the nineteenth century. The scenic route at the end of Chapter 4 is centered in the area where Hwy 64 ends. The route described here remains within West Tennessee, bounded on the east by the Tennessee River and on the west by the Mississippi River.

Headed east out of Memphis on Hwy 64/100, you'll be on the "barbecue road" to quote a friend who has tried them all, so watch for smoke rising behind small general stores and country eating establishments. About an hour outside of Memphis, where 64 and 100 split at **Whiteville**, there is a wonderful Mennonite bakery. If you follow Hwy 100, which deviates toward the northeast, for 13 miles you'll come to **Chickasaw State Park**, an area of high timberland reclamation in the 1930s by the Civilian Conservation Corps. This park has a swimming lake, cabins with

HWY 64, MEMPHIS TO SAVANNAH

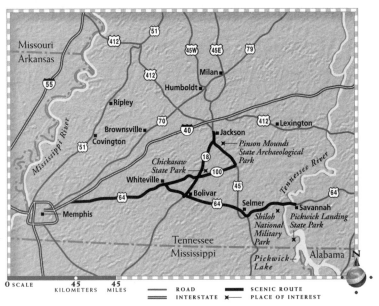

fireplaces, horseback riding, and a campground with hookups, (901) 989-5141.

Another 15 or so miles northeast is **Pinson Mounds State Archeological Park**. A Mississippian Indian ceremonial and burial site dating back earlier than 500 A.D., Pinson contains 12 mounds including Saul's Mound that, at 72 feet tall, is the second tallest in the country. Administered by the Tennessee Department of Conservation, Pinson Mounds and its interpretive museum are well worth going out of your way to see. Phone: (901) 988-5614. About 10 miles north of Pinson is Jackson, the largest city between Memphis and Nashville, located right on I-40.

Jackson, named in honor of Battle of New Orleans hero Andrew Jackson when it was founded in 1821, claims its own local heroes: Casey Jones, Carl Perkins, and Sonny Boy Williamson. You'll find a **Casey Jones Museum and Restaurant Complex** and **Carl Perkins' *Suedes*** restaurant in Jackson, along with a strip of national chain motels and restaurants. If you are lucky enough to arrive in June, you might get to set up your own lawn chairs and taste the homemade barbecue at the **Shannon Street Bluesfest**, held at the West Tennessee Farmer's Market, which honors Sonny Boy Williamson. Call the Jackson Convention and Visitors Bureau to find out the exact dates, (901) 425-8333.

From Jackson, take Route 18 south for 30 miles (the southeasterly Hwy 64 fork at Whiteville also takes you) to **Bolivar** (pronounced BAH-liv-er), an antebellum town that seems almost literally to rise from the cotton fields. This was plantation country, and the early 1800s brick residences in this charming town seem the epitome of the Old South. The courthouse square is intact, and **Magnolia Manor**, now a bed and breakfast, is in the town's historic district, (901) 658-6700. At Selmer, 23 miles east on Hwy 64, you can visit the still-operating **Hockaday Broom Company**, run by Jack Martin, grandson of the founder. Call to let him know you are coming, (901) 645-4823.

Shiloh National Military Park is on the Tennessee River, just southwest of Savannah, and can be reached by Route 142 from Selmer or by staying on Hwy 64 and turning south on Route 22 before you reach Savannah. The eight-day Battle of

Shiloh in April of 1862 engaged a number of famous generals and had an enormous casualty count: 24,000 soldiers or one-fifth of the Union men and one-fourth of the Confederate force. The battle was a major loss for the Confederates, who lost control of important supply lines along the Tennessee River and West Tennessee. The park is open daily. The visitor's center shows a film explaining the complexly orchestrated battle, and the 9-mile driving tour of the battlefield has explanatory markers along the way. South of Shiloh is the enormous Pickwick Lake, created in 1935 by a massive 1½ mile long dam on the Tennessee River. **Pickwick Landing State Resort Park**, which is a very popular vacation spot for Tennesseans and Alabamians, has a modern lodge and cabins and offers boating, swimming, golf, and camping, (901) 689-3135. East of Shiloh is **Savannah**, whose designated "Historic Trail" tells the stories of local American Indians and of those who passed this way on the Trail of Tears. Where it runs along the river, it tells also about the ferry run by Alex Haley's grandfather and points out Civil War sites. The **Tennessee River Museum**, operated by the Chamber of Commerce, is open daily, (800) 552-3866.

From Savannah you can continue across the southern part of the state on Hwy 64, through the picturesque towns of Waynesboro, Lawrenceburg, Pulaski, Fayetteville, and Winchester until you reach Monteagle, a favorite mountain retreat and summer chatauqua for many Tennesseans. Or you can head north to Nashville on the scenic **Natchez Trace Parkway** (no billboards allowed), which intersects Hwy 64 about 25 miles east of Savannah. This two-lane National Park Service road, which runs for 450 miles from Nashville to Natchez, bears interpretive markers describing its history and importance even before it was first documented as an Indian trail by French explorers in 1733. For information, call (800) 305-7417. ◼

3
KNOXVILLE

This hilly city, whose landmarks in the "Old City" bear witness to its prominence as a railroad and manufacturing center, has a fine view of the Great Smoky Mountains, and is home to the state's largest university community, the University of Tennessee. Knoxville was once an American frontier outpost. At the site where the confluence of the Holston and French Broad Rivers becomes the Tennessee River, pioneer James White built a fort in 1786. Visitors will find his 20-by-30-foot cabin, reconstructed from the original hand-hewn logs, plus the 1792 William Blount mansion, right in downtown Knoxville. Blount, who was the first territorial governor of "the United States South of the River Ohio" built a comparatively elegant 2-story frame home near White's trading post and gristmill, and christened the small town Knoxville to honor Major General Henry Knox, Secretary of War under President Washington. Tennessee's constitution was drafted by Blount and Andrew Jackson in Blount's office. In 1796, Tennessee became the sixteenth state, and Knoxville became its first capital.

Today's Knoxville is a city on the move. It boasts the largest and newest art museum in the state and the new Museum of East Tennessee History. Its highways are undergoing a needed expansion, while the watchful eyes of local environmental groups attempt to safeguard the fragile East Tennessee environment. Outdoor recreation abounds in the areas surrounding Knoxville—the Great Smoky Mountains National Park, the Cumberland Plateau of the Appalachian Chain, and the Tennessee River Valley. ◪

DOWNTOWN KNOXVILLE

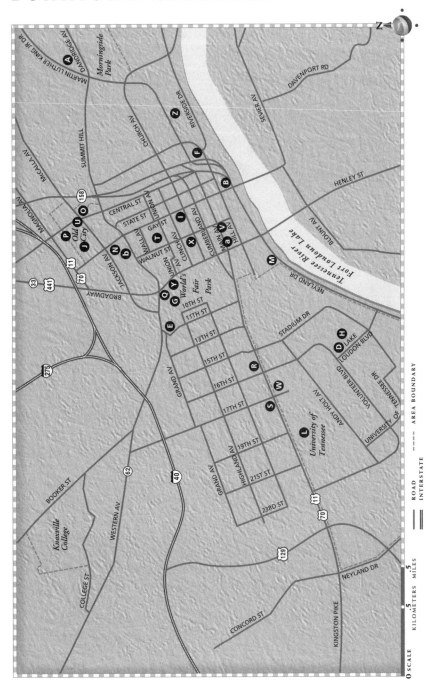

Sights

A Beck Cultural Exchange Center

B Blount Mansion

C Candy Factory

D Ewing Gallery of Art and Architecture

E Fort Kid

F James White Fort

G Knoxville Museum of Art

H McClung Museum of Natural History and Anthropology

I Museum of East Tennessee History

J Old City

K Sunsphere

L University of Tennessee

Q Parisi's

R Sunspot

S The Varsity

T Tomatohead

U Tomo

Lodging

V Blakely House

W Campus Inn

X Hilton

Y Holiday Inn, Downtown

Z Hyatt

a Middleton House Bed and Breakfast

b Radisson

Food

M Calhoun's

N Harold's Deli

O Java

P Lucille's

A PERFECT DAY IN KNOXVILLE

Stop for coffee at Java in the Old City before heading uptown for a visit to the Museum of East Tennessee History, the James White Fort, and Blount Mansion. Look east from the high ground of downtown for a surprisingly good view of the Great Smoky Mountains. Next, the Knoxville Museum of Art will provide late morning edification and a delicious light lunch at the Artist's Palette Café. A few blocks further west is the University of Tennessee (UT) campus. Find the Ewing Gallery in the Art and Architecture Building for a glimpse into an enormous factory-like working art department. Ask at the gallery, which generally has excellent shows, for a guide to the UT Sculpture Tour, a changing exhibit of outdoor sculpture arranged as a walking tour around the campus. While on campus, visit the McClung Museum of Natural History and Anthropology for an indepth look at Tennessee's prehistory. Take a late afternoon walk in Cherokee Park to catch the sunset by the Tennessee River. After dinner at the Sunspot, walk up to the Laurel Theater for the best in traditional acoustic music.

SIGHTSEEING HIGHLIGHTS

✯✯✯ **Blount Mansion**—The home of Governor William Blount, this historic mansion is just a few blocks away from the James White Fort, at the other end of Hill Avenue. The house has original late eighteenth-century furnishings that belonged to this first governor of the Southwest Territory. An admission fee is charged. The mansion is open year-round, closed Monday. Address: 200 W. Hill Avenue. Phone: (423) 525-2375. (1 hour)

✯✯✯ **James White Fort**—This group of original and reconstructed buildings houses authentic artifacts. The fort is closed Monday and January–February. Call for specific hours and admission prices. Address: 205 E. Hill Avenue. Phone: (423) 525-6514. (¾ hour)

✯✯✯ **Knoxville Museum of Art**—Designed by Edward Larrabee Barnes, the museum features traveling exhibits and fine original shows of regional and national contemporary artists. There is also an exploratory gallery for students, a gift shop, and a restaurant. On Friday evenings the museum is open late for "Alive after Five," a radio broadcast of a local jazz performance. Admission is free. Phone: (423) 525-6101.

★★★ **Museum of East Tennessee History**—This museum, sponsored by the East Tennessee Historical Society, has an excellent orientation film that will change the way you see the whole region. An important repository for the region, it contains collections of documents, genealogy materials, works of art, and artifacts that are vital to the history of the area. Address: 600 Market Street. Phone: (423) 544-4318.

★★★ **Old City**—A walk through this district will take you by brick warehouse buildings near the railroad tracks, the JFG coffee roasting plant, and several worthwhile antique stores.

★★ **Marble Springs**—The home of John Sevier, first governor of Tennessee, Marble Springs was built in 1796. It is located outside of Knoxville on the old road leading to Sevierville. An admission fee is charged. Open year-round, closed Monday. Address: 1220 W. Governor John Sevier Highway. Phone: (423) 573-5508.

★★ **Ramsey House**—The first stone house built in Knoxville, Ramsey House dates from 1797 and was designed by an English architect. Closed in winter. Address: 2614 Thorngrove Pike. Phone: (423) 546-0745.

★★ **University of Tennessee**—This scenic campus sprawls on either side of Cumberland Avenue just west of downtown Knoxville. Outstanding sites for visitors are the **Ewing Gallery of Art and Architecture** (423-974-3200), where you can pick up a catalogue and walking map of the campus **Sculpture Tour**, and the **McClung Museum of Natural History and Anthropology** (423-974-2144). The Sculpture Tour, which enables the University to have a changing exhibit of large-scale sculpture on campus, is an innovative idea that has caught on. Sculptors come to Knoxville from all over to leave a piece on site, since opportunities to display outdoor sculpture are rare. UT also purchases one piece every year for its permanent campus collection. The McClung Museum is one of the few resources in the state for the study of the Indian civilizations that preceded the white settlement of Tennessee. Here, and at the Tennessee State Museum in

Nashville, you will see some incredible finds—including two 30-foot-long poplar canoes made from single straight trees. You'll also learn what researchers have interpreted from the implements and ornaments of the Cherokee and the Mississippian Indians, who built towns and ceremonial sites here, and the Woodland Indians, who wandered these lands and owned traded items from as far away as the Gulf of Mexico. Admission is free. Open daily.

✰ **Beck Cultural Exchange Center**—This research facility is dedicated to the achievements of African Americans in Knoxville. Admission is free. Hours: Tuesday–Saturday, 10 a.m.–6 p.m. Address: 1927 Dandridge Ave. Phone: (423) 524-8461.

✰ **Candy Factory**—Located next door to the Knoxville Museum of Art, the Candy Factory was built in 1919 by Littlefield and Steere, makers of Red Seal candy. You can take a tour of the candy manufacturer's quarters (423-546-5707). The building also houses the **Knoxville Arts Council** gallery and several others. Just a block away is the "artist's colony" on 11th Street, where Victorian houses contain art and craft studios. Behind the Candy Factory building is the 1982 World's Fair site, home of the **Sunsphere** observation tower which offers a wonderful view of the mountains on a clear day. Hours: Monday–Friday, 10 a.m.–3 p.m. Across the street from the museum and Candy Factory is **Fort Kid**, an innovative playground that always seems to have a few kids in it, even on weekdays.

DAY TRIPS FROM KNOXVILLE

Since Knoxville is located at the juncture of two natural wonders, the Tennessee River and the Smoky Mountains, and in the midst of historical and present-day pockets of culture such as the Appalachian and Native American, it makes a good base from which to explore. I've listed several daylong itineraries you might wish to try.

✰✰✰ **Norris, Tennessee**—Located about 35 miles north of Knoxville, off I-75, on Hwy 441, Norris is situated in the foothills of the Cumberland Mountains. This small community, established in 1934, was one of the first planned communities in the country. It is the home of **Norris Dam**, the first dam built by the Tennessee Valley Authority (TVA). The Regional Library System in Tennessee, which still sends bookmobiles out over rural roads, started here as a book depository for the workers building the dam. The City Hall/Police/ Fire Department has a map and brochure. You can tour the 1930s chrome-trimmed, Deco-influenced power house and stay in the rustic cabins that are now part of **Norris Dam State Park**. This park has two campgrounds with hookups, and also has beautiful wooded hiking trails. Call ahead to arrange a tour of the power house. Phone: (423) 632-1825.

The **Lenoir Pioneer Museum,** just above the city of Norris before you go into the park, has a collection of artifacts that range in dates from Indian times to the Great Depression. It also has a working gristmill. Admission is free, but call ahead to make sure they are open. Phone: (423) 494-9688 or 494-7461.

If you take Hwy 61 to the park, you'll pass the highly recommended **Museum of Appalachia,** which consists of two large exhibit buildings with a 65-acre working Appalachian farm community attached. There are 30 authentic log outbuildings on the premises. Local resident John Rice Irwin, whose family was among the pioneer settlers in the area, has labored for many years to build his dream—a repository that celebrates the ingenuity of mountain folk. The museum collection, which in places is arranged almost like a flea market, contains many objects that may have never been seen by most people although, in many cases, they are still in use at working rural homesteads tucked back into the hills. There is a relatively new music museum, which celebrates those who come from the upper east Tennessee area in particular. This unpretentious institution is filled with the pride of its creator, who may seem a bit of a promoter to the museum purist—but Irwin's a hardscrabble survivor, and his museum is a public success story. Be sure to inquire about the famous October Homecoming Celebration if you'll be here in the fall. Admission is $6 per adult, $4 for children ages 6–15. Phone: (423) 494-7680. Right across the road from the museum is a nice little barbecue restaurant that's open 7 days a week.

Also nearby is the **Community Crafts Co-op**, where you can purchase contemporary pieces made by artisans in the local area. Phone: (423) 494-9854.

✸ **Oak Ridge**—This infamous little city is located about 25 miles west of Knoxville. You can visit the **Oak Ridge National Laboratory** grounds on a self-guided driving tour, or if you have a group of five, you can arrange for a free guided tour with 30 days advance notice. Phone: (423) 574-4163. The **Oak Ridge Visitor's Center** and the **American Museum of Science and Industry** are both free and open daily. There is sort of a defensive air here, not surprising among folks who have dedicated their lives to something so controversial. But seeing this once-secret place from today's historical perspective might prompt new insights into the endeavors of 50 years ago, and Oak Ridge is an oddly interesting community with an aging population of creative, quirky scientists who support cultural activities with a vengeance.

If you choose to stay overnight, check in at the **Oak Ridge Community Arts Center** or the visitor's center to see if the Oak Ridge Symphony is in performance, or if there are any art, dance, or theater events in town. You can contact the visitor's center for information on hotels and restaurants in Oak Ridge and to inquire if pending security regulations at ORNL have been enacted, which may change the visitor policy. Phone: (423) 482-7821.

FITNESS AND RECREATION

Run, bike, or walk in **Cherokee Park** along the Tennessee River and you will see most of Knoxville's fitness devotees. The rest of them are at the **YMCA** downtown or the **UT climbing gym**. The **Third Creek Bicycle Trail** winds around the town, and more greenways are under construction. There are tennis courts in public parks and on the UT campus (accessible in summer). For organized canoeing and rowing activities, check with local stores such as **Blue Ridge Mountain Sports** (423-588-2638) and **River Sports Outfitters** (423-523-0066). **Willow Creek** and **Whittle Springs** golf courses (423-675-0100 and 423-525-1022, respectively) are two nice ones open to the public. The **Ijams Nature Park** (423-577-4717) offers wildlife observation and nature walks.

If you desire a rewarding half-day uphill hike in isolated woods without going to Great Smoky Mountains National Park, try **House Mountain State Park**, about 15 miles north of town on Rutledge Pike (423-933-6851).

For information about regional geology, flora, fauna, and local outdoor groups, check the bookshelves at the outdoor equipment stores or try the Tennessee-based **Davis-Kidd Booksellers** at 113 North Peters Road, (423) 690-0136.

FOOD

The **Sunspot**, on Cumberland Avenue (known as "The Strip") near the UT campus, is my favorite restaurant in Knoxville. Open for lunch and dinner, it features an unpretentious atmosphere, imaginative cuisine that nods toward healthy but always has a filet mignon special, friendly service, and moderate prices (1909 Cumberland, 423-524-3380). In the Old City, **Tomo** has fine sushi and wonderful udon (423-546-3308). A block away, **Lucille's** has good food and live jazz. This is a Knoxville favorite, so call for reservations, (423) 546-3742.

If it suits your mood, a drive out Hwy 441 Chapman Highway (southeast), about 10 miles toward the mountains, will take you to the wonderful **Ye Olde Steakhouse**, in a rustic log building (423) 577-9328. Budget-conscious travelers or strict vegetarians will like **Tomatohead** (12 Market Square, 423-637-4067) for good eats in the Old City, and **Litton's Market and Restaurant**, an old neighborhood favorite at 2803 Essary Drive, off Broadway in the Fountain City area (423-688-0429). For atmosphere that will appeal to kids, try **Parisi's** in the old L&N depot, (423) 522-8400, or **Calhoun's**, for barbecued ribs and a view of the river, at 400 Neyland Drive, (423) 673-3355.

For breakfast, **Java** coffeehouse in the Old City has excellent baked goods and is open early. So is **Harold's Deli** on Gay Street, which serves a classic lox, eggs, and bagel breakfast, and the **Varsity**, a Greek-style diner near UT, which has been serving great cheap food to students since time began. All three serve lunch. If you want to pack your own picnic, go to the **Fresh Market** on Kingston Pike, a gourmet grocery store with carry-out foods and a bakery.

LODGING

Downtown Knoxville is full of executive hotels, most of which offer weekend specials with the exception of convention bookings and football season. You'll find the **Holiday Inn**, downtown next to World's Fair site and Convention Center, (423-522-2800); the **Marriott Fairfield**, 9 miles west of the city; and the **Hyatt**, **Radisson**, and **Hilton**, all in the center of town. Also downtown are **Middleton House B&B** (new, with 15 rooms), (800) 583-8100 and **Blakely House**, 26 executive suites in a remodeled old hotel, (423)-523-6000.

GREATER KNOXVILLE

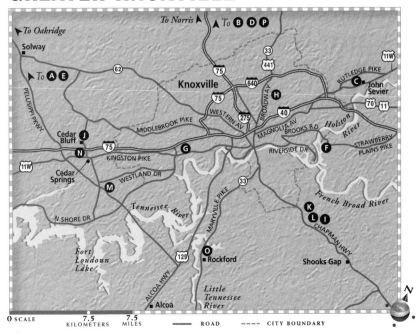

Sights

A American Museum of Science and Industry

B Lenoir Pioneer Museum

C Marble Springs

D Museum of Appalachia

E Oak Ridge Laboratory

F Ramsey House

Food

G Fresh Market

H Litton's Market and Restaurant

I Ye Olde Steak House

Lodging

J Hampton Inn

K Hilltop Inn

J Holiday Inn, Cedar Bluff

L Lakeview Motel

M Maple Grove Inn

N Ramada

O Wayside Manor Bed and Breakfast

Camping

P Norris Dam State Park

Note: Items with the same letter are located in the same town.

Near UT, try the **Campus Inn**, (423) 521-5000, and in west Knoxville at the Cedar Bluff exit are **Hampton Inn, Holiday Inn**, and **Ramada**. Also in the area is the **Maple Grove Inn**, a historic 1799 home that is now a resort and meeting place, (423) 690-9565. If you are headed to the mountains, or if you are flying into Knoxville you might want to stay south of town, on the way to the airport and the south entrance to Great Smoky Mountains National Park, at the **Wayside Manor B&B** (4 rooms, 1 cabin, 1 lodge); call (800) 675-4823. East of the city on Hwy 441 (Chapman Highway), the most direct—and therefore most crowded—route to the Smokies, you might try **Hilltop Inn**, at 4001 Chapman Hwy, (423) 577-1616, or the **Lakeview Motel**, 6133 Chapman Hwy, (423) 577-7621.

CAMPING

Norris Dam State Park has two campgrounds with hookups that are available on a first-come, first-served basis. You can call the park at (423) 632-1825 to check availability. There are many commercial campgrounds in and around Knoxville, but quality varies because this is such a heavily touristed area in summer. I would recommend relying on the state and national parks in the area for satisfactory camping arrangements. Call (800) 421-6683 for a Tennessee State Parks Information Package. The national parks in the area—Big South Fork National Wilderness Area, Obed Wild and Scenic River, Great Smoky Mountains, and Cherokee National Forest—are covered in other chapters of this book.

NIGHTLIFE

Check out the *Metro Pulse* free weekly for listings or tune into WUOT public radio at 91.9 FM to find out what's happening while you're in Knoxville. The **Laurel Community Theater**, built as a church in 1898, is just north of the UT campus in the Ft. Sanders historic neighborhood. Their programs focus on traditional arts of the region, contra dancing, and live acoustic music. They are also headquarters for innovative regional educational programs by Jubilee Community Arts (423-522-5851). The **Bijou Theater**, on Gay Street, is a restored downtown vaudeville theater that offers the best in national and regional music, including jazz, contemporary country, rock, and pop acts as well as ballet and theater, (423) 522-0832. The **Tennessee Theater**, a 1928 silent movie house also on Gay Street, shows movies with a live organ prelude and mounts stage productions and live concerts, (423) 525-1840. The **University of Tennessee** brings in nationally prominent pop, rock, and jazz concerts during the school year, as well as presenting classical and jazz performances from its own School of Music, (423) 974-3241. The **Theater Department** produces both musicals and dramatic performances, (423) 974-5161, and the university also has an outstanding film series. Check at the UT Student Center on Cumberland Avenue for information. Knoxville's **Symphony and Chamber Orchestra**, (423) 523-1178, as well as the **Opera Company**, (423) 523-8712, offer annual concert series. You can find excellent local programming on UT public radio, with the nightly "Improvisations," history of jazz show at 6:30 p.m.; "Unhinged," an eclectic new music show Friday nights at 10:00 p.m.; and "Live at the Laurel Theater" on Sunday at 5:30 p.m.

Knoxville is a mecca for sports lovers, with the nationally ranked **UT Vols** basketball (women's) and consistently strong football teams. The **Knoxville Smokies** play AA baseball for the Toronto Blue Jays.

Nightlife in the Old City revolves around **Java** and **JFG Coffeehouses**, and **Lucille's** outdoor jazz courtyard, while bars on "The Strip" are rowdy student scenes with occaisional live music.

Scenic Route: Hwy 411, from Knoxville to Cleveland, the Tennessee "Overhill"

Hwy 411 is the old main road from Knoxville to Atlanta whose path lay along the railroad route. It passes through what was once the home of the "Overhill" Cherokees, those who chose to settle on the western side of the Great Smoky Mountains. Today the region includes monuments to the Cherokee who lived here before the Indian Removal of 1838 in cities such as Toqua, Citico, Tuskeegee, Chota, and Tanasi (from which the name Tennessee was derived), all of which were inundated when the Tellico Dam project was completed in the late 1970s. Some sites, such as Toqua, were large cities built in the fifteenth century by Mississippian Indians. Further south in Englewood, Athens, Etowah, and Ducktown, you'll see relics and reminders of the late nineteenth- and early twentieth-century industrialization of the rivers, mountainsides, and open pasturelands of the Tennessee River Valley. Head east out of Knoxville on Hwy 129 for 17 miles to Alcoa, then south on Hwy 411. This route, a total distance of 90 miles, could be followed round-trip from Knoxville or could be taken to travel from Knoxville to Chattanooga or Atlanta.

Vonore, site of both the **Sequoyah Birthplace Museum** and the reconstructed **Fort Loudon**, is located just off Hwy 411 about 30 miles south of Alcoa. The Sequoyah Birthplace Museum is owned by the Cherokee and dedicated to Sequoyah, who lived from 1776 to 1843. In 1821, Sequoyah introduced an 86-character alphabet based on the syllables of the Cherokee spoken language. The museum contains artifacts excavated in the Tennessee Valley that provide evidence of pre-Cherokee habitation spanning as far back as 8,000 years, as well as interpretive exhibits explaining Cherokee history and culture. The museum also has a bookstore and shop featuring contemporary Cherokee crafts. On the grounds is a monument to the Cherokees who died in the Removal and remains from burial sites that were flooded by the TVA's Tellico Dam in the 1970s. The museum staff can direct you to monuments nearby that commemorate the flooded towns and ceremonial sites of their ancestors. The museum is open year-round. Phone: (423) 884-6246.

Fort Loudon, a fort built by the British with Cherokee permission and originally intended as protection for the Cherokee, existed from 1756–1760. The convoluted history of relations between the Cherokee leaders, British soldiers, the settlers who were soon to become Americans, and the first United States Indian Agents is clearly and sympathetically explained by Vicki Rozema in *Footsteps of the Cherokees: A Guide to the Eastern Homelands of the Cherokee Nation,* 1995, and also by Carroll Van West in the excellent *Tennessee's Historic Landscapes: A Traveler's Guide,* 1995. The remains of the Tellico blockhouse, built in 1794, can be seen. Here the first Indian Agents were stationed, sent not only for the protection of the Cherokee but also to negotiate any official business between the United States and the Cherokee. Tellico blockhouse also functioned as a trading post and served as an agricultural training center for the Cherokee. Call the Fort Loudon State Historic Site, (423) 884-6217.

Sixteen miles south is Englewood, which was founded in the late nineteenth century as a textile factory town. The **Englewood Textile Museum** has placed the emphasis of its interpretive

HWY 411

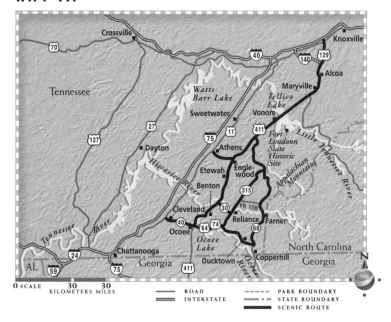

exhibits upon the story of women in the labor force of the Appalachian region. The museum is housed in actual mill buildings donated by the grandson of an early mill owner. (The little-known story of Depression-era labor strikes among women textile workers in Tennessee and surrounding states has been captured in the 1995 documentary film *The Uprising of '34*, directed by George Stoney.) Admission is free. The museum is closed on Sunday and Monday and during the winter months; call (423) 887-5455.

Athens, located about 10 miles west of Englewood, is the largest town in the region, with a population of around 15,000. The **McMinn County Living Heritage Museum** has three floors of exhibits on local culture. Their annual quilt show will surprise visitors with the extent of both tradition and innovation to be seen in this historic art form. Kids will want to tour the **Mayfield Dairy**, whose cheerful yellow trucks are seen all over the vicinity. Tours are free, and they have an ice cream parlor where you can sample their wares. Closed Sunday. Phone: (423) 745-2151. Because it is accessible from I-75, and about halfway between Knoxville and Chattanooga, Athens is a good place to spend the night for those who like to stay outside of the big city. If you want a special treat, try the **Woodlawn B&B**, located downtown in the 1858 Keith Mansion, (800) 745-8213. The **Holiday Motel**, small and locally owned, is also recommended. Athens is also home to a number of good places to eat. Try **Jenkins Restaurant & Deli**, which is known for its catfish, (423) 745-7671.

The town of **Etowah** ("muddy waters" to the Cherokee) was formed by the railroad, with the **L&N Railroad Depot**, built in 1906, as its first permanent structure. Today the beautiful, 3-story Victorian depot has a museum on its first floor; the Chamber of Commerce and Etowah Arts Commission upstairs. A permanent museum installation entitled "Growing Up with the L&N: Life and Times in a Railroad Town" was created by letting Etowah residents tell the story of this planned community of Appalachians, African Americans, and others who helped to build a portion of the modern southern industrial complex. Special events including craft exhibits and train excursions are held throughout the year. Admission is free, depot closed Monday. Call (423) 263-7840.

Further south on Hwy 411 you'll reach **Benton**, where Cherokee leader Nancy Ward, who struggled to make peace between the white settlers and the Overhill Cherokee, is buried. After about 8–10 miles, turn east on Hwy 64, a national forest scenic route winding 26 miles alongside the Ocoee River. The **Ocoee** ("place of the river people"), is a white-water river with Class IV rapids— site of 1996 Olympic trials and events. There are several professional outfitters that run group rafting expeditions on the Ocoee; call (423) 338-4133 for a listing. You'll be well within the **Cherokee National Forest**, a wonderland of outdoor recreational activity that offers wilderness activities, lake swimming and boating, camping, and horseback riding, in addition to white-water sports. Stop by the Ocoee Ranger Station on Hwy 64 or call (423) 338-5201 for information.

Ducktown and Copperhill, sites of major copper mines that operated for roughly 100 years beginning around 1850, offer startling evidence of environmental destruction, although federal reforestation efforts were begun as early as the 1930s. Mining operations at Ducktown's Burra Burra mine and others turned the **Great Copper Basin**—where the Cherokee had known of the rich deposits of copper ore long before they were "discovered" by those who moved in after the Cherokee Removal of 1838—into acres of denuded land covered with reddish residue from open-air copper smelting. Many Cherokee who remained behind became part of the regions labor force, working in mining, railroads, and other industries. The **Ducktown Basin Museum** offers tours of the mine and exhibits explaining the "industrial archaeology" of the region as well as the Cherokee heritage. For information, call (423) 496-5778.

From Copperhill, make a loop north through the Cherokee National Forest on Hwy 68, following 108 and 30 west along the Hiwassee River to Hwy 411. This will take you very near an18.8-mile section of **John Muir Trail** (from Farner to Reliance) that passes through some of the most diverse terrain in the forest, with a 3-mile scenic route beginning at **Reliance**. The historic Reliance community is a designated **trophy trout fishing** area; ask for information at Webb's or Adams Store. ◼

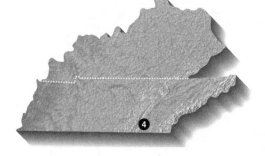

4
CHATTANOOGA

Coca-Cola® was first bottled in Chattanooga, Bessie Smith was born here, and the city's name has been immortalized in popular song. Its name derives from Creek Indians, who described Lookout Mountain as "rock coming to a point." Indians were familiar travelers of the Tennessee Valley long before Spanish explorer Hernando DeSoto "discovered" the area in 1540. By 1816, John and Lewis Ross had established a landing, warehouse, and ferry service in current-day downtown Chattanooga.

Chattanooga was a strategic supply line location during the War Between the States and the site of such major battles as Chickamauga and Lookout Mountain. Chattanooga's manufacturing economy attracted freedmen from all over the South after the war. Many African American entrepreneurs and professionals made their start here.

To hear some local historians tell it, the wealthy economic infrastructure of Chattanooga—one of the first southern cities to get back on its feet after the Civil War—has provided the wherewithal for Atlanta's resurgence. However, decades of exploiting natural resources have taken their toll on Chattanooga. For the past 10 years the city has been taking action to clean up its own air and water.

The Tennessee Aquarium, the first freshwater aquarium in existence, was built in 1992. It is located in Ross's Landing Park and Plaza, which is designed as a microcosmic "History Walk," combining public art and native plantings to tell the story of Chattanooga. ◼

CHATTANOOGA

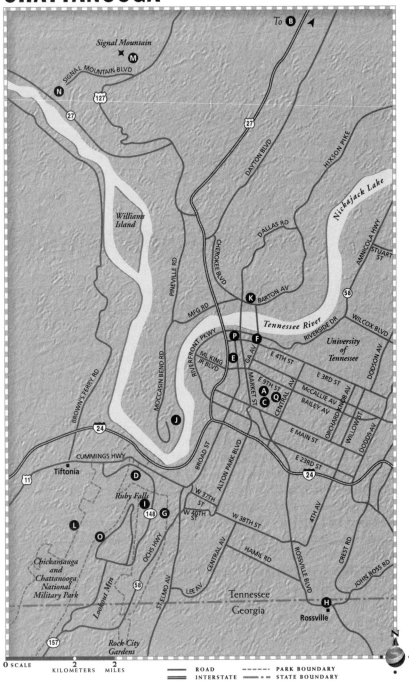

To **B**

Signal Mountain × **M**

SIGNAL MOUNTAIN BLVD

N

(127)

(27)

(27)

DAYTON BLVD

HIXSON PIKE

Williams Island

Nickajack Lake

PINEVILLE RD

CHEROKEE BLVD

DALLAS RD

AMNICOLA HWY

STUART ST

MFG RD

K BARTON AV

(58)

RIVERSIDE DR

WILCOX BLVD

Tennessee River

RIVERFRONT PKWY

P **F**

ML KING JR BLVD

E

GA AV

E 4TH ST

University of Tennessee

DODSON AV

E 3RD ST

MOCCASIN BEND RD

MARKET ST

E 9TH ST

A

CENTRAL AV

McCALLIE AV

KNOB AV

E 9TH ST

Q

BAILEY AV

ORCHARD

WILLOW ST

BROWN'S FERRY RD

C

DODDS AV

E MAIN ST

J

(24)

E 23RD ST

CUMMINGS HWY

(24)

BROAD ST

ALTON PARK BLVD

(11)

Tiftonia ■

D

Ruby Falls

I

(148)

G

W 37TH ST

W 40TH ST

4TH AV

W 38TH ST

OCHS HWY

L

O

CENTRAL AV

HAMIL RD

ROSSVILLE BLVD

CREST RD

Chickamauga and Chattanooga National Military Park

Lookout Mtn

(58)

ST ELMO AV

LEE AV

JOHN ROSS RD

Tennessee

Georgia

H

(157)

Rock City Gardens

Rossville

N

0 SCALE

2 KILOMETERS 2 MILES

——— ROAD   - - - - - PARK BOUNDARY
=== INTERSTATE   — - — STATE BOUNDARY

Sights

A African American Museum and Bessie Smith Music Hall

B Antique Warehouses

C Chattanooga Choo Choo

D Cravens' House

E Creative Discovery Museum

F Hunter Museum of Art

G Incline Railway

H John Ross House

I Lookout Mountain's Point Park

J Moccasin Bend

K North Shore Gallery

L Ochs Museum at Point Park

L Reflection Riding and the Chattanooga Nature Center

M Signal Mountain

N Signal Point Park

O Sunset Park

P Tennessee Aquarium

Q Warehouse Row

Note: Items with the same letter are located in the same place.

A PERFECT DAY IN CHATTANOOGA

After coffee and a pastry at Rembrandt's Coffee House, visit the nearby public sculpture garden overlooking the bluffs of the Tennessee River. One long block back will take you to the Hunter Museum of Art, with its fine Albert Paley iron gateway out front, its magnificent view of the river behind, and the finest collection of contemporary art in the State. The Back Inn Café across the street will serve you a gourmet luncheon on their outside patio. Drive through the Fort Wood neighborhood across the river, stopping at the North Shore Gallery for a peek at some of the South's best. Then move on to the African American Museum and Bessie Smith Music Hall. The innovative and mesmerizing Tennessee Aquarium will take up most of the afternoon but leave time for a quick shop at Warehouse Row. At the end of the day, drive up Lookout Mountain and watch the sunset from pretty little Sunset Park, aptly named, on the west side. Afterwards, have a long, leisurely dinner at the Southside Grill.

SIGHTSEEING HIGHLIGHTS

To get oriented in Chattanooga, you can listen to public radio on the University of Tennessee Chattanooga's WUTC, 90.5; pick up the monthly alternative paper *Chug*; or call the 24-hour "Arts Line" sponsored by Chattanooga's Allied Arts organization at (423) 756-ARTS.

✮✮✮ **African-American Museum and Bessie Smith Music Hall—** Just opened in February 1996, the museum and auditorium are located in a marvelous adaptive reuse building. The museum, which moved from smaller quarters, has both a collection of African Art and a permanent display of Chattanooga history with some fascinating artifacts. Admission to the museum is $1 per adult, 50 cents per child. Address: 200 E. Martin Luther King. Phone: (423) 267-1076. The music hall will feature concert performances, lectures, and special events of relevance to the Chattanooga community—particularly the strong African-American community. Phone: (423) 757-0020.

✮✮✮ **Chattanooga Choo Choo—**That famous old train station is now a Holiday Inn. You can still see the grandeur of its central terminal in the main lobby. The hotel's gourmet restaurant is actually an old dining car.

★★★ **Creative Discovery Museum**—Several blocks away from the aquarium, this museum for children of school-age and above provides indepth treatment and directed learning experiences in areas such as art, music, technology, and history. Any one of these could intrigue a child for an hour or so, according to one parent. The museum provides hands-on docents who help children start on their own particular quest. Admission is $7.75 per adult, $4.75 per child. Address: 321 Chestnut Street. Phone: (423) 756-2738. (2 hours)

★★★ **Hunter Museum of Art**—When touring this museum, be sure to look for James Cameron's circa 1852 portrait of Colonel Whiteside and his family. It includes a Lookout Mountain landscape with Moccasin Bend below and is one of the earliest and best Tennessee landscapes in existence. Don't miss the museum's own sculpture garden, and down the street, the public River Gallery sculpture garden (free admission) contains works by regional and national artists. Across the street from the museum is the River Gallery, which features some regional art but is primarily a craft gallery. Admission to the Hunter Museum is $5 per adult, $2.50 per child. Closed Monday. Address: Bluff View at Fourth and High Streets. Phone: (423) 267-0968. (1½ hours)

★★★ **Lookout Mountain's Point Park**—From here you have a fine view of **Moccasin Bend**, always strategic for controlling river access to points north and south, even prior to the Civil War. On September 20, 1782, a group of militiamen commanded by John Sevier, later the first governor of Tennessee, defeated an Indian party led by Cherokee Chief Dragging Canoe, one of the dissenters in the 1775 Treaty at Sycamore Shoals, in one of the final battles of the Revolutionary War. Also on Lookout Mountain, the **Cravens' House**, built in 1854, served as a headquarters for both sides during the Civil War. The **Ochs Museum at Point Park** (founded by newspaper executive Adolph Ochs, who purchased *The New York Times* in 1896 and whose family still runs it) interprets the battles that took place here for visitors. The "classic" tourist destinations of Rock City and Ruby Falls are located on the east side of the mountain. You might want to go for the kitsch. Tiny **Sunset Park**, a public park with beautiful west-facing views, has become a major rock-climbing destination so don't be surprised to find small groups of intent climbers around the corner of a path. (1½ hours) At the base of the mountain, 3917 St. Elmo Avenue, is the **Incline**

Railway, another popular tourist site. If you want the distinction of having ridden one of the world's steepest cable cars, go for it. Phone: (423) 821-4224.

✮✮✮ **Tennessee Aquarium**—Visitors learn about the history and ecosystem of the Tennessee River from its origins in the Appalachian mountains to its commingling with the Mississippi River at the Gulf of Mexico. The aquarium features a fine folk art exhibit across from the gift shop at the rear—you can see it without going through the aquarium. The plaza outside contains built-in historical and interpretive information. Admission is $9.75 per adult, $5.25 per child. Open daily. Address: Ross's Landing Plaza at the riverfront. Phone: (800) 262-0695. (2 hours)

✮✮ **John Ross House**—Built by his grandfather in 1779, this home is located right outside of Chattanooga. John Ross, who was one-eighth Cherokee, later became the Cherokee Nation's chief, a post he held for 38 years. Ross led his people over Walden's Ridge on the "Trail of Tears" in the forced expulsion of the Cherokee, a journey during which his wife and thousands of others died. Address: Hwy 27 south in Rossville, Georgia.

✮✮ **North Shore Gallery**—Dealing in the work of "outsider" or untrained artists, this gallery, housed in an old brick building, is one of the best places to see this kind of folk art. Address: Just across the river at 101 Frazier Ave. Call ahead to make sure they are open. Phone: (423) 265-2760.

✮✮ **Reflection Riding and the Chattanooga Nature Center**—This 300-acre arboretum, botanical garden, and wildlife- and nature-viewing site also includes Civil War battlefields and identifiable Cherokee paths and cabins. On the grounds is an environmental education center with handicapped access. Admission is $2.50 per adult, $1.50 per child. Phone: (423) 821-1160.

✮✮ **Signal Mountain**—Across the river from Chattanooga, this was a strategic Union supply signal point; visit **Signal Point Park** to learn more. Country music-making is alive and well at the **Signal Mountain Opry**; **Plum Nelly Craft Shop** has a terrific selection of fine art and crafts; and **Waycrazy's BBQ** is a local favorite. The Opry, a gathering of traditional bluegrass musicians, is held every Friday night from 8 p.m.–11 p.m. Admission is free.

✩✩ **Warehouse Row**—Located near the Choo Choo, Warehouse Row is another innovative adaptive reuse of railroad storage buildings. It features the best brand-name shopping that I have encountered anywhere.

Antique Warehouses—There are several of these large warehouses located on Hwy 153 north of town. These dealers hold estate sales in other cities and Saturday auctions in Chattanooga on a regular basis. Call **Clements, Mickey's**, or **Northgate** to see when the next scheduled auction might be.

FITNESS AND RECREATION

Chattanooga is an incredibly rich area for all manner of sports. If you are going to be staying for several days, request the *Southeast Tennessee Outdoor Recreational Guide* from the Chattanooga Visitors Bureau, (800) 322-3344. Outdoor sports enthusiasts should also check with local outfitters like River City Biking, (423) 265-7176, and Rock Creek Outfitters, (423) 265-5969, for advice.

There are biking and walking trails all around the riverfront, especially over the **Walnut Street Bridge** from downtown, which is billed as the longest pedestrian bridge anywhere. The **Riverwalk** includes children's play areas along the way and fishing docks. There are bike paths along **Tennessee Riverpark**, the **Moccasin Bend** loop road, and **North Chickamauga Creek** above the dam. Road biking is allowed in **Chickamauga National Battlefield, Cherokee National Forest**, and **Prentice Cooper State Forest**. Both mountain bikes and road bikes can be used in **Ocoee Ranger District**. Phone: (423)-338-5201.

Rock-climbing is a popular sport in this region, perhaps because there are so many exposed rock bluffs. The **"Tennessee Wall,"** a well-known destination, is close to downtown, and **Sunset Park** on Lookout Mountain has good climbs for beginning as well as intermediate climbers.

The Chattanooga area is the hang-gliding capital of the East and **Lookout Mountain Flight Park & Training Center** is the largest hang-gliding school in the U.S. For information contact Buzz Chalmers at (706) 398-3541.

Water sports, such as canoeing, kayaking, and white-water rafting are a big business on the **Ocoee** and **Hiwassee Rivers.** The summer Olympic events of 1996 were held on the Ocoee in Tennessee. There are lots of outfitters from which to choose; check the *Southeast Recreation Guide,* or call (423) 338-4133 for information.

FOOD

The **Big River Grille** (222 Broad, 423-267-BREW) is a brewpub near the Tennessee Aquarium, which, although sometimes noisy, serves consistently good food and is lively enough to keep youngsters happy. My favorite Chattanooga restaurant is **Southside Grill**, near the Choo Choo off Market Street at 14th and Cowart, (423) 266-9211. Southside serves terrific southern American cuisine (fried green tomatoes with smoked crawfish, for example), has good service, and is moderately expensive ($20–$25 entrees) but worth every penny. The **Back Inn Café**, near the Hunter Museum, has a view overlooking the river, a nice patio for sitting outside, and serves gourmet light lunches and dinners with friendly service. Prices are moderate, and they are almost always open, (423) 757-0108. Upstairs in the same building is the pricier French restaurant **LeDoux's.** Around the corner is **Rembrandt's Coffee House**, which makes great sandwiches and has beautiful pastries, (423) 757-0107. Near UT Chattanooga, at 414 Vine, is the **Vine Street Market**, a friendly, moderately priced restaurant that also has gourmet grocery items for sale in an adjacent room, (423) 267-8165. The **Brass Register**, a cozy fern bar that serves good food and drink at moderate prices and has been around at least 20 years, is near downtown at 618 Georgia Avenue, (423) 265-4121.

Last but not least, let me recommend **Darr's Chow Time BBQ**, a few miles south of town at 801 McFarland Avenue in Rossville, Georgia, (423) 866-7770. This family has owned barbecue places in Chattanooga since the 1950s. The old Chow Time in Tiftonia, a '50s diner kind of place with a neon Chow Time clock, is now closed but was once one of my favorites. Darr's is run by one of the brothers and serves some of the best meat you'll ever eat. They pit cook pork shoulder over hickory coals for 12 hours, never allowing the meat to sit directly above the heat so that it is truly smoked. They serve a red tomato-vinegar sauce on the side, along with a selection of five kinds of beans.

LODGING

Chattanooga's old downtown **Read House Hotel** is now a **Radisson**. Check to see if the **Green Room** is open again for dining and whether their renovation is complete. This and the Choo Choo are Chattanooga's executive hotels, so ask about weekend specials ($75 and up), call (423) 266-4121. The **Chattanooga Choo Choo/Holiday Inn** seems more family oriented, and you can call them at (800) TRACK 29. In the downtown area there are national chain hotels: **Days Inn, Ramada, Quality Inn, Hampton Inn, Marriott**, and the **Chattanooga Clarion** (all of which have 1-800 listings).

If you want to try a fancy bed and breakfast inn, there are several around town in old neighborhoods. The **Bluff View Inn**, (423) 265-5033, and **Adams Hilborne**, (423) 265-5000, have rooms starting around $95. Less expensive is the **Milton House B&B**, a 1915 house in the Fort Wood neighborhood, (423) 265-2800. On Lookout Mountain you can try the **Alford House B&B**, (800) 817-7625, or the **Chanticleer Inn B&B**, which is built of mountain stone, (706) 820-2015.

Chattanooga has become quite a tourist destination in summer, so if you are having trouble finding a place to stay, stop by the visitor's bureau near the Tennessee Aquarium or call them at (800) 322-3344 for an accommodations guide.

CAMPING

Harrison Bay State Park, located 24 miles north of Chattanooga, offers lakefront campsites with hookups from April through October for around $14 per day, (423) 344-6214. **Camp on the Lake**, a privately run campground on Nickajack Lake, is approximately 18 miles from town. It is the smallest of the commercial campsites available, with 49 sites and hookups, (423) 942-4078. **Outdoors Adventures**, located on the Ocoee River, has 20 sites for camping (no hookups), (800) 627-7636.

NIGHTLIFE

You can check in on the 24-hour "Arts Line" at (423) 756-ARTS to find out about performances by the **Chattanooga Symphony and**

CHATTANOOGA

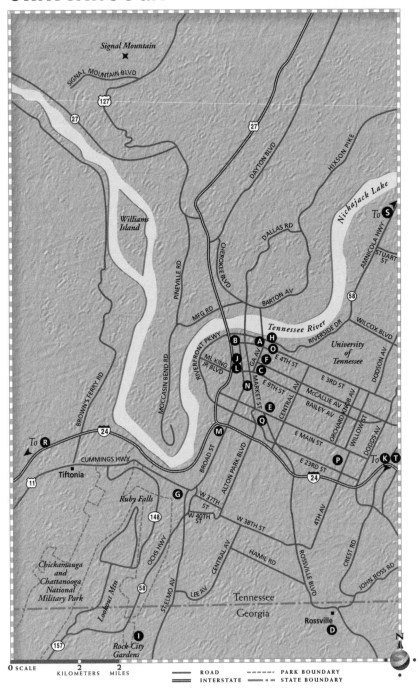

Signal Mountain

SIGNAL MOUNTAIN BLVD

127

27

Williams Island

PINEVILLE RD

DAYTON BLVD

CHEROKEE BLVD

DALLAS RD

27

HIXSON PIKE

Nickajack Lake

To **S**

AMNICOLA HWY

STUART ST

BARTON AV

RIVERSIDE DR

58

WILCOX BLVD

MFG RD

Tennessee River

University of Tennessee

RIVERFRONT PKWY

MOCCASIN BEND RD

ML KING JR BLVD

B **A** **H** **O** **F** E 4TH ST

J **L** GAY AV **C**

N MARKET ST E 9TH ST

E 3RD ST

DODSON AV

McCALLIE AV

CENTRAL AV

BAILEY AV

E

ORCHARD KNOB AV

WILLOW ST

DODDS AV

Q E MAIN ST

M BROAD ST

ALTON PARK BLVD

E 23RD ST

P

To **K** **T**

24

BROWN'S FERRY RD

24

To **R**

CUMMINGS HWY

11

Tiftonia

Ruby Falls

G W 37TH ST

W 38TH ST

4TH AV

148

W 40TH ST

OCHS HWY

CENTRAL AV

HAMIL RD

ROSSVILLE BLVD

CREST RD

JOHN ROSS RD

Chickamauga and Chattanooga National Military Park

Lookout Mtn

58

ST ELMO AV

LEE AV

Tennessee
Georgia

Rossville **D**

157

I Rock City Gardens

N

O SCALE
KILOMETERS   MILES
2   2

ROAD ——— PARK BOUNDARY -----
INTERSTATE ═══ STATE BOUNDARY ─ ·─

Food

A Back Inn Café

B Big River Grille

C Brass Register

D Darr's Chow Time BBQ,

A LeDoux's

A Rembrandt's Coffee House

E Southside Grill

F Vine Street Market

P Quality Inn

L Radisson Read House

Q Ramada

Camping

R Camp on the Lake

S Harrison Bay State Park

T Outdoors Adventures

Lodging

F Adams Hilborne

G Alford House B&B

H Bluff View Inn

I Chanticleer Inn B&B

J Chattanooga Clarion

E Chattanooga Choo
Choo/Holiday Inn

K Days Inn

L Green Room

M Hampton Inn

N Marriott

O Milton House B&B

Note: Items with the same letter are located in the same area.

Opera Association, the **Chattanooga Little Theatre**, or events at the **Tivoli Theater, Soldiers & Sailors Memorial Auditorium**, or **Bessie Smith Music Hall**. The ornate Tivoli, built in 1921, has been restored to its original brilliance. This 1,700-seat downtown venue features Broadway shows as well as dance, opera, classical, and popular music events. Call (423) 757-5042.

If you go for sports, check out the **UTC Mocs**. And Chattanooga's minor league baseball team, the **Lookouts**, is one of the oldest in the country, chartered in 1885. Call (423) 267-2208 to see if they're at home in the newly renovated 1929 Engel Stadium.

On Friday nights, you can get a taste of old-time bluegrass up on Signal Mountain at the **Mountain Opry**. It's free, located in the Walden Civic Center, and starts at 8 p.m. Stop by Waycrazy's BBQ for a bite on the way.

FESTIVALS AND FREEBIES

Chattanooga hosts an annual music and arts festival called **Riverbend**, which lasts for nine days in late June and features outstanding national and regional acts. For information call (423) 265-4112. The **Bessie Smith Jazz Fest** is held in May, call (423) 267-0944. To inquire about the **Southern Literature Festival** held every spring, call Allied Arts at (423) 756-2787.

Miller Plaza in downtown Chattanooga features free musical performances and artists-in-residence year-round. If you are interested in this city's amazing downtown revival, stop by the **Chattanooga Downtown Planning and Design Center** in Miller Plaza and talk to the folks who are making it happen (423-266-5948).

Scenic Route: I-24 Tennessee Backroads, between Chattanooga and Nashville

The eastern half of south central Tennessee quietly boasts two completely different sorts of off-the-beaten-path locales. Located about 30 miles northwest of Chattanooga on I-24 is Monteagle, which sits atop the Cumberland Plateau just as it rises up from the Tennessee Valley below. Monteagle, Altamont, and Beersheba Springs, as you may be able to surmise from the names, are all mountain retreats. About 20 miles further up the interstate toward Nashville, the land to the south and west becomes gently rolling lush pastureland. This is Tennessee's answer to the Kentucky Bluegrass. It is in Lynchburg, Shelbyville, Wartrace, and Normandy that you'll find Tennessee Walking Horses and Tennessee whiskey.

Monteagle got its start as the "Chatauqua of the South" in 1882. High enough to enjoy cooling breezes even in the hottest season, it is still a favorite summering spot and is one of the four remaining chatauqua programs in the country (the original, at Chatauqua, New York, began in 1874).

TENNESSEE BACKROADS

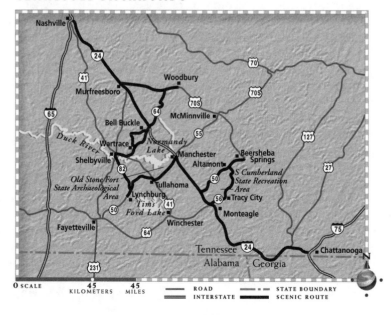

Summer residents from all over the South maintain elaborate houses in the 90-acre area known as the **Monteagle Sunday School Assembly**. Lodging is available year-round at the deluxe **Adams-Edgeworth Inn**, (615) 924-4000, and the **North Gate Inn**, (615) 924-2799.

Monteagle is adjacent to the **South Cumberland State Recreation Area**, a 12,000-acre state wilderness area that includes **Savage Gulf Canyon, Great Stone Door, South Cumberland State Park, Grundy Forest**, and **Foster Falls**. Call (615) 924-2980 or stop by the South Cumberland Visitor's Center on Hwy 41 between Monteagle and Tracy City.

Right on the road as you pass through **Tracy City** is the friendly **Dutch Maid Bakery**, which has been in business since 1902. If you feel like venturing even further away from the main highway, drive through the tiny town of **Altamont** and on to **Beersheba Springs**, which was founded in 1833 at the location of a mineral spring discovered by Mrs. Beersheba Cain. A fashionable place to "take the waters" in the 1840s and 1850s, the 2-story white wooden Beersheba Hotel was taken over by the Methodist Assembly after the Civil War, and public access to it is limited. Beersheba is a charming community of private summer cabins and cottages which looks out over the western edge of the Cumberland Plateau and is located very close to the Great Stone Door entrance to the South Cumberland State Recreation Area.

From Beersheba and Altamont you can either head back to Monteagle on Hwy 56 or (if you're heading northwest, toward Nashville) take Hwy 50 to a point approximately 7 miles further north on I-24. Driving north on I-24, you'll come to **Manchester**, where **Old Stone Fort State Archeological Park** is located along the Duck River. The "fort" is a 50-acre enclosure bounded by mounds, wall, cliffs, and two forks of the river. It is thought to be a Woodland Indian ceremonial site. Visitors can walk the perimeter on an interpretive trail and learn about the fort's makers in an exhibit hall. Programs and activities further interpreting the site are scheduled on weekends during the summer. Campsites with hookups are available only on a first-come, first-served basis. Call (615) 723-5073 for information. From Old Stone Fort, continue on Hwy 55 to **Tullahoma**, where you'll find the elegant old **Holly Berry Inn B&B**, which also serves delicious meals to nonguests by appointment, (615) 455-4445. Continue south and west on Hwy 55 to **Lynchburg**, and you'll have entered **Jack Daniel's** country.

The world-famous **Jack Daniel's Distillery**, founded in 1866 by Jasper Newton Daniel, offers free tours daily, from 8 a.m. to 4 p.m.—but there's no tasting, as this is a "dry" county, (615) 759-6180. A visit to Jack Daniel's is not complete without a family-style lunch at **Miss Mary Bobo's Boarding House**. Reservations are a must, and Miss Mary's is closed on Sunday, (615) 759-7394. Not far up the road (here, as in the Kentucky Bluegrass, the limestone-filtered water is ideal for brewing purposes) is "the other" Tennessee sour-mash whiskey distillery, George Dickel, founded in 1867. **George Dickel Distillery** offers free tours Monday–Friday from 9 a.m.–3 p.m. Call (615) 857-3124 for information.

Shelbyville, the Walking Horse Capital of the World, is located about 20 miles north of Lynchburg, in the midst of beautiful gently rolling farmland. Shelbyville has a classic town square, which dates from 1810. The very formal **Tennessee Walking Horse Celebration** is held every year in late August in Calsonic Arena. Inquire at the **Walking Horse Museum** about tickets to the different events and about stable tours around Shelbyville. The museum is open Monday–Friday on the Celebration Grounds, (615) 684-0314. The Shelbyville Chamber of Commerce will send you a guide to area horse farms, (615) 684-3482.

About 10 miles east is Wartrace, where if you turn north on Route 269, you'll find the tiny town of **Bell Buckle** sitting along the railroad tracks. Bell Buckle has become a mecca for Tennessee craft artists. Stop in at the **Bell Buckle Café** on Railroad Square for delicious smoked-out-back barbecue and live music on the weekends. Call the café at (615) 389-9693 or call **Bell Buckle Crafts**, also on Railroad Square, at (615) 389-9371 to find out more. Either Hwy 82 west from Bell Buckle or Hwy 64 north from Wartrace will lead you back out to the same entrance to I-24, where you will find yourself about 60 miles south of Nashville.

However, if you haven't quite had enough of the wonderful Tennessee backroads, cross over the interstate on Hwy 64 and head north until you reach Hwy 70S. A right on 70S will take you to **Woodbury**, in Cannon County, the white oak basket capital of Tennessee. Stop in at the **Arts Center of Cannon County**, open Tuesday–Saturday, 10 a.m.–4 p.m. to see their current exhibit and inquire about visiting craft artists in the vicinity. Phone: (615) 563-ARTS or (800) 235-9073.

You can take 70S northwest to **Murfreesboro** when you are ready to head back in the direction of Nashville. Stop and look around this charming town, which has one of the prettiest old courthouses in the state. On Main Street leading into the square are many lovely old brick homes dating from the mid- to late-1800s (Murfreesboro was the state capital for a brief period). If you are hungry, stop in at the **City Café** on Main Street, one block from the courthouse, for great fried chicken and homemade pie. Or circle the square to **Kebab Cuisine**, also on Main Street. At this tiny, family-owned Syrian restaurant, you'll be served excellent, inexpensive, cuisine in a friendly atmosphere. Murfreesboro is approximately 35 miles southeast of Nashville. Tune your radio dial to 89.5 as you leave Murfreesboro so that you can lock in Middle Tennessee State University's fine WMOT jazz format public radio station. ◼

5

NORTHEAST TENNESSEE

O nce the great stage road between Nashville and Washington, and then a major pre-Civil War railroad route between Knoxville and Wytheville, the over-mountain passage roughly paralleling Interstate 81 runs through mountain country. By the time one reaches Bristol, whose State Street is the Tennessee-Virginia line, the great peaks of the Smokies have become visible to the south, and the Shenandoah range to the north has receded into the distance. This wide corridor through the mountains, which brought the Scots-Irish pioneer settlers into Tennessee and was one of the major entry points for railroad industrialization in the South, has—because of its isolated location and rugged terrain— remembered more of its pioneer heritage and retained more of the original character of the land the settlers first saw than any other part of the state.

The Appalachian Trail runs the length of this region, and several of the best preserved towns in Tennessee—Jonesborough, Greeneville, and Rogersville—can be seen very much as they were in the early days of Tennessee's battles for statehood. Later history is represented by the towns the railroad built: Newport, Johnson City, Erwin, and Elizabethton. These towns have no central square. Their linear arrangements not only mimicked the Shenandoah Valley towns on which they were modeled, but also allowed easy railroad access for loading raw materials and manufactured goods and for unloading supplies. ◼

NORTHEAST TENNESSEE

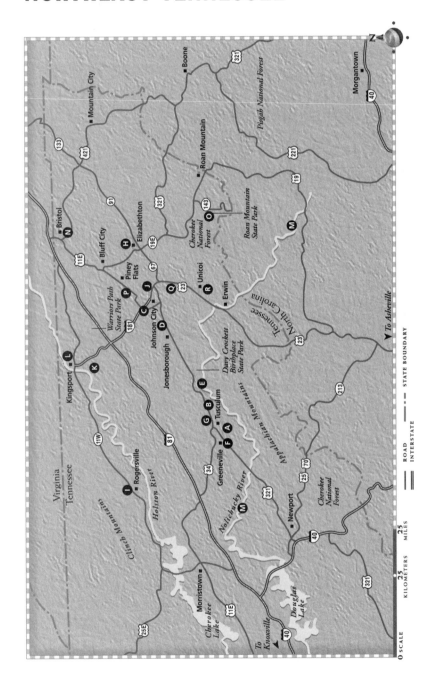

Virginia
Tennessee

Tennessee
North Carolina

Bristol
Mountain City
Boone
Morgantown

Roan Mountain
Pisgah National Forest

Bluff City
Elizabethton
Cherokee National Forest
Roan Mountain State Park

Piney Flats
Unicoi
Erwin

Kingsport
Johnson City
Jonesborough
Warriors Path State Park
Davy Crockett Birthplace State Park
Appalachian Mountains

Rogersville
Tusculum
Greeneville
Nolichucky River

Clinch Mountains
Holston River

Newport
Cherokee National Forest

Morristown
Cherokee Lake
Douglas Lake

To Knoxville
To Asheville

SCALE
0   25 KILOMETERS
0   25 MILES

ROAD
INTERSTATE
STATE BOUNDARY

Sights

A Andrew Johnson Home and Tailor Shop

B Andrew Johnson Museum and Library

C Archives of Appalachia

C Carroll Reese Museum

D Chester Inn

E Davy Crockett Birthplace State Park

F Dickson-Williams Mansion

G Doak House

H Doe River Covered Bridge

I Hale Springs Inn

J Hands On! Regional Museum

K Harry V. Steadman Mountain Heritage Farmstead Museum

D Jonesborough and Washington County History Museum and Historic District Headquarters

L Long Island of the Holston

F Nathaniel Greene Museum

L Netherland Inn

M Nolichucky River

N Paramount Theater

O Roan Mountain State Park

P Rocky Mount Historic Site

I Rogersville Depot Museum

H Sycamore Shoals State Historic Area

Q Tipton-Haynes Historic Site

R Unicoi County Heritage Museum

Note: Items with the same letter are located in the same town or area.

A PERFECT DAY IN NORTHEAST TENNESSEE

After an overnight stay at one of the many charming B&Bs in Jonesborough, take a walk around the beautifully preserved historic district, visiting the Washington County History Museum. Indulge in the Jonesborough Times and Tales Tour, an award-winning history brought to life in Jonesborough's historic homes and buildings, even if you don't generally do that sort of thing. After all, this is the headquarters of the National Storytelling Festival, and unless you are fortunate to have planned a visit during October, this may be your only taste of the ancient word craft. Visit the craft artist shops and studios in historic downtown, then travel back into pioneer times, visiting Sycamore Shoals, the Carter Mansion, and Rocky Mount, with a stop for lunch at the Ridgewood Restaurant in Bluff City. Then on to Kingsport to see the Long Island of the Holston River, from which Daniel Boone's Wilderness Road commenced (see Chapter 7). Stop for dinner in Johnson City and stay for outstanding acoustic music at the locally famous Down Home club.

SIGHTSEEING HIGHLIGHTS—JONESBOROUGH

★★★ **Chester Inn**—This frame stucture dates from 1797 and is home to the **National Storytelling Association**. Address: Main Street. Phone: (423) 753-2171. (½ hour)

★★★ **Jonesborough and Washington County History Museum and Historic District Headquarters**—Learn about Tennessee's oldest town and its fascinating history. The Tennessee state seal was created by local jeweler/engravers, Andrew Jackson was admitted into law practice here, and the first antislavery newspaper, *The Manumission Intelligencer*, later *The Emancipator*, was published here. Address: 117 Boone Street. Phone: (423) 753-1015. You can sign up at the museum for the highly recommended **Jonesborough Times and Tales Tour**, available year-round by reservation. Phone: (423) 753-1010. (1 hour)

SIGHTSEEING HIGHLIGHTS—GREENEVILLE

★★★ **Andrew Johnson Home and Tailor Shop**—Dating from around 1830, this was the home and business establishment of the seventeenth president of the U.S., both before and after his term in office. Address: College and Depot Streets. Phone: (423) 638-3551. (1 hour)

✩✩ **Andrew Johnson Museum and Library**—At Tusculum College, this museum which contains Johnson's personal library, papers, and artifacts and also creates changing exhibits. Phone: (423) 636-7348. (½ hour)

✩✩ **Davy Crockett Birthplace State Park**—The park features a reconstruction of his 1786 birthplace cabin, a small museum, and hiking and camping along the Nolichucky River. Address: Limestone, between Jonesborough and Greeneville. Call to make sure it's open. Phone: (423) 257-2061. (1 hour)

✩✩ **Dickson-Williams Mansion**—When it was built in 1815–1821, this mansion was considered "the showplace of East Tennessee." The historic home hosted Davy Crockett, Andrew Jackson, and the Marquis de Lafayette. Address: Irish Street. Phone: (423) 638-4111. (1 hour)

✩✩ **Doak House**—Now preserved as a museum by Tusculum College, Doak House was built in 1818 by Reverend Samuel Doak, a pioneer educator who founded the first school west of the Allegheny Mountains in 1780 (Washington College Academy) and Tusculum College in 1794. Call for an appointment. Phone: (423) 636-8554. (½ hour)

✩ **Nathaniel Greene Museum**—This small museum focuses on the local history of Greeneville and Greene County. Address: 101 West McKee. Phone: (423) 636-1558. (1 hour)

SIGHTSEEING HIGHLIGHTS—KINGSPORT

✩✩✩ **Long Island of the Holston**—This was the point of departure for Daniel Boone and the 30 men who set out to blaze a trail through the wilderness and establish boundaries for the claim of Richard Henderson's Transylvania Land Company in 1775. Nearby, the **Netherland Inn**, dating to 1818, was a key stage stop in close proximity to the important flatboat yard on the river. The inn is authentically furnished and includes a children's museum. Visitors can walk the distance to imagine portage from one mode of transport to another in those days. Phone: (423) 246-6262. (1 hour)

✿✿ **Harry V. Steadman Mountain Heritage Farmstead Museum**—
Located at Bays Mountain Park, this museum collects artifacts of sub-
sistence farming and mountaineer heritage. Displays illustrate the
importance of conservation of resources. Open weekends throughout
the year, daily in summer. Phone: (423) 229-9447. (1½ hours)

SIGHTSEEING HIGHLIGHTS—BRISTOL

✿✿ **Paramount Theater**—Dating from 1931, this newly restored
theater is headquarters to the **Birthplace of Country Music
Alliance**, a group dedicated to the early history of country music as it
evolved in and around this area, beginning with the 1927 Bristol
Sessions, which produced the first professional country music recordings. The Alliance holds monthly Thursday evening concerts that
emphasize the living tradition of southwest Virginia and northeast
Tennessee music. For information about the Alliance, which is a newly
formed membership organization, or to obtain a schedule, write P.O.
Box 216, Bristol, TN/VA 37620. Phone: (423) 968-7136.

SIGHTSEEING HIGHLIGHTS—JOHNSON CITY

East Tennessee State University, located in Johnson City, provides a
variety of cultural activities for the city. Listen to campus public radio
station WETS, 89.5, for happenings in and around the Johnson City
area. ETSU has a strong music department, which features no less
than five student bluegrass bands along with its classical music program. The university is also home to CASS, the Center for
Appalachian Studies and Services, which is dedicated to research and
public outreach in the Appalachian region.

✿✿ **Carroll Reese Museum**—Also a part of the CASS, the museum
is devoted not only to conserving the historical and artistic heritage of
the region but also to bringing in historical and artistic influences
from outside the region in its changing exhibits. Phone: (423) 929-
4392.

✿✿ **Hands On! Regional Museum**—Twenty exhibits on topics that
kids are interested in are combined with activities designed to rein-
force learning. An admission fee is charged. Closed Monday. Address:
315 Main Street. Phone: (423) 928-6915.

⋆⋆ Rocky Mount Historic Site—In Piney Flats, Tennessee, this living history museum interprets the year 1791 when William Blount, who was visiting the Cobb Family, made this the first headquarters of the Southwest Territory. Address: 200 Hyder Hill Road. Phone: (423) 538-7396. (1½ hours)

⋆⋆ Tipton-Haynes Historic Site—This is the home of Colonel John Tipton, which was built in 1783. The house and its grounds, which include ten original and restored buildings, will give visitors insight into life before Tennessee was a state—the Battle for the "Lost State of Franklin" took place here. While on the premises, visitors can see demonstrations and look inside a cave. Address: 2620 Roan Street. Phone: (423) 926-3631. (2 hours)

⋆ Archives of Appalachia—This division of CASS houses over 5 million manuscripts and a collection of photographs and sound and image recordings an all aspects of Appalachian history and culture. The archives are open to the public. Hours: Monday–Friday, 8:30 a.m.–4 p.m. Phone: (423) 929-4338.

SIGHTSEEING HIGHLIGHTS—ELIZABETHTON

⋆⋆⋆ Roan Mountain State Park—This scenic park includes Roan Mountain, which at 6,285 feet is the fifth highest peak in the Appalachian chain (fourth highest in the Smokies). The park is justly famous for its massive stand of rhododendrons and its beautiful high country scenery. Blueberries thrive here in late summer, and this is Tennessee's only park to offer cross country skiing. Lodging is available either in cabins or tents. Address: Hwy 143. Phone: (423) 772-3303.

⋆⋆ Sycamore Shoals State Historic Area—Featuring the reconstructed Fort Watauga, this historic area was one of the first settlements outside the 13 colonies. The story of the Transylvania Purchase and the involvement of land speculator Richard Henderson and explorer Daniel Boone in opening up the Wilderness Road in 1775 is told. Address: 1651 W. Elk Avenue. Phone: (423) 543-5808 (2 hours).

⋆ Doe River Covered Bridge—This is one of the four covered bridges still in use in Tennessee. It was built in 1882. Address: Near Elizabethton on Hwy 19E at the Doe River. Phone: (423) 547-3850.

SIGHTSEEING HIGHLIGHTS—ERWIN

✩✩ **Nolichucky River**—The 2,800-foot gorge of the Nolichucky River near Erwin affords spectacular views and churning white water and is a popular sport kayaking and rafting destination.

✩✩ **Unicoi County Heritage Museum**—"Unaka" Indian displays and railroading memorabilia along with other aspects of this mountain community's heritage are exhibited here. Address: Hwy 107 in Erwin. Phone: (423) 743-9449. (1 hour)

SIGHTSEEING HIGHLIGHTS—ROGERSVILLE

✩✩✩ **Hale Springs Inn**—Located on the town square of this historic town on the Wilderness Road, the Hale Springs Inn opened in 1824. It is the oldest continuously operated inn in Tennessee. The inn has ten rooms with fireplaces for overnight stays, and their Colonial Dining Room is highly rated. Reservations are needed. Phone: (423) 272-5171.

✩✩✩ **Rogersville Depot Museum**—This restored 1890s train station now houses a collection of historic Rogersville memorabilia. You can pick up a brochure describing a self-guided tour of Rogersville here or at the Hale Springs Inn. Hours: Monday–Friday. Phone: (423) 272-2186.

FITNESS AND RECREATION

This rugged landscape offers the opportunity for a number of challenging outdoor activities, from hiking the Appalachian Trail, to cross-country skiing, to white-water rafting. Travelers might wish to plan a longer stay while in this part of the country to take advantage of the many unique recreational attributes of northeast Tennessee.

The **Appalachian Trail** enters the area north of Bristol, touches Watauga Lake at Laurel Fork Gorge, and traverses Roan Mountain State Park, Cherokee National Forest, and Mount Pisgah National Forest. It crosses the Nolichucky River near Erwin and straddles the Tennessee/Kentucky line all the way through the Great Smoky Mountains National Park. Highways 421, 321, 19E, 23, 19W, 70, and 25/70 intersect the trail, providing access points for short hikes. For information, contact the Appalachian Trail Conference at (304) 535-6331. Just across the North Carolina line where Hwy 25/70 parallels the French Broad River is the tiny town of **Hot Springs**, which still has at least one operative bathhouse.

Roan Mountain State Park, very near the North Carolina line, is best known for Catawba rhododendron plantings covering 600 acres that bloom in June. This spectacular park has cabins, camping, hiking, and cross-country skiing. The park is located on Hwy 143. For information, call (423) 772-3303.

Bays Mountain Park and Planetarium, outside of Kingsport, is a mecca for those with kids. In addition to the ever-popular planetarium, Bays Mountain has hiking trails, a barge ride, and an outstanding nature interpretive center, which includes the **Mountain Heritage Farmstead Museum** and illustrates pioneer methods of resource conservation, (423) 229-9447.

Steele Creek Park in Bristol is a municipal park of 2,000 acres, which includes a golf course, nature center, 25 miles of hiking trails, children's train ride, and a mountain lake, (423) 989-4850.

In Johnson City, **Buffalo Mountain Park** will provide a rewarding place to stretch the legs after a day of historic homes and museums. Its hiking trails have scenic overlooks, (423) 283-5815. Both the **Davy Crockett Birthplace State Park**, outside of Greeneville, and **Warriors Path State Park**, in Kingsport, have swimming pools. Warriors Path also offers resort amenities such as horseback riding, boating, fishing, and golf. Call (423) 239-8531 for reservations and information.

If you want to arrange a white-water rafting expedition, you might check out the following list with an outdoor outfitter, such as **Mahoney's** in Johnson City, 702 Sunset Drive, (423) 282-5413; or companies like **B-Cliff White-Water Rafting**, Watauga River, Elizabethton, (800) 592-2262; **Cherokee Adventures White-Water Rafting**, Nolichucky River, Erwin, (800) 445-7238 or (800) 838-7238; **Nantahala Outdoor Center** includes Nolichucky and handles four other rivers as well, Bryson City, NC, (800) 232-RAFT; **USA Raft**, Nolichucky and French Broad Rivers, Erwin, (they have a retreat with lodging beside the Nolichucky River), (800) USA-RAFT.

There are lots of golf courses in the area besides those mentioned in conjunction with public and state parks. The **Roan Valley Golf Course** on Hwy 421 near Mountain City is a public course that is noted for its spectacular views, (423) 727-7931.

Cavers will be interested in **Bristol Caverns**, the largest cave in the eastern Smoky Mountains, located on Hwy 421 South, (423) 878-2011, and **Appalachian Caverns**, near Bluff City, (423) 323-2337, which has one area that opens up to a height of more than 100 feet. Bristol Caverns was reportedly found in 1863, but it is likely that various nomadic Indian groups had used it for several centuries as they had Appalachian Caverns and Mammoth Cave.

FOOD

In Jonesborough the **Parson's Table** is an 1870s church that has been converted into a restaurant. It's an odd feeling at first, but the romantic setting works and the chef-owner does a nice job. It's worth a splurge at 102 Woodrow Street in downtown Jonesborough. Call for reservations at (423) 753-8002. Another unusual conversion is that of plank-front, rural grocery store to fine restaurant, as at **Harmony Grocery**, in the little community of Harmony just outside of Jonesborough. Specialties include Creole cuisine. It's closed on Monday; call (423) 348-6183 for directions. I was also surprised to find a Mexican menu being served in a 100-year-old home overlooking the Nolichucky River at the **Chucky Trading Company**, located at 3937 Hwy 81 South. Local musicians perform on weekends. Call (423) 753-5611 to see if you should come for dinner or just enjoy the music afterwards. The **Main Street Café**, which makes healthy sandwiches, is a reliable lunch choice in downtown Jonesborough, at 117 W. Main. Call ahead and get them to fix a picnic lunch, (423) 753-2460.

In Johnson City **Galloway's Restaurant** is located in a bungalow on Roan Street. Their specialty is pasta, and the food is good. Call (423) 926-1166 to see if you need reservations for dinner. The **Peerless** is an old steakhouse that is well liked by the locals. It can be found at 2531 N. Roan Street, closed Sunday. The **Firehouse**, at 627 W. Walnut, is a 1900s firehouse where a 1925 fire engine is on display—a must. You'll find both barbecue and steaks on the menu, (423) 929-7377.

In Kingsport **Skoby's**, on Konnarock Road, is a popular spot for upscale dining with its "theme" rooms—a diner or a butcher shop. You might want to call and find out if you have a choice of "atmosphere," (423) 245-2761. Two Italian restaurants that offer good food at good value are **Giuseppe's**, 2530 E. Stone Drive, which is open every day, (423) 288-2761; and **Amato's Pasta Palace**, 4340 W. Stone Drive.

In Bristol **Bristol Bagel & Bakery Co.**, 501 State Street, makes their bagels on the premises and serves espresso and cappuccino in an historic downtown neighborhood, (703) 466-6222. They also have locations in Kingsport and Johnson City. The **Troutdale Dining Room**, at 412 Sixth Street is in a Victorian house. They have been well-reviewed for their fine regional food at moderate prices, (423) 968-9099.

In Bluff City the **Ridgewood Restaurant**, at 900 Elizabethton Highway, has been serving its famous barbecue for many years and is included in lots of BBQ guidebooks. Call to make sure they are open, since this is a bit out of the way, (423) 538-7543.

In Greeneville, for plain country cooking, residents rely on **West Main Restaurant**, at 915 West Main, (423) 638-8818. In Erwin try the **Elms** restaurant, at 202 S. Elm, for fine home cooking, (423) 743-6181. And in Rogersville a candlelight dinner at the **Colonial Dining Room** in the Hale Springs Inn is a memorable experience both for the regional cuisine and the historic ambiance; call (423) 272-5171.

LODGING

Jonesborough has a multitude of bed and breakfast accommodations, many in historic homes. Among those downtown are: the 1850s **Aiken-Brow House**, 104 Third Avenue South, (423) 753-9440; the **Hawley House**, which dates from the late 1800s, at 114 E. Woodrow, (423) 753-8869; the **Bowling Green Inn**, built in 1824 as a stagecoach stop (this is about ½ mile out of town at 901 W. College, 423-753-6356); and the **Tea Room B&B**, a Victorian house with a restaurant downstairs and three bedrooms upstairs. It's at 130 W. Main, (423) 753-0288.

Outside of town, you'll find the **Bugaboo B&B** (two bedrooms with private baths) about a mile away, located on 15 acres with a mountain view, (423) 753-9345. Also on the outskirts are the **Country Charm B&B Inn**, which has an indoor heated pool, as well as separate log cabins, 1604 Boone's Creek Road, (423) 753-5163; and the **Inn at Sheppard Springs**, which is in an 1860s farm house about 4½ miles out in the country. They offer hot-air balloon rides and next door is the Sheppard Springs Barn and Playhouse, a family entertainment venue, which is open April–November. To find out what's playing and the cost of a balloon ride, call the inn at (423) 753-6471.

Rogersville's **Hale Springs Inn**, a restored stage stop on the Wilderness Road, has been in continuous operation since 1824. Ten

NORTHEAST TENNESSEE

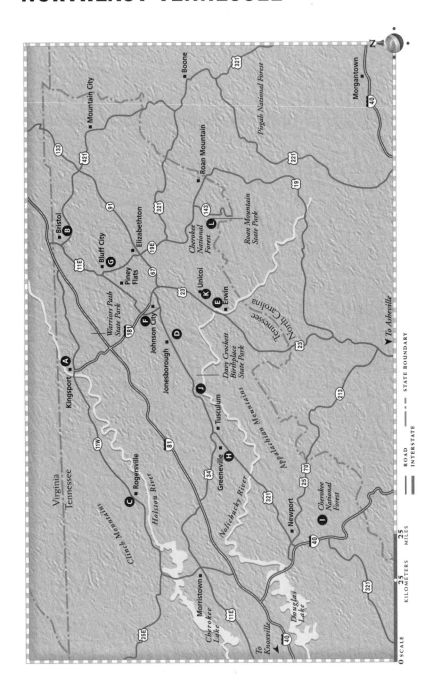

Morgantown

Boone

Pisgah National Forest

Roan Mountain

Mountain City

Roan Mountain State Park

Bristol

Bluff City

Elizabethton

Cherokee National Forest

Piney Flats

Unicoi

Erwin

Kingsport

Warriors Path State Park

Johnson City

North Carolina

Tennessee

To Asheville

Jonesborough

Davy Crockett Birthplace State Park

Tusculum

Virginia

Tennessee

Rogersville

Appalachian Mountains

Greeneville

Nolichucky River

Holston River

Clinch Mountains

Newport

Cherokee National Forest

Morristown

Cherokee Lake

Douglas Lake

To Knoxville

SCALE

25 KILOMETERS

25 MILES

ROAD — INTERSTATE ⸗ STATE BOUNDARY

Food

A Amato's Pasta Palace

B Bristol Bagel & Bakery Co.

C Colonial Dining Room

D Chucky Trading Company

E The Elms

F The Firehouse

F Galloway's Restaurant

A Giuseppe's

D Harmony Grocery

D Main Street Café

D Parson's Table

F The Peerless

G Ridgewood Restaurant

A Skoby's

B Troutdale Dining Room

H West Main Restaurant

Lodging

D Aiken-Brow House

D Bowling Green Inn

D Bugaboo B&B

D Country Charm B&B Inn

C Hale Springs Inn

D Hawley House

D Inn at Sheppard Springs

H General Morgan Inn

H Snapp Inn B&B

D Tea Room B&B

Camping

I Cherokee National Forest

J Davy Crockett Birthplace State Park

K North Indian Creek Campground

L Roan Mountain State Resort Park

A Warriors Path State Park

K Woodsmoke Campground

Note: Items with the same letter are located in the same town or area.

rooms with fireplaces await. Call in advance for reservations, (423) 272-5171, so you won't miss the opportunity to stay here. In Greeneville the **General Morgan Inn**, originally four interconnecting 1890s railroad hotels, has been turned into a historic luxury hotel (111 North Main, 423-787-1001). Near Davy Crockett's birthplace at Limestone, you'll find the **Snapp Inn B&B** in an early 1800s Federal-style home. It features two bedrooms with private baths, and a full breakfast is included. Call (423) 257-2482.

CAMPING

Tennessee State Parks in the vicinity include the **Davy Crockett Birthplace State Park**, at Limestone, which has a campground and hookups, (423) 257-2167. **Roan Mountain State Resort Park**, on Roan Mountain, has cabins and tent camping, (423)772-3303. **Warriors Path State Park**, in Kingsport, has campsites and hookups, (423) 239-8531. There are lots of commercial RV parks and campgrounds in the area. Two that sound especially nice for RV travelers are the **North Indian Creek Campground**, in Unicoi near the Nolichucky River Gorge, which has 27 sites with hookups, (423) 743-4502; and the **Woodsmoke Campground**, also in Unicoi, which is located in the woods with a small stream and has 24 sites with hookups, (423) 743-2116. The **Cherokee National Forest** borders this entire area.

NIGHTLIFE

The **Down Home** is a well-loved acoustic music club in Johnson City. Call (423) 929-9822 to find out who's in their lineup. If you are in the mood for traditional country music, check the **Paramount** in Bristol to see what they have scheduled, (423) 968-7456. In the summertime, kids will enjoy the novelty of seeing the outdoor theater performance of *The Wataugans*, a dramatic reenactment of the events that took place at Sycamore Shoals when Richard Henderson negotiated the Transylvania Purchase with the Cherokee in 1775. For details, contact the Watauga Historical Association at Elizabethton by calling (423) 543-5808.

6

WESTERN WATERLANDS OF KENTUCKY AND TENNESSEE, REELFOOT LAKE AND PADUCAH

The far western portions of both Kentucky and Tennessee offer nature lovers the unforgettable experience of a vast wetlands ecosystem, and historians and folk culture aficionados get a look at Mississippi river life, past and present. Reelfoot Lake, one of the largest lakes in the country at 18,000 acres, is located near the shared border of Kentucky and Tennessee, about 10 miles from the Mississippi River. The lake, which was formed by a cataclysmic earthquake in the winter of 1811–1812, is now a Tennessee State Park offering facilities for fishing in spring, summer, and fall and for eagle watching in the winter. For the curious visitor, local experts and interpretive museum displays in the nearby towns of Tiptonville and Samburg can provide a wealth of information about duck calling, stump-jumper boats, and the eventful history of Reelfoot Lake, dominion over which has been the subject of heated dispute since early in its history.

Journeying north to historic Paducah—a town that is proudly restoring its heritage as a center of commerce at the confluence of the Tennessee and Ohio Rivers—takes one past the important Mississippian Indian ceremonial and trade center at Wickliffe Mounds, the strategically critical Columbus-Belmont Civil War battle site, and several Kentucky state wildlife preservation areas. ◼

WESTERN WATERLANDS

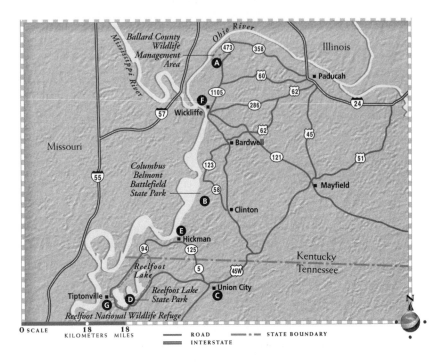

Sights

- **Ⓐ** Ballard Public Wildlife Area
- **Ⓑ** Columbus-Belmont State Park
- **Ⓒ** Dixie Gun Works
- **Ⓓ** Ellington Interpretive Museum
- **Ⓓ** Reelfoot Lake
- **Ⓓ** Reelfoot Lake State Park
- **Ⓔ** Warren Thomas Museum
- **Ⓕ** Wickliffe Mounds

Food

- **Ⓓ** Boyette's Dining Room
- **Ⓓ** Pier Restaurant
- **Ⓓ** Airpark Inn

Lodging

- **Ⓓ** Airpark Inn
- **Ⓓ** Boyette's Resort
- **Ⓒ** Cultra Motor Inn
- **Ⓕ** Grassy Lakes Hunting Resort
- **Ⓒ** Hampton Inn
- **Ⓓ** Spillway Motel
- **Ⓖ** Sweet Dreams Cottage
- **Ⓕ** Wickcliffe Motel

Camping

- **Ⓑ** Columbus-Belmont State Park

Note: Items with the same letter are located in the same town or area.

A PERFECT DAY IN THE WESTERN WATERLANDS

Arrive at Reelfoot Lake State Park the night before in order to be in place for a 10 a.m. eagle-watching tour in winter or a 9 a.m. scenic boat cruise on the lake in summer. After experiencing the lake first-hand, learn more about its early history at the Ellington Museum at the Park and more about contemporary Reelfoot Lake culture at Dale Calhoun's Boat Shop across the road. For more local color, try the catfish at Boyette's Dining Room next to Calhoun's or the Pier in Samburg. Drive north, paralleling the Mississippi River, and stop by Hickman, Wickliffe Mounds (at the confluence of the Ohio and Mississippi), and the Columbus-Belmont Civil War site. End the day in Paducah, letting a carriage ride take you back into Paducah's glory days as an important nineteenth-century river and railroad town. Find your lodging in historic downtown quarters.

REELFOOT LAKE AREA HISTORY

Obion County, where both the Obion (an Indian word meaning prongs or forks) River and Reelfoot Lake are located, was settled after the land was "purchased" from the Indians in the Jackson Purchase of 1818. Davy Crockett, who lived in neighboring Gibson County, is said to have achieved his record hunt of 103 bears in Obion County. Crockett helped to layout the first capital at Troy in 1825 and represented the district in the U.S. Congress from 1827 to 1831 and from 1833 to 1835.

SIGHTSEEING HIGHLIGHTS

✰✰✰ **Market House Museum**—Located in what was a turn-of-the-century drug store, this museum features local history and tributes to Paducah's favorite sons, Alben W. Barkley, vice-president under Harry S. Truman; and humorist Irvin S. Cobb, 1876–1944. Admission is $1.50 per adult, 50 cents per child. Closed Monday and January–February. Address: Between Broadway and Kentucky Avenues. Phone: (502) 443-7759.

✰✰✰ **The Museum of the American Quilter's Society**—One of Paducah's newest attractions, the society has a permanent collection of 200 quilts and also mounts temporary exhibits of regional quilts and related arts. The museum sponsors the AQS National Quilt Show in late April. Admission is $4 per adult, $3 per student. Closed Monday; call for specific hours and seasonal closings. Address: 215 Jefferson Street. Phone: (502) 898-7903.

★★★ **Paducah**—This city was founded by explorer William Clark in 1827. As the story is told, Clark "purchased" older brother George Rogers Clark's 37,000-acre Revolutionary War land grant for $5 from his brother's estate, after returning from his famous 1804–1806 expedition with Meriwether Lewis. The younger Clark laid out a town 12 blocks square and gave one block to the city for community use—it soon housed a courthouse, a jail, and a market house. Prior to Clark's arrival, the settlement was known as Pekin. Clark named his new town in honor of Chief Paduke, a leader of the Chickasaw. A 1909 sculpture of Chief Paduke by classicist Lorado Taft can be seen at 19th and Jefferson Streets. Following Clark's plan, Paducah had a central marketplace where farmers could trade produce for goods until as recently as 1960. The 1905 brick **Market House** that stands today replaced a wooden structure built in 1836 and a brick structure from 1850. The revitalized downtown historic district begins at the Market House Square. A detailed historic self-guided walking tour brochure is available from the Paducah Tourist and Convention Commission. Phone: (800) PADUCAH or (502) 443-8783.

★★★ **Reelfoot Lake**—Reelfoot is rumored to have gotten its name from Chickasaw chieftain Reelfoot, who kidnapped a Choctaw maiden and brought her back to his Chickasaw home territory near the Mississippi. Legend has it that the earth swallowed Reelfoot and his warriors, and water covered their burial ground. (The Indian lore obviously staked its claim long before the legend of Paul Bunyan explained the lake as one of Babe's footprints.) **Reelfoot Lake State Park** offers guided eagle-watching tours and cruises on the lake, as well as the **Ellington Interpretive Museum**. Reelfoot Park is the only Tennessee park to feature its own landing strip. It has both lakeside motel accommodations and the Airpark Lodge and Restaurant. Address: Route 1, Tiptonville, TN. Phone: (901) 253-7756.

★★ **Market House Theater**—This theater, in the Market House, holds 250 for a six-show annual series by one of Kentucky's fine regional theater groups. Tickets are reasonable at $6–$8. Call for a schedule of performances. Address: 141 Kentucky Avenue. Phone: (502) 444-6828.

★★ **Players Bluegrass Downs**—It functions as a thoroughbred racing track in October and November, and as a simulcast, inter-track betting facility for the rest of the Kentucky racing season. Address: 32nd and Park Avenue. Phone: (502) 444-7117 for details, or (800) 755-1244 for post times.

★★ **Wickliffe Mounds**—Located at the joining of the Ohio and Mississippi Rivers, Wickliffe Mounds was a ceremonial and trade site for the Mississippian Indians, who inhabited this area from around A.D. 800–1350. The state of Kentucky now operates an interpretive site here. Admission is $3.50. Handicapped accessible. Hours: Open daily, 9 a.m.–4:30 p.m., closed December–February. Phone: (502) 335-3681.

★★ **Yeiser Arts Center**—A part of the Market House complex, this center was founded in 1957 as an art museum housing a nineteenth- and twentieth-century collection and an arts center featuring exhibits of regional, national, and international contemporary artists. Admission is $1 per person. Closed Monday. Phone: (502) 442-2453.

★ **Dixie Gun Works**—Located in Union City, the Dixie Gun Works began in 1954 as a supplier of antique muzzle-loading guns and parts. It now features an antique car museum, a display of small antique tools, and an 1850 log gun shop. Phone: (901) 885-0211.

★ **Union City**—Obion county's largest town, it got its name from the crossing of the Mobile & Ohio and the Nashville & Northwestern rail-roads in 1854. The area of small farms around Union City is among the highest producing in the state for corn, wheat, and apples. On Saturday, you can still find the **Farmer's Market** opening at 7 a.m. The **Annual Fall Festival**, in September, celebrates the harvest with a variety of events for the whole community, including white bean and barbecue cook-offs, a "fishing rodeo," and the Round House reunion, which re-creates the Bluebank Round House music-making of the 1950s and 1960s at Reelfoot Lake.

Ballard Public Wildlife Area—Located in the curve of the Mississippi River near the town of Monkey's Eyebrow, Ballard Public Wildlife

Area and **Swan Lake PWA** both have observation towers. The **West Kentucky PWA** is near Paducah. (A word of warning, supervised water-fowl hunting is allowed at Ballard.) Phone: (502) 564-4336.

Columbus-Belmont State Park—This park commemorates the Civil War battles for the western frontier that took place in late 1861 and early 1862. The Federal soldiers, led by General U.S. Grant in his first foray as commander, burned the Belmont encampment and managed to overtake Columbus, with its anchor-chain blocking the Mississippi to Union gunboats, after an initial repulsion by a 10,000–19,000 strong Confederate force. Before these confrontations, troops were amassed at

Mary Entrekin

Union City, a bitter staging ground of divided loyalties. A museum, containing both Indian and Civil War artifacts, is located in the park. Picnic areas and a self-guided hiking trail located on the bluffs overlook the river and earthen bunkers built by the Confederates. A nominal admission fee is charged. Open April–October. Phone: (502) 677-2327.

Paducah Steamboat Dock at Shultz Waterfront Park—The dock is now port for three Mississippi River luxury steamers, the *Mississippi Queen*, the *Delta Queen*, and the new *American Queen*. Call the Paducah Visitors Bureau for more information. Phone: (800) PADUCAH.

Warren Thomas Museum—Located in one of Mark Twain's favorite towns, Hickman, Kentucky, this museum reflects the city's African-American community. Admission is free, but you must have an appointment. Phone: (502) 236-2191 or (502) 236-2535.

Whitehaven Visitor's Center—This 1860 house is now being used as a welcome center at the I-24 entrance to the city. It has an upstairs filled with Alben W. Barkley memorabilia. Hours: Open 24 hours a day. Phone: (502) 554-2077.

FITNESS AND RECREATION

Boating, fishing, and hiking are all available at **Reelfoot Lake State Park**, as are hiking trails and paths at **Columbus-Belmont State Park** and the **Kentucky Public Wildlife Areas**. In and around this flat countryside, running suggests itself as a popular form of recreation. Bicycling information for the Paducah area can be obtained from Hutch Smith c/o **Bike World**, 848 Joe Clifton Drive, Paducah 42001, (502) 442-0751. **Paducah's Paxton Park Golf Course** is an 18-hole public course, (502) 444-9514. **Paducah's Nautilus Swim and Racquet Club** allows visitors with area motel keys full access for a $5 fee. **Noble Park**, at 2915 Park Avenue in Paducah, has tennis courts and a public pool open mid-June through August, (502) 444-8539.

FOOD

Reelfoot Lake State Park Airpark Inn (901-253-7756) provides breakfast, lunch, and dinner year-round. Across the road from the

PADUCAH

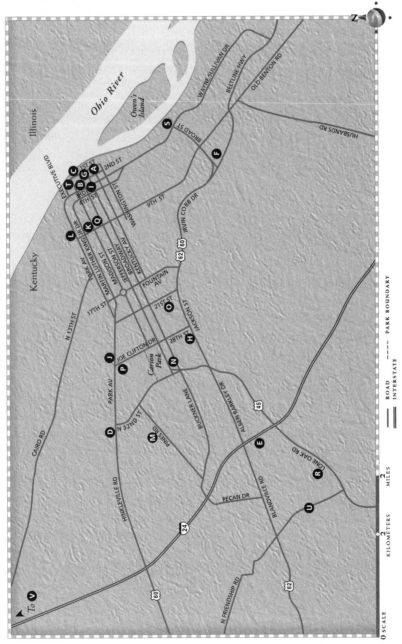

Sights

Ⓐ Market House Museum

Ⓐ Market House Theater

Ⓑ The Museum of the American Quilter's Society

Ⓒ Paducah Steamboat Dock at Shultz Waterfront Park

Ⓓ Players Bluegrass Downs

Ⓔ Whitehaven Visitor's Center

Ⓐ Yeiser Arts Center

Food

Ⓕ B.B. Whiskers

Ⓖ C.C. Cohen

Ⓗ Chong's

Ⓖ Cynthia's

Ⓘ Downtown Diner

Ⓙ Holman House

Ⓚ Ninth Street House

Ⓛ Oldtown Restaurant and Bar

Ⓜ The Pines

Ⓝ Prices Bar-B-Q

Ⓞ Skinhead's

Ⓟ Starnes

Lodging

Ⓖ 1857 B&B

Ⓠ 1868 B&B

Ⓡ Denton's

Ⓢ Farley Place

Ⓣ J.R.'s Executive Inn

Ⓖ Paducah Harbor Plaza

Ⓤ Rosewood Inn

Camping

Ⓥ Fern Lake Campground

park is **Boyette's Dining Room**, a locally popular restaurant, (901) 253-7307; and in the town of Samburg, also on the lake, is the **Pier Restaurant**, (901) 538-2803.

Paducah offers a number of fine restaurants, several of which are in historic buildings. The **Oldtown Restaurant and Bar**, 701 Park Avenue, which used to be a stagecoach stop and tavern, features steaks and ribs, (502) 442-9616. **Ninth Street House**, located in a 1886 Victorian home at 323 N. Ninth Street, has a reputation for fine food, (502) 442-9019; and **C.C. Cohen** is in an old store at Second and Market Streets (502-442-6391). Also recommended are **The Pines**, 900 N. 32nd Street, (502) 442-9304; **Cynthia's**, at 127 Market House Square, whose menu of Italian gourmet dishes changes weekly, (502) 443-3319; and **Chong's**, a popular Chinese American restaurant so well-loved by local folks that it now has four restaurant locations, (502) 898-6402. **Holman House**, 2714 Park Avenue, is another well-liked, casual family restaurant (no liquor) that serves buffet-style, (502) 444-3903.

For breakfast try the **Downtown Diner**, 308 Broadway, (502) 443-1288, or **Skinhead's** (what can I say? I ate there years ago when passing through Paducah just because of the name), 1020 S. 21st Street, (502) 442-6471, where the parking lot is always packed.

Barbecue, western Kentucky-style, is close kin to northwest Tennessee's hot pepper, vinegar, and tomato-sauced and hickory-smoked, chopped pork shoulder. **Prices Bar-B-Q**, at 3001 Broadway, has been in business for 50 years, (502) 444-9256; **Starnes**, 1008 Joe Clifton Drive, also cooks beef and mutton and bottles its sauce for sale, (502) 444-9555; and **B.B. Whiskers**, 2701 Irvin Cobb Drive, gets high marks for local catfish and barbecue, (502) 443-7076.

LODGING

Reelfoot Lake State Park has modern facilities at its **Airpark Inn** ($56 double rooms) and the **Spillway Motel** on the banks of the lake ($56 and $66 double rooms, many of which have kitchenettes and can be rented by the week). Call (800) 250-8617 or (901) 253-7756 for reservations. Across the road from the park, **Boyette's Resort** has cabins for rent, (901) 253-6523. In Tiptonville there is a private cottage B&B behind a historic home at 431 Wynn Street, call (901) 253-7653 to ask about **Sweet Dreams Cottage**. There is also a **Hampton Inn** in Union City, (800) HAMPTON, as well as the

Cultra Motor Inn, (901) 885-6610, both located on Reelfoot Avenue.

Between Reelfoot and Paducah, you'll find the 19-unit **Wickcliffe Motel**, (502) 335-3121, and the **Grassy Lakes Hunting Resort**, also at Wickliffe, which provides meals and lodging in the company of fishermen and waterfowl hunters, (502) 335-5143.

Paducah is the place to stay, with a number of bed and breakfasts housed in historic structures. The **1857 B&B**, at 127 Market House Square, (800) 264-5607, and the **Paducah Harbor Plaza**, at 201 Broadway, which was an old hotel, (800) 719-7799, are both downtown. The **1868 B&B**, at 914 Jefferson Street, (502) 444-6801, and **Farley Place**, an 1850 Victorian house, (502) 442-2488, are also fairly close to the historic district. The **Rosewood Inn**, just outside of town, is in a turn of the century home as well, (502) 554-6632.

There are also a number of motels in Paducah, including national chains such as **Hampton Inn**, **Holiday Inn Express**, **Days Inn**, **Quality Inn**, and **Ramada Inn**. **Denton's** is a locally owned 34-room motel that has suites with kitchenettes, (800) 788-1626. **J.R.'s Executive Inn**, which is located at the Riverfront near the Convention Center, features regularly scheduled performances by major country music stars, just like its counterpart (now a Ramada) in Owensboro, (800) 866-3636.

CAMPING

Columbus-Belmont State Park, located 36 miles south of Paducah, has both hookups and primitive camping. It is open April–October, but does not accept reservations, (502) 677-2327. **Fern Lake Campground**, outside of Paducah at 5535 Cairo Road, is open year-round with 50 sites and full hookups, (502) 444-7939.

NIGHTLIFE

Paducah has a variety of evening offerings, including a sunset carriage ride and a surprising number of performing arts events. Call **Annie's Horse-Drawn Carriage** to reserve a 7 p.m. or later slot in spring, summer, and fall. The fee is $6 per adult, $3 per child. Phone: (618) 524-3272.

If you are a contemporary country music fan, check with **J.R.'s Executive Inn** to see who they are bringing to town, (800) 866-3636.

The **Market House Theatre** offers six plays per year at $6–$8 a seat, (502) 444-6828; the **Paducah Community College Focus Series** includes national professional groups in their annual series with tickets at just $12, (502) 554-9200; and the **Paducah Symphony** plays a five-concert season, (502) 444-0665. **Players Riverboat Casino**, located 7 miles from Paducah at Metropolis, Illinois, has daily cruises. Call (800) 935-7700 to find out about riverboat gambling, Illinois-style.

7

HENDERSON
AND OWENSBORO

Henderson and Owensboro are located on the northern border of Kentucky, which is formed by the Ohio River. These two western Kentucky towns, approximately 30 miles apart, were and still are ports for the exportation of Kentucky goods to the outside world. Henderson, whose wealth came from tobacco, has a row of old brick mansions downtown on Main Street to testify to its former prominence. Henderson's downtown Central Park is complete with gazebo, conjuring visions of Sunday promenades at the turn of the century.

In Owensboro, Kentucky's third largest city, one can still watch barges laden with Kentucky coal moving down the swift river towards the Mississippi. Henderson's most famous citizen was John James Audubon, who owned a gristmill near the river. In addition to that historic commemorative site, there is a museum complete with a collection of his works and personal artifacts, as well as a bird habitat in the state park that bears his name.

Both Henderson and Owensboro are cities on the move. They are well kept and are so proud of their history that they hold festivals celebrating their musical and culinary heritage: Henderson's W.C. Handy Blues and Barbecue Festival and Bluegrass in Central Park, and the International Bluegrass Music Association Festival and International Bar-B-Q Festival in Owensboro. ◾

OWENSBORO

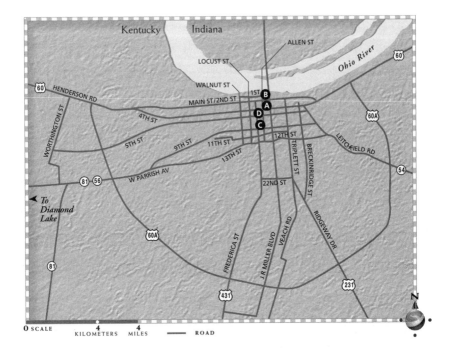

Sights

- **A** Andria's Homestyle Candies
- **B** International Bluegrass Music Association and Museum
- **A** Owensboro Area Museum of Science and History
- **C** Owensboro Museum of Fine Art
- **D** Raines Drive-Thru Shoe Hospital
- **B** Riverpark Center

Note: Items with the same letter are located in the same area.

HENDERSON

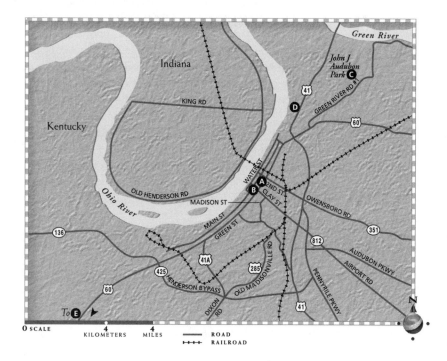

Sights

Ⓐ Audubon Mill Park

Ⓑ Central Park

Ⓒ John J. Audubon Museum and Nature Center

Ⓓ River Park/Walk

Ⓔ Sloughs Wildlife Management Area

A PERFECT DAY IN OWENSBORO/HENDERSON

After touring the International Bluegrass Museum and watching the river traffic pass by from Owensboro's new Riverpark Center, stop in at the Museum of Art to see its Kentucky craft collection. Then grab a sandwich at Moonlite BBQ on the way out of town before departing on Hwy 60 for a drive through beautiful Kentucky farmlands to Henderson. Drive or walk around downtown. Visit the Audubon grist-mill and the fine new museum at Audubon State Park before setting out for your own bird-watching walk in Sloughs Wildlife Management Area. Dine and spend the night in the historic downtown area, listening for the strains of W.C. Handy's music as you take an after-dinner walk in Central Park.

SIGHTSEEING HIGHLIGHTS—HENDERSON

★★★ **John J. Audubon Museum and Nature Center**—A beautiful new facility, this center includes not only works of art and artifacts related to one of the town's best-known citizens but also a wild bird habitat. Open daily. Address: Audubon State Park, a few miles west of town. Phone: (502) 827-1893.

Unicorn/Jean Higgins

✯✯ **Audubon Mill Park** is located downtown at Water and Second Streets; its millstone remains on location.

✯ **Central Park**, located downtown within a block of the Ohio River, was built in 1797. It is the oldest city park west of the Allegheny Mountains.

✯ **River Park/Walk** is a 1-mile jogging and exercise trail located in Atkinson Park near the Ohio River boat ramps.

✯ **Sloughs Wildlife Management Area** contains a 10,000-acre waterfowl refuge. Both hunting and camping are allowed in designated areas, which include wetlands, fields, and woodlands. Phone: (502) 827-2673.

SIGHTSEEING HIGHLIGHTS—OWENSBORO

✯✯ **Owensboro Area Museum of Science and History**—Relocated in spring 1995 to a large former clothing store, the museum exhibits are not yet fully installed. It does include, however, natural history, local and regional history, exploratory science displays for children, and a good gift and book shop. Address: 220 Daviess Street, downtown. Phone: (502) 683-0296.

✯✯ **Owensboro Museum of Fine Art**—This museum is housed in a restored Carnegie Library building attached to a historic house and bound together by a new addition on the back. It features changing exhibits and a Kentucky folk art collection. The permanent installation of stained glass windows from a now-demolished Catholic church reflects the German Catholic heritage of this and nearby river cities, such as Louisville and Cincinnati. Address: 901 Frederica Street, downtown. Phone: (502) 685-3181.

✯✯ **Riverpark Center**—This performance hall and culture center offers great views of the J.R. Miller Bridge and Yellow Bank Island. It features the Owensboro Symphony Season, touring dance and theater companies, local and regional theater, a "First Night" community New Year's Eve celebration, and a variety of children's theater productions. For schedules, phone: (800) 285-ARTS. The **International Bluegrass Music Association and Museum** is also headquartered here. Phone: (502) 684-9025.

Andria's Homestyle Candies—Founded in 1910, this is a tiny candy factory that specializes in Kentucky Bourbon Candy, which makes great take-home gifts and can be shipped all over the U.S. Address: 217 Allen Street, downtown. Phone: (502) 684-3733.

Raines Drive-Thru Shoe Hospital is surely a one-of-a-kind. It's still "operating," and you'll find its classic neon sign downtown on Frederica Street.

FITNESS AND RECREATION

In Henderson, walking tours of downtown, including **Central Park**, **Audubon Gristmill Site**, and **River Park/Walk**, are available anytime. **Audubon State Park** offers hiking, fishing, tennis, and golf. **Sloughs Wildlife Management Area**, which has hiking and walking trails and allows hunting and fishing as well, can be reached by following Hwy 60W to KY 136 to KY 268 (about 6 miles). Phone: (502) 827-2673.

In Owensboro, hike the nature trails at **Ben Hawes State Park**, Hwy 60, 4 miles west of Owensboro, (502) 684-9808; walk the elevated wetlands trails at **Panther Creek Park** (handicap access), or find **Yellow Creek Park**, which has a climbable fire tower, to see more of the flat landscape in this region. Owensboro has a sizable parks and recreation program. Call (502) 281-5346. There are tennis courts available in the parks, (502) 687-8700, and also at **Ramey Sport and Fitness Center**, (502) 771-5590. Ramey also offers horseback riding. The **Owensboro Ice Arena** is open October–March, (502) 687-8720, and Owensboro has a **Family YMCA**, (502) 926-9622.

FOOD

In Henderson **Wolf's Tavern** is open for lunch and dinner at moderate prices in an historic building downtown, (502) 826-5221. Also downtown are **Planters Coffeehouse**, at 130 N. Main Street, open for morning coffee and lunch, and **Mezzaluna Garden Café**, open for lunch and dinner and located on the river at 104 North Water Street, (502) 826-9401.

Owensboro bills itself as the barbecue capital of the world. The **Moonlite Bar-B-Q Inn**, 2840 W. Parrish, is a tourist attraction but quite wonderful nonetheless. It is famous for its spicy mutton, although beef, pork, and chicken are also available. Try the mutton—it tastes like lamb—and is served sliced or chopped. This large three generation family-owned restaurant has a cozy feel and a sizable local following, (502) 684-8143. **Old Hickory BBQ Inn**, off Frederica Street at 25th, (502) 926-9000, which advertises "five generations of quality BBQ," has the same fare as above on the site where local blacksmith Pappy Foreman began to barbecue mutton in 1918. This is a smaller restaurant that serves no liquor but has equally good BBQ. **George's BBQ**, on the east side of town, is also open for breakfast and is always crowded, but it's closed Sunday.

Two other Owensboro breakfast spots are the **Gem Café**, 1006 E. Fourth Street, and **Jay Dee's**, at 1420 Breckenridge. Both serve plate lunches and homemade pies. The **Famous Deli Ltd.**, in downtown Owensboro at 102 W. Second, has Greek-style sandwiches and dishes. Phone: (502) 686-8202. Just down the street is the **Pastalotta Café and Wine Cellar**, 118 W. Second, a locally owned Americanized-Italian restaurant with some interesting specialties. Phone: (502) 684-3752. A few blocks away in an old building is **Colby's Fine Food and Spirits**, 202 W. Third, which has a fern bar ambiance with its wood and tile interior and serves an upscale menu of fresh fish and beef entrees. Phone: (502) 685-4239. **Trotter's Restaurant and Lounge**, located in the Cigar Factory complex in midtown, at 1100 Walnut Street, is popular for lunch with a variety of daily specials and salads. Closed Sunday. Phone: (502) 683-4755.

LODGING

In Henderson highly recommended is the **L&N B&B** at 327 N. Main Street, in the historic district next to the old railroad trestle (502-831-1100). **Audubon State Park** has five nice cabins, (502) 826-2247. On the east side of Henderson are a number of discount chain hotels.

In Owensboro the **Ramada** (formerly Executive Inn Rivermont) on Second Street, has the best view of the Ohio River in town. This is a convention center type hotel, which has indoor and outdoor pools and well-known entertainers performing regularly (502-926-8000 or 800-625-1936). Rates are $75–$85 for a double room, and weekend packages often include show tickets and rooms at savings. Their weekend buffet breakfast is a good buy at $5.95. The **Cadillac Motel**, on W. Second Street, has 40 rooms and is locally owned, (502) 684-2343. A

OWENSBORO

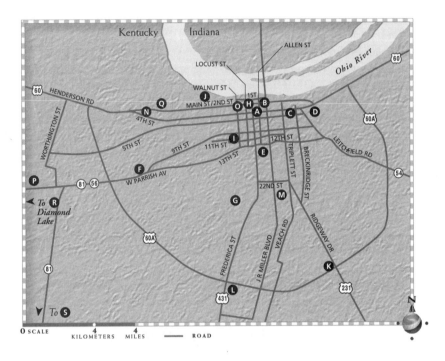

Food

- **Ⓐ** Colby's Fine Food and Spirits
- **Ⓑ** Famous Deli Ltd.
- **Ⓒ** Gem Café
- **Ⓓ** George's BBQ
- **Ⓔ** Jay Dee's
- **Ⓕ** Moonlite Bar-B-Q Inn
- **Ⓖ** Old Hickory BBQ Inn
- **Ⓗ** Pastalotta Café and Wine Cellar
- **Ⓘ** Trotter's Restaurant and Lounge

Lodging

- **Ⓙ** Cadillac Motel
- **Ⓚ** Days Inn
- **Ⓛ** Hampton Inn
- **Ⓜ** Helton House
- **Ⓝ** Holiday Inn
- **Ⓞ** Ramada
- **Ⓟ** Trail's End
- **Ⓠ** Weatherberry

Camping

- **Ⓡ** Diamond Lake Campground
- **Ⓢ** Windy Hollow Campground

HENDERSON

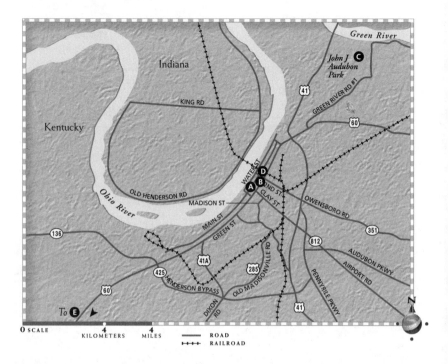

Food

Ⓐ Mezzaluna Garden Café
Ⓐ Planters Coffeehouse
Ⓑ Wolf's Tavern

Lodging

Ⓒ Audubon State Park
Ⓓ L&N B&B

Camping

Ⓒ Audubon State Park
Ⓔ Sloughs Wildlife Management Area

Note: Items with the same letter are located in the same area.

Holiday Inn, a **Hampton Inn**, and a **Days Inn** are located out near the Hwy 60 bypass. Owensboro has several bed and breakfasts including the **Weatherberry**, in an 1840s house on Second Street (Hwy 60) just west of town, (502) 684-8760; the **Helton House** at 103 E. 23rd Street, (502) 926-7117; and **Trail's End**, which has three cottages, on Hwy 56 West, (502) 771-5590.

CAMPING

Audubon State Park in Henderson has 71 sites with amenities but no hookups. They take no reservations. Call (502) 826-2247.

Donnie Beauchamp

Sloughs Wildlife Management Area offers primitive camping only; call (502) 827-2673.

Owensboro's **Windy Hollow Campground**, 10 miles southwest on Hwy 81 has hookups, a swimming lake, and a restaurant. The Windy Hollow Speedway is nearby, with stock car and drag racing on Saturday and Sunday nights, April–October. Call (502) 785-4150 for information. **Diamond Lake Campground** is located 12 miles west on Hwy 56; call (502) 229-4961.

FESTIVALS

Both towns are big on festivals, and visitors might well want to plan accordingly. Because these are relatively small cities, the festival atmosphere could add just the right spice to your trip along Kentucky's northern riverfront.

Henderson has three cultural heritage events of interest to out-of-town visitors. The **W.C. Handy Blues and Barbecue Festival**, which brings in major-name entertainers to concert venues citywide, takes place in June. Handy, who married Hendersonian Elizabeth Price, lived here for 10 years in the 1850s while he traveled the minstrel show circuit. Call the Convention and Visitors Bureau at (502) 826-3128 for information. **Bluegrass in the Park**, held in Central Park, takes place in August. Either the Henderson Area Arts Alliance, (502) 826-5916, or the visitor's bureau can fill in this year's schedule for you. The **Big Rivers Arts & Crafts Festival**, which takes place in early October, is one of the largest crafts fairs in Kentucky, often drawing as many as 40,000 visitors. It is held in Audubon Park. Call (502) 926-4433 for more information.

Owensboro sponsors a big Fourth of July Summer Festival and a First Night (New Year's Eve) Arts Festival. Call the Owensboro Tourist Commission for more information at (800) 489-1131. Best-known is the **International Bar-B-Q Festival**, which happens in mid-May at the riverfront and includes competitive teams with names like Blessed Mother, Our Lady of Lourdes, St. Pius X, Precious Blood (last year's champion), and the Telephone Workers. What a photo opportunity! You can get in the serving line for $7. Call the festival organizers at (502) 926-6938. The **International Bluegrass Music Association FanFest** takes place in September at English Park, overlooking the Ohio River. For a preliminary idea of the talent lineup, call the association at (502) 684-9025.

NIGHTLIFE

Henderson has a new Fine Arts Center on the campus of Henderson Community College that features a yearly schedule of music, dance, and theater events. Call (502) 830-5324, or call the visitor's bureau at (502) 826-3128 for more information. Ellis Park, across the river, features thoroughbred racing late June–August and inter-track wagering the rest of the year, (800) 333-8110.

Owensboro holds a lively schedule of performing arts events at **Riverpark Center**, (800) 285-ARTS, and the nearby **Ramada Executive Inn** has regularly scheduled country music acts. Call (502) 926-8000 or (800) 626-1936 for information.

8

BOWLING GREEN
AND MAMMOTH CAVE

This area of south-central Kentucky is approximately one hour north of Nashville, just off I-65 headed north to Louisville. Its most spectacular natural feature is Mammoth Cave. Once a tourist destination second only to Niagara Falls in popularity, Mammoth Cave is now an international biosphere reserve and national park interpretive and recreation site. This is cave country—nearby towns are named Horse Cave and Cave City.

Bowling Green, home to Western Kentucky University, offers the visitor a central point from which to explore a wide range of activities—from the quiet ingenuity of the early nineteenth-century Shaker settlement at South Union to the style and innovation of the Corvette, America's best-known sports car, at its assembly plant and newly opened museum. Bowling Green has a surprisingly cosmopolitan air for a city its size. One finds serious theater at the Capitol Arts Centre, located in a historic building downtown along with a public art gallery. An 82-mile scenic driving tour of the region touts both its natural and historic attributes. WKU houses an impressive museum of state and local history, and an archeological collection related to the exploration of Mammoth Cave.

East of Bowling Green, the countryside is flat, rich farmland—once prime tobacco-raising ground. Smoking barns dot the landscape, and small towns like Franklin, Auburn, and Smith's Grove are filled with Victorian architecture and antique shops. ◣

BOWLING GREEN AND MAMMOTH CAVE

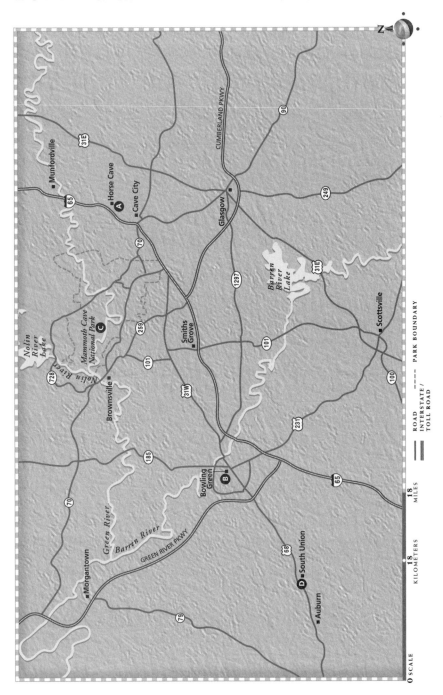

Sights

Ⓐ American Cave Museum and Hidden River Cave

Ⓑ Bowling Green Walking Tours

Ⓑ Capitol Arts Center

Ⓐ Horse Cave Theater

Ⓑ Kentucky Museum and Library

Ⓒ Mammoth Cave

Ⓑ National Corvette Museum and GM Corvette Assembly Plant

Ⓑ Riverview at Hobson Grove

Ⓓ Shaker Museum at South Union

Ⓓ Shaker Tavern

Note: Items with the same letter are located in the same area.

A PERFECT DAY IN BOWLING GREEN

After an overnight stay at one of the Mammoth Cave Hotel cabins, strike out early on one of the ranger-led guided tours of the Cave (tours begin as early as 8 a.m., and crowds can be a problem). Pack a picnic and explore the wonders of Mammoth Cave National Park, perhaps taking a boat ride on the Green River. Or head into Bowling Green for a tour of the Corvette Factory—the museum across the street is a one-of-a-kind. Lunch in historic downtown at the Parakeet Café. The Kentucky Museum at WKU has a wonderful exhibit about Victorian childhood that kids will love. Drive out to South Union and wander leisurely through the Shaker museum and grounds. Dine on regional specialties and spend the night at the 1869 Shaker Tavern. If you are up for some nightlife, check to see if the Phoenix Theater or the Capitol Arts Centre has anything in production.

SIGHTSEEING HIGHLIGHTS

Listen to WKYU for excellent public radio that serves all of western Kentucky and ties into the statewide public radio network. Some of the most exceptional programming comes from the eastern Kentucky town of Whitesburg, home of Appalshop, a non-profit entity that promotes Appalachian culture.

★★★ **Mammoth Cave**—Rediscovered by frontier-era Kentuckians around 1800, this series of caves, which snakes underground for about 350 miles, was named for its sheer size. Evidence exists of extensive site use by nomadic bands of Archaic Indians, which decreased as agriculture was later developed by the Woodland and Mississippian peoples. Park rangers offer a number of fine explanatory tours covering a wide range of topics, from geology to history to biology. At least four tours are offered daily, year-round, while others can be arranged by advance reservation. Caving trips can also be arranged. Reservations are highly recommended during the busy period of June through August and can be made up to five months in advance. Mammoth Cave offers a wide range of park concessions, from lodging, camping, and dining to boat excursions and horseback riding. For information, write or call the park. Address: Mammoth Cave National Park, Mammoth Cave, KY 42259. Phone: (502) 758-2328 for information or (800) 967-2283 for tour reservations.

★★★ **Shaker Museum at South Union**—The settlement at South Union, located about 10 miles southwest of Bowling Green, was started in 1807 by a band of 30 Shakers who traveled west to Kentucky under the leadership of Brother Benjamin Seth Youngs and Sister Molly Goodrich. At its height in 1827, South Union numbered 350 converts from the surrounding communities, and its furniture-making industry was at peak production. Six thousand acres of land and 250 buildings made up the original community, which lasted until 1922. The Centre House is beautifully interpreted and historically intact, with a museum store containing a fine selection of books by and about the Shakers. Informative tours are available. Admission is $3 per adult, $1 per child. The museum is open March 1–December 15, and programs, including workshops in making Shaker-style furnishings, are held throughout the year. Phone: (502) 542-4167. (2 hours)

Near the railroad tracks just to the south stands the 1869 **Shaker Tavern**, constructed as a business venture in hopes of attracting visitors from the outside world who would continue to patronize Shaker industries. The Tavern is now operated as a bed and breakfast that also serves lunch and dinner Tuesday–Saturday. Phone: (502) 542-6801.

Peggy Schaefer

✯ **American Cave Museum and Hidden River Cave**—This is a favorite with kids, and it presents a clear environmental message that parents will appreciate. It is a project of the American Cave Conservation Association. Address: P.O. Box 409, Main Street, Horse Cave, KY 42749. Phone: (502) 786-1466.

✯ **Capitol Arts Center**—Located in a restored theater building on the main square, the center features an art gallery and a full schedule of music and dance performances, film, theater, and other activities sponsored by the Bowling Green/Warren County Arts Commission. Open Monday–Friday. Address: Bowling Green. Phone: (502) 782-2787.

✯ **Horse Cave Theater**—This well-known regional theater offers a June–December season during which it is possible to see three plays in two days. Recent offerings include *All the King's Men*, Robert Penn Warren's classic based on the life of Louisiana governor Huey Long; and *The Dancers of Canaan*, a new play with authentic Shaker music. The theater is dark (no plays) on Monday; matinees Saturday and Sunday. Address: P.O. Box 215 Horsecave, KY 42749. Phone: (800) 342-2177.

✯ **Kentucky Museum and Library**—This museum of regional and state history was founded in 1931 with the creation of an archive for significant materials relating to Kentucky history. The library holds important collections of Kentucky books, manuscripts, and information on folk life. The museum facility presents an impressive yearly schedule of changing exhibits as well as semi-permanent interpretive exhibits, such as "Growing Up Victorian" and "Main Street: Mirror of Change," designed to bring local and regional history to life. The **Nelson Collection** of artifacts from Mammoth Cave National Park is housed at the museum, and cooperative research projects between the two entities are ongoing. Many exhibits place a special emphasis on children as the audience and a number of interactive interpretive activities are used. Closed Monday. Address: Western Kentucky University, Bowling Green. Phone: (502) 745-2592.

✯ **National Corvette Museum** and **GM Corvette Assembly Plant**—Admission to the museum is $8 per adult, $6 per senior, $4.50 per child. Open daily, year round. Phone: (502) 781-7973. (1 hour)

The Corvette Assembly Plant offers free daily tours at 9 a.m. and 1 p.m. (The plant will be closed to tours in late 1996 and early and early 1997 preceding a model change. (502) 745-8419

✶ **Riverview at Hobson Grove**—A grand circa 1870 brick home, Riverview is located just west of Bowling Green. An award-winning interpretive tour presenting the perspective of Victorian servants can be requested. Admission is $3.50 per adult, $1.50 per student, children under 6 free, or $6 per family. Closed Monday and the month of January. Phone: (502) 843-5565. (1 hour)

Bowling Green Walking Tours—The Landmark Association sponsors tours of four significant historic areas. Arrangements should be made in advance. Address: 912½ State Street. Phone: (502) 782-0037.

FITNESS AND RECREATION

Mammoth Cave National Park offers a wonderland of outdoor activity for the whole family. For information and to make reservations for guided hikes, cave adventures, or a trip on the *Miss Green River* boat, call park information at (502) 758-2328 or (800) 967-2283. To rent canoes for outings on the **Green River**, contact the **Green River Canoe Outfitter**, (502) 597-2031, and **Salings Canoe Outfitters**, (502) 286-8323.

Fishing within the park requires no license. Horseback riding can be arranged by **Double J Stables**, (502) 286-8167—one of the park's campgrounds has facilities for overnight horse-boarding if you book an extended trailride. The gently rolling terrain and paved country roads make this perfect biking territory. Call the **Bowling Green League of Bicyclists** for maps to Shakertown and Mammoth Cave, (502) 781-2729. If indoor workouts are more your style, Bowling Green has a new **YMCA** with gymnasium, indoor pool, and racquetball courts.

FOOD

Bread and Bagels Bakery, located at 871 Broadway in Bowling Green, features baked from scratch breads by Al Baker (no kidding), who won Small Businessman of the Year honors in 1995. **Yoder's Mennonite Bakery**, a place to be sought out in the Mennonite community near

BOWLING GREEN AND MAMMOTH CAVE

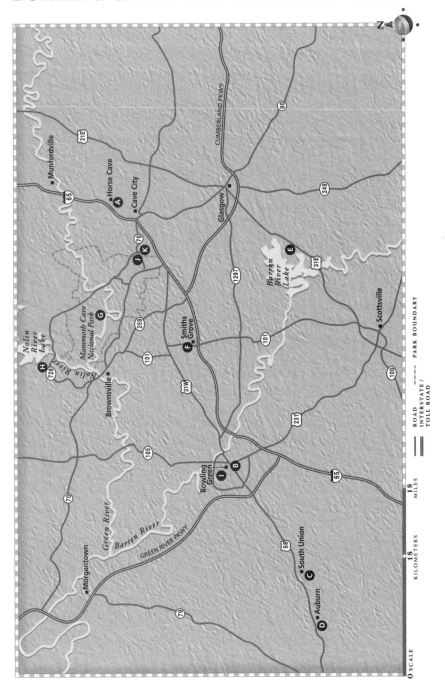

Food

- **Ⓐ** The Bookstore and Café
- **Ⓑ** Bread and Bagels Bakery
- **Ⓑ** 440 Main Restaurant and Bar
- **Ⓐ** Hal's Restaurant
- **Ⓑ** Parakeet Café
- **Ⓒ** Shaker Tavern
- **Ⓑ** Smokey Pig BBQ
- **Ⓓ** Yoder's Mennonite Bakery

Lodging

- **Ⓔ** Barren River Lake State Resort Park
- **Ⓑ** Best Western
- **Ⓕ** Bryce Motel
- **Ⓖ** Cave Spring Farm
- **Ⓑ** Comfort Inn
- **Ⓑ** Days Inn
- **Ⓑ** Fairfield Inn/Marriott
- **Ⓓ** Federal Grove B&B
- **Ⓑ** Hampton Inn
- **Ⓑ** Holiday Inn

- **Ⓖ** Mammoth Cave National Park
- **Ⓗ** Mello Inn B&B
- **Ⓑ** News Inn of Bowling Green
- **Ⓑ** Plaza Hotel
- **Ⓑ** Ramada Inn
- **Ⓒ** Shaker Tavern
- **Ⓕ** Victorian House
- **Ⓘ** Walnut Lawn B&B
- **Ⓙ** Wayfarer B&B
- **Ⓐ** Wigwam Village #2
- **Ⓖ** Woodland Cottages

Camping

- **Ⓔ** Barren River Lake State Resort Park
- **Ⓖ** Double J Stables & Campground
- **Ⓖ** Mammoth Cave National Park
- **Ⓚ** The Oakes

Note: Items with the same letter are located in the same area.

Auburn, is acclaimed by locals. **Shaker Tavern**, in South Union, features fresh local ingredients and regional cuisine, and is open for lunch and dinner Tuesday–Saturday, (502) 542-6801.

Downtown Bowling Green's **Parakeet Café**, a local favorite open for lunch and dinner, has moved around the corner from its original location on the square, (502) 781-1538. Also downtown in a historic building is **440 Main Restaurant and Bar** (closed Sunday), (502) 793-0450. Right on Hwy 31 just east of downtown is **Smokey Pig BBQ**, if you want a quick BBQ to go.

In Horse Cave, try the **Bookstore and Café**, 111 Water Street, (502) 786-3084 which brags about their coffee and sandwiches, and **Hal's Restaurant**, a plain, family-style restaurant, open early every day for breakfast and featuring catfish on Friday, Hwy 31W, (502) 768-4949.

LODGING

To fully experience **Mammoth Cave National Park**, stay overnight at one of the rustic **Woodland Cottages** (open May–October). They are within easy walking distance of the cave mouth so you can take advantage of evening and early morning activities at the park. The park also offers a hotel, motor lodge, and hotel cottages available year-round at reasonable rates. June–August are the busiest months, so try to make reservations before April if you will be there during the prime season. Call (502) 758-2225, or fax (502) 758-2301.

Just outside the entrance to the park you will find a beautiful old white house with a craft shop and folk-style Floyd Collins Museum on the ground floor and the newly remodeled **Wayfarer B&B** above, 1240 Old Mammoth Cave Road, (502) 773-3366. Open all year, off-season rates are available. (Floyd Collins was a local man who became lost in the cave in 1925, attracting national attention. An outdoor drama based on his story is performed at the Green River Amphitheater during the summer months—see Nightlife section.) The **Mello Inn B&B**, (north, on Nolin Lake), (502) 286-4126, and **Barren River Lake State Resort Park** (south, at Lucas, Kentucky), (800) 325-0057 offer alternatives to staying in Mammoth Cave National Park. Barren River Lake has a lodge with 51 rooms, 22 lakeside cottages, RV hookups, golf course, tennis courts, and horseback riding. The 10,000-acre lake also offers a variety of watersport activities. Another fun option is **Wigwam Village #2** (#1 is in Holbrook, Arizona) in Cave

City. The rooms are individual concrete wigwams. Don't miss it. For information, call (502) 773-3381.

There are many historic homes being used for bed and breakfast accommodations in the area surrounding Bowling Green. My first choice would be the **Shaker Tavern**, built in 1869 by the Shakers to accommodate visitors who arrived by train. It is located just east of the settlement at South Union, (502) 542-6801. Several miles further west on Hwy 68 at Auburn is **Federal Grove B&B**, built circa 1886, (502) 542-6106. Twelve miles north of Bowling Green is the community of Smith's Grove, which features at least nine antique stores; bed and breakfasts **Victorian House**, (502) 563-9403, and **Cave Spring Farm**, (502) 563-6941; and the small, locally-owned **Bryce Motel**, (502) 563-5141. **Walnut Lawn B&B** is located northwest of Bowling Green, on Morgantown Road, (502) 781-7255.

Bowling Green has a number of motels, many of which are located off I-65, at Exit 22. The **News Inn of Bowling Green** is locally owned, (800) 443-3701, and the **Plaza Hotel**, a convention center hotel with 219 rooms, is the newest in town, (502) 745-0088. **Best Western, Comfort Inn, Days Inn, Fairfield Inn/Marriott, Hampton Inn, Holiday Inn**, and **Ramada Inn**, for which one can find telephone numbers in the national 1-800 directory, are also located at Exit 22.

CAMPING

Mammoth Cave National Park offers primitive camping year-round for $5. Three other campgrounds are open from March–November, and one accommodates horses, (502) 758-2251. The **Double J Stables & Campground**, (502) 286-8167 is the park's concessionaire for horseback riding in the park. Near the park entrance on Old Mammoth Cave Road is a neatly kept establishment named **The Oakes**, which offers both camping and cabins. **Barren River Lake State Resort Park** has RV hookups, (800) 325-0057.

NIGHTLIFE

Ask at the **Shaker Museum** for a schedule of their occasional interpretive activities, including holiday dinners and musical performances, (502) 542-4167. Or drive 12 miles south on 31W to **Dueling Grounds Racetrack**, which offers thoroughbred racing in September, year-round simulcast, and off-track betting for thoroughbred racing at other times. They also offer the **Turf Club Restaurant and Bar**, and are located in Franklin, (502) 586-7778.

For live theater, call to see what's playing at the **Horse Cave Theater** in Horse Cave, which features both the works of new playwrights and classic dramatic productions. For information call (800) 342-2177. In Bowling Green, the **Capitol Arts Centre** offers not only theater performances but nationally known music and performing arts groups, (502) 782-ARTS, and the **Phoenix Theater** runs a fine yearly dramatic series, (502) 781-6233. Families might enjoy the experience of outdoor theater at **Green River Amphitheatre**, north of Mammoth Cave National Park in Brownsville, where *The Floyd Collins Story* runs from June to September, (800) 624-8687. **O'Pawley's Pub** is the venue for live music in Bowling Green, (502) 842-6349.

9

BARDSTOWN AND HISTORIC CENTRAL KENTUCKY

The counties surrounding Bardstown form the historic center of Kentucky. Bardstown, home of Federal Hill, the mansion that inspired Stephen Foster's ballad "My Old Kentucky Home," is a charming town that merits a several-day visit. Located in the heart of Kentucky's distillery country, this is the place to learn about Kentucky's traditional Southern hospitality. The surrounding small towns and historic sites will easily take two days to explore. Located southwest of Lexington, this area contains the first settlements west of the Allegheny Mountains. Fort Harrod, now reconstructed in a park on its original location, was built in 1774 as a shelter for pioneer families.

Bardstown was founded from a Virginia land grant in 1780. The Kentucky state constitution was written in nearby Danville in the years before Kentucky was granted statehood in 1792. The Shaker Village at Pleasant Hill, active from 1805 to 1910, was the third largest Shaker community in the United States, with as many as 500 residents at its height. Visitors to Perryville and its surrounding landmarks of the War Between the States will experience the divided loyalties of Kentucky and Tennessee firsthand. South of Bardstown can be found Abraham Lincoln's 1809 birthplace at Hodgenville and his boyhood home at Knob Creek. ◨

BARDSTOWN

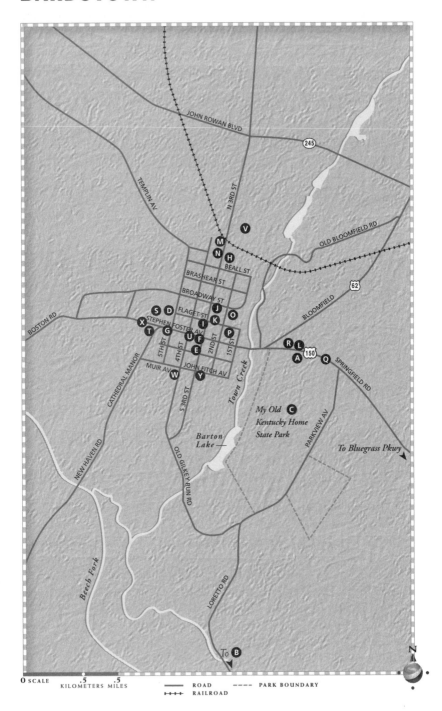

Sights

- Ⓐ Federal Hill
- Ⓑ Maker's Mark Distillery Tour
- Ⓒ My Old Kentucky Home State Park
- Ⓓ Oscar Getz Museum of Whiskey History/Bardstown Historical Museum
- Ⓔ Old Talbott Tavern
- Ⓕ Quisenberry's
- Ⓖ St. Joseph Proto-Cathedral

Food

- Ⓗ The Bardstonian
- Ⓘ Beall's Row Coffee and Ale House
- Ⓙ Dagwood's
- Ⓕ Hurst Drug Store's Old Fashioned Soda Fountain
- Ⓚ Hurst's
- Ⓛ Kurtz Restaurant
- Ⓜ My Old Kentucky Dinner Train
- Ⓔ Old Talbott Tavern
- Ⓝ Tom Pig's

Lodging

- Ⓞ 1790 House
- Ⓟ Amber Lee-Ann
- Ⓠ Bardstown Inn
- Ⓡ Bardstown Parkview Motel
- Ⓢ Beautiful Dreamer
- Ⓣ Best Western General Nelson Motel
- Ⓤ Jailer's Inn
- Ⓥ The Mansion
- Ⓦ McLean House
- Ⓧ Old Kentucky Home
- Ⓔ Old Talbott Tavern
- Ⓨ Victorian Lights
- Ⓜ Wilson Motel

Note: Items with the same letter are located in the same place.

A PERFECT DAY IN AND AROUND BARDSTOWN

Walk the old streets of central Bardstown, stopping at Beall's Row Coffee and Ale House for coffee and a muffin and dawdling in some of the antique and craft shops. The several block walk to the Bardstown Historical Society Museum takes you past beautiful, early 1800s houses that are still private residences. Enjoy the Oscar Getz Museum of Whiskey History, which will whet your appetite for a taste of the real thing. Lunch early at the historic Old Talbott Tavern—try the famous Kentucky Hot Brown—and then move on to My Old Kentucky Home for a guided tour. A leisurely drive out into the rolling countryside will take you through Perryville and Harrodsburg on the way to Pleasant Hill. Spend the afternoon musing over Shaker exhibits and demonstrations before a quiet supper in the Trustee's Office Dining Room.

SIGHTSEEING HIGHLIGHTS—BARDSTOWN

Bardstown was founded in 1780 when William Bard came to claim his brother David's Virginia land grant. A courthouse of hand-hewn logs was built in 1785, and the town was incorporated in 1788 as part of Virginia's "Kentucky district." Kentucky's distillery industry, whose records date it as far back as 1776 in this vicinity, arose here because of the high limestone content of the water.

★★★ **Federal Hill**—Often better known as **"My Old Kentucky Home,"** Federal Hill was built in 1818 by Judge John Rowan Sr. It was after a visit here in 1853 that Stephen Foster penned his famous song. Tours are led by guides dressed in period costume. Admission is $4 per adult, $2 per child. Phone: (800) 323-7803. (1 hour)

 My Old Kentucky Home State Park surrounds the historic site. From June until Labor Day *The Stephen Foster Story* outdoor drama is performed in the amphitheater here. Tickets are $12 per adult, $6 per child and can be ordered in advance. Phone: (800) 626-1563.

★★★ **Old Talbott Tavern**—Opened in the late 1770s, the tavern began as a stagecoach stop and is still a restaurant and inn offering overnight lodging and plenty of tales to tell of its many early visitors. George Rogers Clark and John James Audubon stayed here, and an upstairs room contains a late eighteenth-century mural painted by one of Louis Philippe's entourage. Visitors are welcome. Phone: (502) 348-3494. (¼ hour)

★★ **Maker's Mark Distillery Tour**—This tour is highly recommended by those who have toured them all. Open daily. Call for directions and tour times. Phone: (502) 865-2099. (1½ hours)

Also located in and around Bardstown are the **Heaven Hill** (Evan Williams, Elijah Craig), **Barton Brands**, and **Jim Beam** distilleries. These other distilleries also offer free tours—it might be fun to see them all.

★★ **Oscar Getz Museum of Whiskey History** and **Bardstown Historical Museum**—Housed in beautiful old Spalding Hall behind the cathedral, these museums are not to be missed. There is a bookstore downstairs that carries a large selection of publications by Thomas Merton. You can call or fax them to request a booklist, (502) 348-6488 or fax (502) 349-1920. Admission is free. Open daily. Phone: (502) 348-2999. (1 hour)

★★ **St. Joseph Proto-Cathedral**—Built in 1819, this was the first Catholic church west of the Alleghenies. The Cathedral has a fine collection of European paintings. (½ hour)

★ **Antiques and Crafts**—While in Bardstown, be sure to visit **Harman's** for antiques, and **Wetherby's** and **Quisenberry's** for crafts. Wetherby's also has works by local artists, and the owner can recommend artists' studios in the area.

SIGHTSEEING HIGHLIGHTS—HARRODSBURG

Harrodsburg was founded by Captain James Harrod and 32 men who traveled from Pennsylvania to stake out land. They arrived at the site in July 1774 and built a blockhouse fort, the first permanent English settlement west of the Allegheny Mountains.

★★★ **Old Fort Harrod State Park**—Inside this reproduction of James Harrod's fort you can see a "Living History" interpretation with working craftspersons and animals on site, from mid-April to mid-October. The site is authentic, as confirmed by the presence of the pioneer cemetery nearby dating back to the earliest days. Admission is $3.50 per person. It is not handicapped accessible. Closed December to mid-March.

In the summer months, two plays are offered in the park amphitheater, *The Legend of Daniel Boone* and *Shadows in the Forest*, which tells

BARDSTOWN AREA

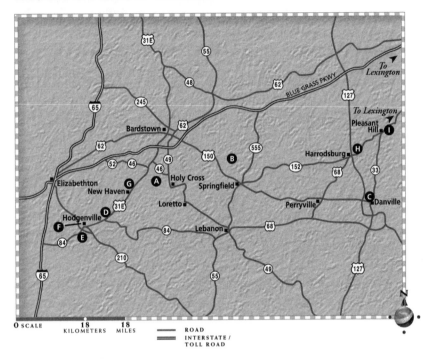

Sights

A Abbey of Gethsemani

B Berry House

C Centre College

C Constitution Square
State Historic Site

C Danville-Boyle County
Historical Society Museum

D Knob Creek

E Lincoln Birthplace
National Historic Site

B Lincoln Homestead State Park

F Lincoln Museum

G Kentucky Railway Museum

H Old Fort Harrod State Park

I Shaker Village at
Pleasant Hill

Note: Items with the same letter are located in the same town or area.

the same story from the Shawnee Indian perspective. Tickets are $12 per adult, $6 per child. Phone: (800) 852-6663 for reservations.

★★★ **Shaker Village at Pleasant Hill**—Located just outside of Harrodsburg, the Shaker Village weaves an almost magical spell over visitors. Excellent explanatory tours are offered, along with demonstrations of daily activities, and a ride on a river steamer that shows how the Shakers loaded and transported their wares to export markets down river. This serene spot is located on a high, bare hill and the yellowish cut-limestone buildings form an austere contrast to the rolling bluegrass fields surrounding the village. Visitors can sample the simple but excellent Shaker recipes in a summertime tearoom, or take meals in the Trustee's House Dining Room. There is also a fine gift and book shop here, and lodgings are available. Admission is $8.50 per adult, $4 per youth, $2 per child. There is an additional charge for the *Dixie Belle* riverboat excursion. Open daily. Phone: (606) 734-5411.

★★ **Perryville**—Named after Oliver Hazard Perry, this town was founded in 1817. It has become well-known because of the Battle of Perryille, fought here in 1862. With troops on both sides arriving from the south through Tennessee, this battle was considered the "Battle for Kentucky." More than 7,500 men died, and although the battle was not a clear victory or loss for either side, the Confederates retreated. A reenactment of the battle is held in early October, on the Sunday closest to the anniversary date of October 8th. Before the war, Perryville was a prosperous town with a number of homes and historic businesses built on what was known as **Merchants Row** along the Chaplin River during the 1840s and 1850s. Many of these are still standing, offering visitors a look at an intact city street from the period. The **River House Café**, a neighborhood restaurant that will give you a walking tour map of the town, is in a building that had been used as a casket-making shop, a post office, and a general store, (606) 332-8101. **Elmwood Inn**, formerly Elmwood Academy, was used as a hospital after the famous battle. It is now a bed and breakfast and serves afternoon tea, (606) 332-2400.

★ **Abbey of Gethsemani**—Twelve miles south of Bardstown, founded in 1848, the abbey is home to the largest order of Cistercian (Trappist) monks in the country. Scholar and religious mystic Thomas Merton lived and wrote here for many years. The abbey is open to the public for daily vespers at 5:30. It is also possible to arrange for a retreat stay at the monastery. The monastic vow of silence is observed, and contributions for room and board are voluntary. Reservations may be made through their Louisville office by writing to: Abbey of Gethsemani, Trappist, KY 40051, or by calling (502) 549-4133 or (502) 584-7866.

✯ **Hodgenville**—This town is home to the **Lincoln Birthplace National Historic Site**, in which the actual cabin has been enclosed inside a granite monument. About 10 miles away, at **Knob Creek**, a period reconstruction of the cabin in which young Lincoln lived until he was around 8 years old has been set at the documented site, in a valley next to the creek, so that visitors can see the landscape as he might have experienced it. The cabin was rebuilt from a cabin on a neighboring farm and, in fact, the boy who lived in this cabin was a friend of young Lincoln's. There is also a **Lincoln Museum** in downtown Hodgenville on the town square ($3 admission, open daily but closed in January).

Danville—Another very early town, Danville was critical to Kentucky's formation because the first constitution was drafted here between 1788 and 1792. Visit **Constitution Square State Historic Site** and the **Danville-Boyle County Historical Society Museum** to learn more, (606) 236-5089. Open daily, the museum is closed in winter. **Centre College**, founded in 1819, is also here. Its oldest building can be toured Monday–Friday. Centre's **Norton Center for the Arts**—music, theater, and visual—is the cultural center of the community. Call for a schedule of performances. Phone: (606) 236-4692.

New Haven—Just south of Bardstown on Hwy 31 is the departure point for the **Kentucky Railway Museum's** 22-mile ride behind a 1905 steam locomotive. There are vintage railcars and memorabilia at the depot. The train runs April–October and is handicapped accessible. The cost is $11 per person. Call to make reservations. The museum is open year-round except the month of January. Phone: (800) 272-0152.

Springfield—The 1816 Springfield courthouse contains the marriage bond of Lincoln's parents. The **Lincoln Homestead State Park** houses a replica of Thomas Lincoln's boyhood cabin and the actual **Berry House**, in which Nancy Hanks grew up. The two families lived in the area after arriving here in the 1780s and 1790s over the Wilderness Road. Don't miss the antique store downtown in the Springfield Opera House, which dates from 1900.

FITNESS AND RECREATION

Daily walking tours of downtown Bardstown, old Harrodsburg, or Shaker Village at Pleasant Hill will keep you both mentally stimulated and well-exercised during your stay in the area. The **Dixie Belle Riverboat** makes hour-long trips from **Shaker Landing** (enter through Shaker Village), April–October. The prices are reasonable ($5.50 per adults, $3.50 per youth), and the boat is a real sternwheeler (handicapped accessible). **My Old Kentucky Home State Park** offers an 18-hole golf course and so does the **Lincoln Homestead State Park** in Springfield, (606) 336-7461.

Running through these historic towns would be fun, as they are fairly flat and there is a lot of see. Horseback riding at **Big Red Stables** in Harrodsburg makes a great day out, especially for families. The stables are located on more than 2,000 acres and offer guided rides for those who prefer to ride with a group. They open every day at 9 a.m. Call (606) 734-3118 to make reservations. Biking on country roads is even possible as a means of transportation because the distances between towns are not great. There is an annual two-day ride between Louisville and Bardstown called "My Old Kentucky Home Tour," held in mid-September. It's sponsored by the Louisville Wheelmen. For registration information, call (502)-893-4232. The Louisville Wheelmen, a biking club, was founded in 1897.

FOOD

In Bardstown the **Old Talbott Tavern**, on one corner of Court Square, has rough stone walls and big fireplaces. The upstairs rooms list to one side. The food is hearty and based in regional specialties, the service is friendly, and the prices are moderate. Don't miss it. Phone: (502) 348-3494. A mile or so from downtown is a tiny place named **Tom Pig's**. They serve a good plate lunch, and the place is always packed with local folks. Across from My Old Kentucky Home, at 418 E. Stephen Foster Avenue, you'll find **Kurtz Restaurant**, a charming establishment made of cut stone. Kurtz serves great food with a regional emphasis at moderate prices. The atmosphere is informal and the staff is knowledgeable and friendly. Call for reservations, as this place is a local favorite, (502) 348-8964.

The Bardstonian, 521 N. Third, is also recommended by locals as one of the best in town. Located in a restored antebellum home, the

Bardstonian's kitchen ranges well beyond regional fare and its wine list is keyed to the entrees, which range in price from $10–$20, (502) 349-1404. **Beall's Row Coffee and Ale House**, on Third Street in the heart of downtown, offers informal dining in a charming storefront for breakfast, lunch, and dinner. Inexpensive for breakfast and lunch, dinner prices range from $10–$15, (502) 348-9594. You could spend your evening out riding on **My Old Kentucky Dinner Train**. The cost of the meal, supposedly quite good, is $55 for lunch and $60 for dinner. Children under 5 are not allowed to board (handicapped accessible). Open April–October, call (502) 348-7300.

For lunch, stop in at **Hurst Discount Drug Store's Old-Fashioned Soda Fountain**, on Court Square. Phone: (502)348-9261. You can sit at the counter and they'll even make you a Brown Cow (rootbeer float). Up the street at 119 N. Third is **Hurst's**, a steak house that also serves great breakfasts. Phone: (502) 348-8929. Nearby is **Dagwood's**. Try the Elijah Craig steak for lunch one day. In Harrodsburg the **Beaumont Inn** serves outstanding meals in the dining rooms of what was constructed as a girl's school in 1845. Regional specialties such as fried chicken, country ham, and corn batter cakes are featured. Reservations are a must for nonguests, (606) 734-3381, (not handicapped accessible). The **Trustee's Office at Shaker Village** serves country ham, roast turkey, catfish, and other regional foods with assorted fresh vegetables and their famous lemon pie. Prices, all inclusive, range from $13–$18. Breakfast, lunch, and dinner served, but no liquor. Reservations are often necessary, (606) 734-5411.

In New Haven the **Sherwood Inn**, an old railroad hotel right by the tracks, gets good reviews for food and drink, providing a nice evening out for local Bardstonians. They also have rooms available. Call for dinner or room reservations, (502) 549-3386.

LODGING

The list of bed and breakfasts in and around Bardstown is extensive. **The Mansion**, on N. Third Avenue, is such a gorgeous old antebellum home that everyone will want to stay there. Its only drawback is that it's close but not within walking distance to downtown. The rooms, all with private baths and furnished with antiques, rent for $85 and up. Even if they're full, they do offer public tours, call (502) 348-2586. The **Amber Lee-Ann**, on Stephen Foster Street, is in a Victorian house downtown, (800) 828-3330. **Victorian Lights**, 112 S. Third, is

BARDSTOWN AREA

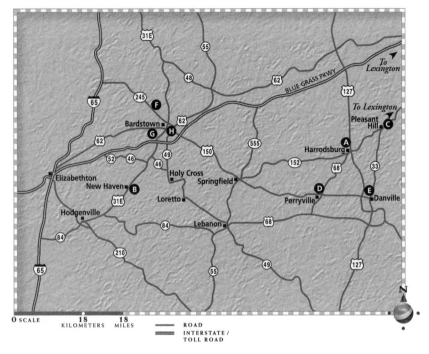

O SCALE   18   18
         KILOMETERS MILES

━━━ ROAD
═══ INTERSTATE /
     TOLL ROAD

Food

Ⓐ Beaumont Inn

Ⓑ Sherwood Inn

Ⓒ Trustee's Office at
    Shaker Village

Ⓑ Sherwood Inn

Ⓒ Trustee's House in the
    Shaker Village

Ⓔ Twin Hollies Retreat

Lodging

Ⓐ Beaumont Inn

Ⓓ Elmwood Inn

Ⓔ Randolph House

Camping

Ⓕ Holt's Campground

Ⓖ My Old Kentucky Home
    State Park

Ⓗ White Acres Campground

Note: Items with the same letter are located in the same town or area.

also very close to downtown, (502) 348-8087. **1790 House**, at 110 E. Broadway, is in a nice neighborhood just off the main streets—Third and Stephen Foster cross at Court Square, (800) 229-1790. **Jailer's Inn**, near Court Square, really was the old jail until about 10 years ago. The front portion of the building dates from 1819. It has three rooms with private baths; call (502) 348-5551. The **Old Talbott Tavern** has seven rooms at reasonable rates, (502) 348-3494, and the **McLean House**, next door, is operated by the same management. A fairly recent addition to the roster is **Beautiful Dreamer**, a new Federal-style house fairly close to My Old Kentucky Home.

If you just want a simple motel, try the clean and quiet **Wilson Motel** on N. Third. It is locally owned and has only 15 units, (502) 348-3364. The **Bardstown Parkview Motel**, next to Kurtz Restaurant, across the street from My Old Kentucky Home would also be a safe choice, (800) 732-2384. The **Bardstown Inn**, a locally owned motel at 510 E. Stephen Foster, is only three years old, (800) 894-1601. **Old Kentucky Home**, at 414 West Stephen Foster is small with seven rooms, (800) 772-1174, and across the street is the **Best Western General Nelson Motel**, (800) 225-3977. On the outskirts of town are **Holiday Inn**, **Ramada**, **Hampton**, and **Red Carpet Inn**.

In Harrodsburg the **Beaumont Inn** has been operated by four generations of the Dedman family since it opened in 1919. It was built in 1845 to house a girl's school and is highly recommended, (800) 352-3992. The **Trustee's House in the Shaker Village** at Pleasant Hill offers lodging in sparsely furnished but comfortable historic quarters. Staying here would guarantee a peaceful night's rest. Room rates vary from $65–$100 for a double room; call (606) 734-5411.

In Danville **Twin Hollies Retreat**, 406 Maple, (606) 236-8954, and **Randolph House**, 463 W. Lexington, (606) 236-9594, both offer bed and breakfast in antebellum homes. In Perryville the **Elmwood Inn**, 205 E. Fourth Street, is a massive brick home built circa 1850 and a lovely place to stay. Stop by for afternoon tea and take a look, (606) 332-2400. And in New Haven, the **Sherwood Inn** offers rooms in an old railway hotel, (502) 549-3386.

CAMPING

My Old Kentucky Home State Park has 39 sites with hookups, (502) 348-3502 or (800) 323-7803. There are two commercial campgrounds outside of Bardstown: **White Acres Campground**

on Hwy 62, (502) 348-9677, and **Holt's Campground** on Hwy 1430 at Hwy 245, (502) 348-6717.

NIGHTLIFE

During the Christmas season, many Bardstown attractions, including My Old Kentucky Home and some of the distilleries, offer candlelight tours on weekends. This is not only very festive, but also true to history, as many of the homes in Bardstown once had only candlelight illumination. The pre-Christmas season is a nice time to be in Bardstown, as the small shops are filled with gift ideas, the brick sidewalks might have a dusting of snow, and the old-time pace might be just what you need to get you into a truly joyful Christmas spirit. In summer, *The Stephen Foster Story* is offered nightly at 8:30 at My Old Kentucky Home State Park's outdoor theater. Mondays are dark, and Saturday matinees are held at 2 p.m. in the indoor facility, which also serves as a rain venue. Call for tickets: (800)626-1563.

You'll find music here, too, in the form of bluegrass and Irish-influenced acoustic performers at **Beall's Row** every Friday and Saturday during the summer. Live contemporary music can be heard on the weekends at the **Old Talbott Tavern**. The **Bardstonian Restaurant** has an upstairs piano bar with a friendly atmosphere, where you'll hear lots of old standards. They also know a lot about whiskey. We tasted several hard-to-find "top shelf" local bourbons and talked about their merits with some local aficionados there. We learned, for example that Booker Noe, grandson of Jim Beam, is much revered in these parts for his single batch whiskey, Booker's, which is indeed a smooth sipping whiskey. Bardstown has begun holding a **Bourbon Festival** the third week of September, which is sure to attract the many connoisseurs of this Kentucky national treasure.

10
LOUISVILLE

L ouisville, Kentucky's largest city, is located at the historically unnavigable Falls of the Ohio. Long before white settlers arrived, rocky outcroppings in the river formed a natural barrier that snagged plant life and provided a crossroads for the ancient men and animals of the last Ice Age. The city of Louisville was founded in 1788 by Revolutionary War general George Rogers Clark as a settlement on the portage site of Corn Island, a strategic position which controlled British troop movement on the river and served as a base of operations for the exploration of the Northwest Territory. In 1804, Clark's brother William departed with Meriwether Lewis to explore the lands that had been acquired in Thomas Jefferson's Louisiana Purchase of 1803. In 1808, John James Audubon began his career as a shop owner in Louisville, doing some of his earliest studies of nature at the Falls of the Ohio before he settled downriver at Henderson, Kentucky, in 1810. Always a center of river trade and a transportation hub, by the late nineteenth century Louisville had reached the height of prosperity. The 3-story brick townhouses of Old Louisville's Belgravia and St. James Court neighborhoods and the 4- and 5-story warehouse buildings of Main and Market Streets testify to that financial prominence.

Today the still-thriving hotels, restored theaters, active Kentucky Center for the Arts, and post-modern Humana and Providian Center skyscrapers attest to downtown Louisville's continued cultural and financial health. ◪

A PERFECT DAY IN LOUISVILLE

Arrive at Lynn's Paradise Café early (to avoid the line at this popular spot) for a hearty and healthful breakfast amidst eclectic folk-art decor. You might be inspired to wander Bardstown Road for some antique and junk browsing afterwards—ask for some good leads at Lynn's. Drive across the river to the Falls of the Ohio Interpretive Center where you can "see" Louisville long before it was a city and understand its relationship to the Ohio River that formed its northern boundary and, for over 150 years, has been its lifeline to the rest of the world.

Stroll down Main Street looking at the architectural details on these hundred-year-old buildings. There are several galleries in the neighborhood; pick up a Louisville Gallery Guide at the elegant Kentucky Art and Craft Foundation Gallery for addresses. Try Check's in Germantown for lunch. Afterwards drive out to the Watertower Gallery, a former water plant whose pump rooms now serve as exhibit spaces. Don't miss the Kentucky Derby Museum (and Churchill Downs in season). Have an early dinner at one of Louisville's renowned new American cuisine restaurants and move on to Actor's Theatre. End your evening with a top-shelf bourbon in the Old Seelbach Bar.

SIGHTSEEING HIGHLIGHTS

★★★ *Belle of Louisville*—For a closer look at river life, take an afternoon cruise on this sternwheeler, first chartered as the packet boat *Idlewild* in 1914 and now the oldest operating steamboat on the Ohio. Tickets are $8 per adult, $4 per child. Cruises daily 2 p.m. and 4 p.m.; sunset cruises from 7 p.m.–9 p.m. on Tuesday and Thursday. Phone: (502) 574-2355.

★★★ **Churchill Downs**—Kentucky's best-known horse racing track, Churchill Downs has hosted the Kentucky Derby on the first Saturday in May since 1875. Seating in the clubhouse, built in 1895, can be enjoyed for a $3.50 ticket during the racing season, late April to July 1 and late October through November. Grandstand seats go for $2.50. With the exception of the Derby, tickets can usually be purchased on the day of race. Phone: (502) 636-4400.

Next door, the **Kentucky Derby Museum** is open daily and includes tours of Churchill Downs in the admission ticket: $5 per

LOUISVILLE

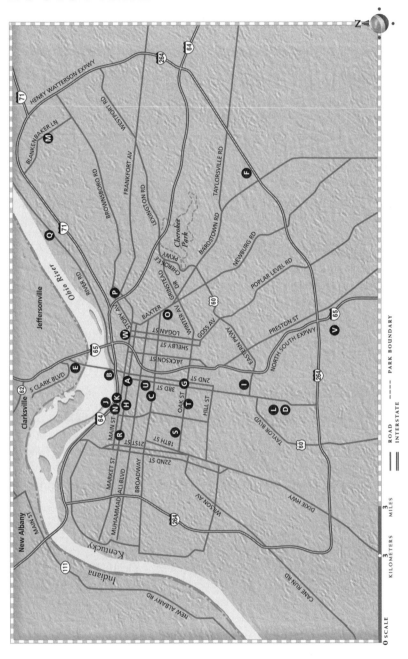

Sights

- **A** Actor's Theater
- **B** Belle of Louisville
- **C** Brennan House
- **D** Churchill Downs
- **E** Falls of the Ohio Interpretive Center
- **F** Farmington
- **G** Filson Club
- **H** Hillerich and Bradsby Company
- **I** J.B. Speed Art Museum
- **J** Kentucky Art and Craft Foundation
- **K** Kentucky Center for the Arts
- **L** Kentucky Derby Museum
- **M** Locust Grove
- **N** Louisville Science Center
- **O** Louisville Stoneware
- **P** Hadley Pottery
- **Q** Louisville Visual Art Association
- **R** Main Street
- **S** Old Louisville
- **T** Old Louisville Information Center
- **U** Palace Theatre
- **V** Pegasus Gallery
- **W** Thomas Edison House

adult, $2 per child. In addition to one of the most powerful slide pre-sentations you will ever see and interactive stations that provide Derby history, there are also semi-permanent changing exhibits. On current view is an exposition of the important early role of African-Americans in thoroughbred racing. Phone: (502) 637-1111

★★★ **Falls of the Ohio Interpretive Center**—Located a stone's throw from downtown Louisville, the center provides the visitor with a thorough introduction to the amazing geologic history of the area and kindles the observing spirit of any nature lover. More than 265 species of birds and 125 species of fish have been recorded in this 1,400-acre wildlife preserve. The superb orientation film begins with a fine explanation of the Devonian age, 400 million years ago, when the southern part of the North American continent was covered by warm seas. Due to a series of geological events, not the least of which was the scraping effect of the glaciers that created the Ohio River Valley, fossils of marine life from the Devonian period can still be found outside on the shoals of the river. The center also contains a fine historical museum. Admission is $2 per adult, $1 for children under 12. Hours: Open daily, 9 a.m.–5 p.m. Address: 2nd Avenue in Clarksville, Indiana. Phone: (812) 280-9970.

★★★ **J.B. Speed Art Museum**—The museum was founded in 1927 by Hattie Bishop Speed in memory of her husband, James Breckenridge Speed. Hattie Speed intended for the museum to be open free of charge to the public, and it still is today. The museum's strengths are its collections of old master and medieval paintings, but it has been steadily acquiring important works by contemporary American artists over the past 20 years or so. Address: 2035 S. Third. Phone: (502) 636-2893. (1 hour)

★★★ **Louisville Visual Art Association**—This multifaceted orga-nization reflects the enthusiastic spirit of Louisville's ecumenical arts community. It is located in the oldest (dating from 1858), tallest, and most ornamented watertower in the country. The association is responsible for the **Pegasus Gallery** at the Louisville International Airport and for exciting child and adult art programming, including the "Boat Race Party" on Kentucky Derby weekend and Waterside Music and Arts Festival in July. Changing exhibits of contemporary local and regional art are displayed. Donations are requested.

Address: 3005 Upper River Road. Phone: (502) 896-2146 for a schedule of events. (1 hour)

★★★ **Main Street**—This historic downtown business district contains the second largest number of cast iron building facades in the country. Look for the **Kentucky Center for the Arts**, 6th and Main, and the post-modern Humana Headquarters Building across the street designed by Michael Graves. Phone: (502) 562-0100. The **Louisville Science Center**, 727 W. Main, (502) 561-6100 is open daily. Admission is $6.75 per adult, $5.75 per child. The **Kentucky Art and Craft Foundation**, 609 W. Main, (502) 589-0102, features changing exhibits and a sales room. **Actor's Theater**, 316 W. Main, is in an 1830s bank building designed by Gideon Schyrock, an important early Kentucky architect who also designed the original state capitol building in Frankfort (now the Kentucky Historical Society). Phone: (502)584-1208.

    Hillerich and Bradsby Company, makers of Louisville Slugger bats, has just moved onto Main Street and will soon be open for tours, (502) 585-5229. A walking tour of Main Street is available from the Main Street Association. They also conduct guided tours on Tuesday and Thursday at 11 a.m. and 2 p.m. The cost $5 per person. Address: 627 W. Main. Phone: (502) 562-0723.

★★ **Brennan House**—Occupied by a single family since its construction in 1868, this historic home contains original Victorian furnishings. Closed Sundays and January–February. Address: 631 S. Fifth Street. Phone: (502) 540-5145.

★★ **Farmington**—This fine Federal-style, 14-room home was built in 1810 from a design by Thomas Jefferson and has been restored to its original interior color scheme. Open daily, with guided tours. Admission is $4 per adult, $2 per student, children free. Address: 3033 Bardstown Road. Phone: (502) 452-9920. (1 hour)

★★ **Filson Club**—A historical and genealogical society founded in 1884, the Filson Club has its museum and library in a 1901 Beaux Arts building that is open to the public. Hours: The library, which charges a $3 fee for research assistance, is open Monday–Friday. The free museum is open Monday through Friday, and Saturdays 9 a.m.–12 noon. Address: 1310 S. Third Street. Phone: (502) 535-5083.

✯✯ **Locust Grove**—The home of George Rogers Clark, Locust Grove was built in 1790 on 55 acres located east of the city. Admission is $4 per adult, $2 per student, children free. Open daily. Address: 561 Blankenbaker Lane. Phone: (502) 896-2146. (1 hour)

✯✯ **Old Louisville**—This well-preserved historic district includes the Brennan House and Filson Club. It can be explored with the aid of a walking tour map distributed by the **Old Louisville Information Center** in Central Park. Open Monday–Friday. Address: Between Second and Fifth Streets, several miles south of downtown. Phone: (502) 635-5244.

✯✯ **Thomas Edison House**—Edison lived in this Butchertown row house in 1866–1867 while he worked for Western Union Telegraph. Tours of the house and museum are available. Call for specific times. Admission is $4 per adult, $2 per student, children free. Hours: Open for tours, Tuesday, Thursday, and Saturday. Address: 729–31 E. Washington. Phone: (502) 585-5247. (1 hour)

✯ **Palace Theatre**—Newly restored to its 1928 glory, the Palace serves as a concert venue for popular acts. Designed by John Ebersole for vaudeville productions and silent films, the Palace still has its original private boxseats and is nothing short of wonderfully gaudy. Call for information or tickets to performances. Tours are available for $2 per person. Tours are given Tuesday–Saturday from 10 a.m.–2 p.m. for $2. Address: 625 Fourth Street. Phone: (502) 583-4335. (¾ hour)

Louisville Stoneware and **Hadley Pottery**—These establishments feature different versions of folk-style blue figured stoneware. Unique souvenir dog dishes and baby gifts with a unique Louisville look are available. Both are open for tours Monday–Friday, with showrooms open Saturday morning. Louisville Stoneware is at 731 Brent Street. Phone: (502) 582-1900. Hadley Pottery, 1570 Story Avenue. Phone: (502) 584-2171. (½ hour)

Art Galleries—In addition to the Kentucky Art and Craft Foundation and the Louisville Visual Art Association, Louisville has a number of art galleries that show contemporary local and regional artists. Interested visitors should seek out **Gallerie Hertz**, 636 E. Market, (502) 584-3547; **Images Friedman**, 833 W. Main, (502) 584-7954; and **Zephyr**,

812 W. Main, (502) 585-5646, in the downtown area; as well as
Swansson-Cralle, 1377 Bardstown Road, (502) 452-2904; and **Yvonne Rapp**, 2007 Frankfort Road, (502) 896-2331.

FITNESS AND RECREATION

The paved **Riverwalk** along the Ohio River from 4th to 18th Streets
makes a good short jogging trail close to downtown.

The **Louisville Wheelmen**, founded in 1897, sponsor bicycling
events and can give information about good bike rides in the area.
They can be contacted via the Internet: www.thepoint.net/~kycycle/

Louisville is a town that loves festivals. The **Kentucky Derby Festival**, complete with a boat race between the *Belle of Louisville* and
the *Delta Queen*, begins in mid-April and lasts until the Derby in early
May. The **Humana Festival of New American Plays** has gained a
reputation for artistic excellence. It takes place in late February–March,
and some of the downtown hotels offer special festival packages to
encourage visitors. For information, call (502) 584-1208. The 20-year-
old **Corn Island Storytelling Festival** is held in several city park locations and focuses on the passing down of history through storytelling.
The **Kentucky Shakespeare Festival** is held during June and July in
Old Louisville. Call the Louisville Convention and Visitors Bureau at
(502) 584-2121 for schedules.

FOOD

For breakfast, grab a cup and a breakfast pastry at **John Conti Gourmet Coffee**, next to the Seelbach Hotel downtown. This is a Louisville coffee company, and they also have a coffee museum on Bardstown Road.
Call (502) 499-8602 for information. Also try **Lynn's Paradise Café**,
984 Barret Road—you'll recognize it by the large metal coffee pot out
front and the gaily decorated exterior. Lynn's serves the freshest produce
(she works with the Kentucky Organic Growers Association and the
Farm Growers of America) and whips up famous scones, pancakes, and
French toast chock full of fruits and nuts (prices range from $5–$8). Also
open for lunch and dinner, (502) 583-EGGS.

For lunch in the downtown area, stop by **Herby's**, 631 S. Fourth,
for a filling, moderately priced meal, (502) 585-HERB. Or step up the
street to **J. Graham's** (a casual dining spot) at the Camberley Brown
Hotel, 335 W. Broadway, (502) 583-1234, to try the original Kentucky

Hot Brown, an open-faced turkey sandwich with Mornay sauce, topped with cheese, tomato, and bacon. Try it with Oldenburg ale, brewed in northern Kentucky. Local favorites for lunch include the **Bristol Bar and Grille** at 1321 Bardstown Road (known as "restaurant row"), phone: (502) 456-1702; **Check's Restaurant**, in Germantown; and **Cunningham's** at Fifth and Breckenridge.

For an inexpensive, unusual dinner downtown, try **Café Kilimanjaro**, 649 S. Fourth St., where you can often find Jamaican jerk chicken ($5) or Ethiopian Doro Wat ($5) cooking outside in a metal barrel, along with World Music on Friday and Saturday nights, (502) 583-4332. The Seelbach Hotel's **Oakroom** offers a $19.95 prix fixe meal in the evening. Address: 500 S. Fourth Avenue, (502) 585-3200. For great seafood try **Mike Linnig's**, located about 20 minutes west along the river with extensive outdoor seating. Sample the artistry of Louisville's trend-setting chefs at **Shariat's**, 2901 Brownsboro Road, (502) 899-7878 (entrees: $15–$23), where you can sample regional specialties like poached pears and Kentucky Ham, after a starter of Kentucky Bibb lettuce with Bourbon vinaigrette. Also try **Lilly's**, 1147 Bardstown Road, (502) 451-0447, which might offer wild mushrooms over grits as an appetizer, free-range chicken pot pie, or Kentucky lambchops with mint pesto. **Jack Fry's**, 1007

Mary Entrekin

Bardstown Road, (502) 452-9244, and **Azalea**, 3612 Brownsboro
Road, (502) 895-5493, are slightly less expensive with entrees in the
$10–$25 range; and **Café Metro**, 1700 Bardstown Road, (502) 458-
4830, which features grilled fish and a hand-written menu that
changes daily, are three more exciting Louisville restaurants. Any one
of these will be worth the splurge for an adventure in cutting-edge
regional haute cuisine.

Louisville restaurants serve large portions, so two people can
eat very well if some dishes are shared. An excellent Louisville
restaurant that serves variations on classical European cuisine is **Le
Relais**, on Taylorsville Road at old Bowman Field Airport, (502)
451-9020, whose dishes rely on authentic French preparation but
whose English-language menu displays a self-confident air. At Le
Relais you might wish to sample the smoked salmon profiterole with
créme fraîche and a caper relish or a New York strip with a cognac
and green peppercorn sauce (entrees: $14–$20). Another excellent
restaurant is **Vicenzo's**, 150 S. Fifth, (502) 580-1350, an Italian
restaurant that offers a Eurospa menu along with risottos, pastas,
and the largest number of veal entrees I've seen on a menu in some
time (entrees: $16–$26).

LODGING

Louisville has two elegant old hotels downtown, the **Seelbach**, Fourth
and Muhammad Ali, (800) 333-3399, and the **Camberley Brown**,
Fourth and Broadway, (800) 866-ROOM. While both charge upwards
of $120 for standard, beautifully appointed rooms, they do give AAA
and AARP discounts when rooms are available and offer special theater
packages and regular weekend packages. The **Galt House**, another
fine hotel of more recent vintage, is located at Fourth Street and River
Road, facing the river, (502) 589-5200.

The **Old Louisville Inn B&B**, 1359 S. Third, is a 1901 house
with 11 guest rooms that comes highly recommended, (502) 635-1574.
Other recommended, delightful historic homes offering bed and breakfast accommodations in Old Louisville are the **Rose Blossom**, 1353 S.
Fourth, an 1884 3-story Victorian, (502) 636-0295 after 6:00 p.m. only;
Magnolia Place, 1421 S. Third, also a 3-story Victorian, with four
rooms available and an award-winning pastry chef in the kitchen, (502)
634-9252; and **Inn at the Park** (facing Central Park), an 1886
Richardsonian Romanesque mansion, with six rooms with private baths

LOUISVILLE

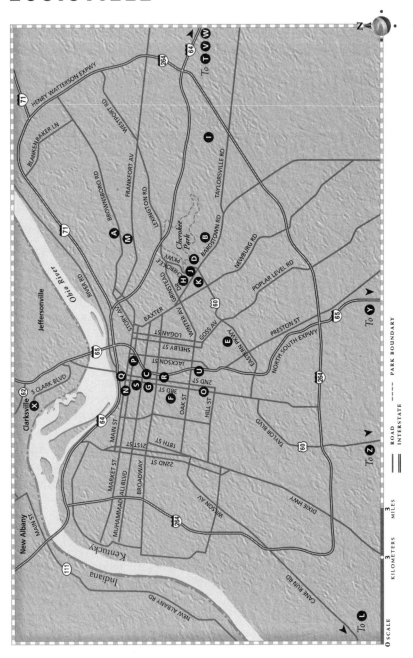

Food

(A) Azalea

(B) Bristol Bar and Grille

(C) Café Kilimanjaro

(D) Café Metro

(E) Check's Restaurant

(F) Cunningham's

(G) Herby's

(G) J. Graham's

(H) Jack Fry's

(G) John Conti Gourmet Coffee

(I) Le Relais

(J) Lilly's

(K) Lynn's Paradise Café

(L) Mike Linnig's

(G) Oakroom

(M) Shariat's

(N) Vicenzo's

Lodging

(G) Camberley Brown Hotel

(O) Columbine

(P) Days Inn

(Q) Galt House

(R) Holiday Inn

(S) Hyatt Regency

(O) Inn at the Park

(O) Magnolia Place

(T) Marriott

(O) Old Louisville Inn B&B

(O) Rose Blossom

(G) The Seelbach

(O) Towne House

(U) Towne House Annex

(V) Travelodge

Camping

(W) Guist Creek Lake

(X) KOA Metro

(Y) KOA South

(Z) Otter Creek Park

Note: Items with the same letter are located in the same area.

ranging in price from $80–$120, (800) 700-PARK. **Towne House**, which has four guest rooms priced at $85–$95, is located at 1460 on treelined St. James Court in a turn-of-the-century home, (502) 636-5673 or (502) 585-4456, and **Towne House Annex** at 105 W. Ormsby offers suites at $85–$145. The **Columbine**, 1707 S. Third, which has five guest rooms with private baths, is also in a circa 1900 house, (800) 635-5010. **Hyatt Regency, Holiday Inn, Days Inn**, and **Travelodge** all have hotels downtown and **Marriott** has just taken over the Inn at Jewish Hospital, located at Jefferson and First.

CAMPING

There are two KOA campgrounds located outside of Louisville: **KOA Metro** in Southern Indiana (just across the Ohio River), (812) 282-4474; and **KOA South** (near Brooks Road, approximately 25 miles south on I-65), (502) 543-2041.

On the way to Frankfurt, near Shelbyville, at I-64 exit 35, is **Guist Creek Lake**, open April–October, which has both primitive camping and full hookups, (502) 633-1934. Thirty-five minutes south of Louisville, on the way to Fort Knox (Hwy 31W) you'll find **Otter Creek Park**, a city park with a view over the Ohio River. There are more than 200 campsites here, first-come, first-served only, both tent camping and full hookups ($10–$14 range), (502) 583-3577.

NIGHTLIFE

The **Palace Theater**, a newly renovated downtown venue at 625 Fourth Avenue, books popular music acts; call for a schedule, (502) 583-4555. **Coyotes**, at Second and Liberty Streets downtown, offers big-name country music acts in a club setting, (502) 589-FUNN, and at **Anthony's by the Bridge**, 131 W. Main Street, you can hear live music nightly beginning at 8:30 p.m. These are two of Louisville's liveliest nightspots. Phone (502) 584-7720.

Actor's Theatre, which presents an exciting yearly schedule in two theaters downtown, hosts the Humana Festival of New American Plays in late February–March. Located in a historic building at 316 W. Main, you can stop by the box office or call (800) 4ATL-TIX or (502) 584-1208 for tickets. The **MacCauley Theater**, Fourth and Broadway, (502) 562-0194, and the **Kentucky Center for the Arts** also offer plays and musical events. On the three stages of the Kentucky Center for the Arts, you'll find the **Louisville Orchestra**, the **Louisville Ballet**, the **Kentucky Opera**, and much more. For schedule information, call (502) 562-0100, and for tickets, (800) 775-7777. Two of Louisville's favorite bars featuring live music are the **Butchertown Pub** and the **Phoenix Hill Tavern.**

Scenic Route: Louisville to Lexington via Frankfort

Hwy 60 from Louisville to Lexington passes through the historic Kentucky countryside and leads into the capital city of Frankfort, located at what was once Frank's Ford across the Kentucky River. Since it closely parallels I-64, Hwy 60 allows travelers easy access to interesting stops as it detours off and on the highway. At Exit 28 is **Simpsonville**, where one can have a meal or late afternoon tea at an 1817 stagecoach inn that was one of the first stone houses in Kentucky, the **Old Stone Inn**, which also offers lodging, (502) 722-8882. About 7 miles down the road is **Shelbyville**, whose late Victorian-era downtown is listed on the National Register of Historic Places. Antique stores abound in this small town, and the historic **Science Hill Dining Room** is located here; call (502) 633-2825 for reservations. Just outside of Frankfort, near Graefenburg, is **Cedar Rock Farm**, a bed and breakfast that offers three rooms with private baths on a 110-acre sheep farm, (502) 747-8754.

Named capital in 1792, **Frankfort**, a beautiful small city right on the river, has preserved a number of distinguished Federal-style homes and public buildings dating from the early 1800s. Remnants of Frankfort's historical past can be found all over the city. Daniel and Rebecca Boone are buried in Frankfort; the exquisite 1831 state capitol building designed by Gideon Schyrock now houses the **Kentucky History Museum**; Bibb lettuce is named after an early citizen-horticulturist; the only Frank Lloyd Wright house in Kentucky is here; and you can take a tour of the old-fashioned kitchens of **Rebecca-Ruth Candy**, where the "bourbon ball" was invented. Stop by the visitor's center, at Gooch House on Capital Avenue, to pick up a walking tour map. They will also give you a local restaurant guide that features no less than six diners—the one I wish I'd tried was **Sweet Nectar**, at 205 Steele Street. Make sure you find the charming **St. Clair Mall** in old downtown Frankfort. Speaking of the river that started it all, **Canoe Kentucky**, headquartered in Frankfort, offers access to 12 of the state's best paddling streams, (1-800-K-CANOE).

From Frankfort follow Hwy 60 to **Versailles** or Hwy 62 to **Midway**, and you'll see beautiful horse country all along the way. Midway, a railroad town founded in 1832, has antique shops in what were once houses and stores running down both sides of the railroad track. Midway can easily be reached by taking Exit 65 from I-64. Shops are open Monday–Saturday. Try the **Depot Restaurant**'s trackside pie at lunch or dinner, (606) 846-4745, or call for reservations to dine at the historic **Holly Hill Inn** on N. Winter Street, (606) 846-4732. Hwy 62 between Midway and Versailles is bisected by Old Frankfort Pike, which has one of the densest groupings of horse farms around Lexington. Follow Old Frankfort Pike into Lexington, where it becomes Manchester Street. The history of Versailles, which was founded in 1793, can be explored at the **Woodford Country Historical Society Museum**, open Tuesday–Saturday until 4 p.m. Admission is free. Hwy 60 coming from Versailles will bring you right past Keeneland on the way into town before it becomes High Street. ◣

LOUISVILLE TO LEXINGTON

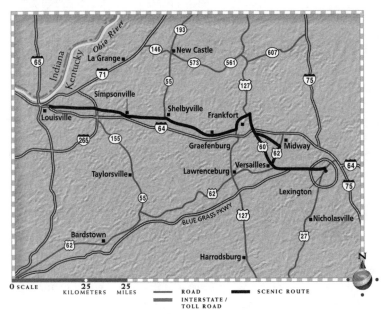

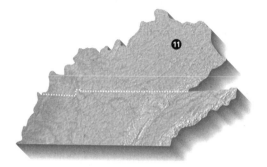

11
LEXINGTON

The Kentucky bluegrass region, centered around Lexington, nourishes the world's champion thoroughbreds. The famous lush grass is fed by a water table that runs through the limestone underlying the softly rolling terrain. The beneficial effects of this same water are just as well-known to the Kentucky bourbon distillers nearby. A drive along Paris Pike or Iron Works Road passes some of the loveliest horse farms in the country. Driving onto the well-manicured grounds of Keeneland Race Course will make anyone feel a member of the privileged elite.

Lexington, Kentucky's second largest city, was founded in 1775. In its beautiful old neighborhoods one finds small British-style parks, like Gratz Park, that function as green spaces for the early 1800s Federal-period brick houses that are the size of city blocks. In the midst of the historic district sits Transylvania University, dating from 1780, the first institution of higher learning in the western United States. Stroll the labyrinth of streets around Gratz Park and Transylvania that bear names like Upper, Limestone, Cheapside, Mill, and Market, and you will absorb some of Lexington's early history. The girlhood home of Mary Todd Lincoln is here, as are the law offices of one of Abraham Lincoln's mentors, the "Great Compromiser" Henry Clay.

Activities at the University of Kentucky are an important part of Lexington life. The Singletary Art Center provides outstanding cultural offerings and an excellent art museum. Rupp Arena, the well-known home court for UK's powerful Wildcat basketball team, is part of Lexington's convention center in the heart of downtown. ◨

A PERFECT DAY IN LEXINGTON

An early morning drive west out Versailles Road to Keeneland for a glimpse of the morning workouts and breakfast at the Track Kitchen are the closest most of us will come to feeling like a bluegrass horse owner. Later drive along Rice Road to Old Frankfort Pike and Yarnalltown Road. Stop at the Kentucky Horse Park on Iron Works Pike and spend a couple of hours in the museums and open stables. To see how thoroughbreds are trained to race, continue on Iron Works Pike to the Kentucky Center for the Horse, where tours are available. Head back into Lexington's historic Gratz Park neighborhood for lunch and a walking tour that includes visits to historic homes or a stop at the lively, interactive Lexington Children's Museum. In the late afternoon, wind down with a quiet hour at UK's Art Museum. A carriage ride around downtown Lexington makes a nice end to the day. Afterwards, dine on regional specialties at the highly esteemed Merrick Inn, and attend an evening performance at UK's Singletary Center for the Arts, the restored 1890s Lexington Opera House, or the 1920s Kentucky Theater in downtown Lexington.

KENTUCKY HORSE CULTURE

Horse racing events are surprisingly accessible to visitors. Keeneland's hedge-lined racecourse and beautiful limestone grandstands are available during the 15-day race seasons in spring and fall to anyone with the price of a basic ticket (well under $10, and parking is free). Race-goers can bring their own picnics, purchase BBQ and Burgoo at the track, or make reservations to dine on higher-priced fare at one of the several enclosed dining rooms at Keeneland. There is no charge to watch the daily morning workouts held there year-round, and visitors are welcome at the Track Kitchen cafeteria for a reasonably priced breakfast with Keeneland employees and visiting trainers.

The Red Mile harness racetrack provides equally low-cost seats and a variety of dining options for its series of races for two months in late spring and two weeks in fall. No two courses run simultaneous events and Kentucky's system of inter-track wagering and simulcast racing at many of its major racecourses ensures a statewide audience for every event.

GREATER LEXINGTON

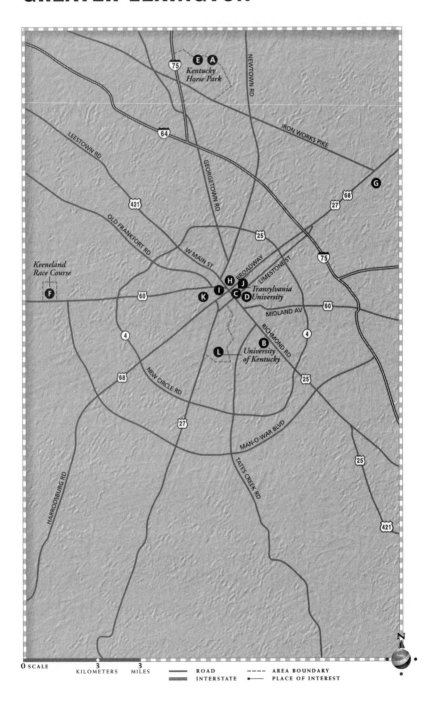

75 Kentucky Horse Park **E** **A**

NEWTOWN RD

IRON WORKS PIKE

64

LEESTOWN RD

GEORGETOWN RD

421

OLD FRANKFORT RD

68

27

G

25

W MAIN ST

BROADWAY

LIMESTONE ST

75

Keeneland Race Course **F**

60

K **I** **H** **J**
C **D** Transylvania University

60

MIDLAND AV

4

RICHMOND RD

4

L **B** University of Kentucky

27

NEW CIRCLE RD

68

25

MAN-O-WAR BLVD

25

HARRODSBURG RD

TATES CREEK RD

421

N

0 SCALE 3 3
KILOMETERS MILES

ROAD   ---- AREA BOUNDARY
INTERSTATE   •— PLACE OF INTEREST

Sights

(A) American Saddle Horse Museum

(B) Ashland, the Henry Clay Estate

(C) Henry Clay's Law Office

(D) Hopemont, the Hunt-Morgan House

(E) International Museum of the Horse

(F) Keeneland

(G) Kentucky Center for the Horse

(E) Kentucky Horse Park

(H) Lexington Children's Museum

(I) Mary Todd Lincoln House

(J) Morlan Gallery

(K) Red Mile Harness Racetrack

(J) Transylvania University

(L) University of Kentucky Art Museum

(L) University of Kentucky, Singletary Center for the Arts

Note: Items with the same letter are located in the same area.

SIGHTSEEING HIGHLIGHTS

The Lexington Convention and Visitors Bureau, (606) 233-7299 or (800) 845-3959, located at Rose and Vine, distributes a terrific bluegrass driving tour map that shows the location of the more than 100 horse farms in and around Lexington. I highly recommend driving this circuit as a general orientation to the area. Turn the map over and you have a walking tour of Lexington's center. Entering the city via one of the old roads, such as Old Frankfort Pike and Versailles Road from the west, or Richmond Road from the south, will also whet your appetite for Kentucky horse culture. To get a good sense of the temper of the town's intellectual community, pick up the free monthly paper *Arts Community Entertainment*.

★★★ **Keeneland**—A must see, this racecourse opened in 1936 and is Kentucky's most beautiful. The motto of Keeneland's founders is "racing as it was meant to be," and that means there is no public address system, so the twice-yearly race meetings (15 days in April and in October) are conducted without the roar of announcers. Call for tickets and information. Address: 4201 Versailles Road. Phone: (800) 456-3412.

★★★ **Kentucky Center for the Horse**—This is a real training facility for thoroughbreds who are being taught the rigors of the race. An extensive and thorough tour is available for $10. Reservations are needed. Hours: Monday–Saturday, 9 a.m. and 10:30 a.m. Address: At the intersection of Iron Works Pike and Paris Pike. Phone: (606) 293-1853. (1½ hours)

★★★ **Kentucky Horse Park**—The park is run by the state of Kentucky. The **International Museum of the Horse** is located on the grounds, as are stables and exhibits that demonstrate many aspects of horse breeding and training. The grounds are extensive and beautiful. Kids of all ages will feel privileged to have been able to see the real thing at such close range. Admission is $9.95 per adult, $4.95 for children over 6. Parking is free. Hours: Open daily, year-round. Address: 4089 Iron Works Pike. Phone: (606) 233-4303 or (800) 568-8813. (2 hours minimum)

★★ **American Saddlebred Museum**—The museum is also part of the Kentucky Horse Park complex, although it is maintained by its own nonprofit organization. The museum displays chronicle the history and development of the American horse, which was created from the lineage of the earliest horses in this country, from English thoroughbreds to Indian ponies, to become fine saddle horses for show and pleasure riding. This museum will be of tremendous interest to anyone who owns a horse. Admission is $3 per adult, $2 per child. It is possible to buy a combined ticket at a discount for both the Kentucky Horse Park and the Saddlebred Museum. Hours: Open daily. Phone: (606) 259-2746. (1 hour)

★★ **Red Mile Harness Racetrack**—This track features the kind of racing that used to be common all over the South, with a single horse hitched to a streamlined sulky from which a lightly perched jockey leans back gracefully. The Red Mile holds racing meets in May–June and late September–early October. Phone: (606)255-0752

SIGHTSEEING HIGHLIGHTS—HISTORIC LEXINGTON

A walk through historic Lexington will take you past these sites and more.

★★ **Hopemont, the Hunt-Morgan House**—Hopemont was built in 1814 by Kentucky's first millionaire, John Wesley Hunt. His grandson, General John Hunt Morgan, who had attended Transylvania University and, as a confederate general, terrorized Union generals with his erratic attacks, stayed here often during the Civil War. Another distinguished relative who also inhabited the house was Thomas Hunt Morgan, who won the Nobel Prize for his research in science and genetics in 1933. The house is a beautiful example of early Kentucky architecture. Admission is $4 per person. It is closed Monday and in January and February. Address: 201 N. Mill. Phone: (606) 253-0362. (1 hour)

★★ **Mary Todd Lincoln House**—This is the home where Mary Todd grew to adulthood after her family moved to Lexington in 1832. Lincoln visited her here three times. Both Todd and Lincoln artifacts are on display. Admission to the Mary Todd Lincoln House is $5 per person. It is closed Monday and January–March. The last tour is given daily at 3:15 p.m. Address: 578 W. Main. Phone: (606) 233-9999. (1 hour)

★★ University of Kentucky, Singletary Center for the Arts—
Singletary is a modern facility for the performing arts. Call for schedule and ticket information. Phone: (606) 257-4929.

Located within the center is the **University of Kentucky Art Museum,** an impressive museum that has both well-curated permanent collections and three large galleries for changing exhibits. Admission is free. Closed Monday. Address: Rose Street and Euclid Avenue. Phone: (606) 257-5716. (1 hour)

★ Ashland, the Henry Clay Estate—Ashland is a bit of an architectural hybrid since it was remodeled by his son after Clay's death. Nonetheless, the home and memorabilia that belonged to Kentucky's great statesman will be of interest. Admission is $5 per adult, $2 for children 6 and over. The house is open May–October. Address: 120 Sycamore Road, not far from the University of Kentucky. Phone: (606) 266-8581.

★ Lexington Children's Museum—This hands-on museum is always filled with lively young visitors—the exhibits are designed primarily for children from 12 months to 12 years. The museum has grown from community interest and has both semi-permanent and permanent exhibits (a multicultural series changes once a year—the current one is on China). Admission is $3 per adult, $2 per child. Hours: Open daily, but closed Monday during the school year. Address: In the Victorian Square complex downtown at Main & Broadway. Phone: (606) 258-3256. (1½ hours)

★ Transylvania University—This first college of higher learning west of the Alleghenies was founded in 1780. The **Morlan Gallery** in Mitchell Fine Arts Center features changing exhibits and is open Monday–Friday, 12 noon–5 p.m. with free admission. Campus tours are available by appointment. Address: 300 N. Broadway. Phone: (606) 233-8210

Henry Clay's Law Office—Although it is not open to the public, you'll want to be sure to pass by this historic building. Address: 178 N. Mill.

FITNESS AND RECREATION

Besides taking a walking tour of historic neighborhoods, the next most natural form of exercise around Lexington—unless you have access to a horse—would be biking or running along the beautiful horse country roads. The **Raven Run Nature Sanctuary**, located southeast of Lexington along the palisades of the Kentucky River, offers extensive hiking and biking opportunities along with wildlife watching. Golf is widely popular in the area, and there are a number of courses available for public use. One of the best-known is **Kearney Links**, a British-style course that has been used for national golf events, (606) 253-1981. On Richmond Road right in town is the **Lakeside Golf Course**, (606) 263-5315, and **Connemara**, which was once a horse farm, is highly touted for its beauty, (606) 885-4331.

If visiting horse country makes your kids want to try it for themselves, the **Kentucky Horse Park** offers a 50-minute trail ride for $10. A 45-minute drive from Lexington will reach several stables that can provide a more extensive horseback riding outing: **Big Red Stables**, Harrodsburg, (606) 734-3118; **Deer Run**, Richmond, (606) 527-6339; and **Wildwood Stables**, Ft. Boonesborough (just outside of Richmond), (606) 527-6602.

FOOD

Breakfasts come highly recommended at **Linda's Sandwich Shop**, 214 S. Limestone, downtown, (606) 252-6264. For fresh-baked goodies and strong coffee, try **Magee's Bakery**, 726 E. Main. **Coffee at the Gratz**, located in the Gratz Park Hotel, 120 W. Second, (606) 231-1777, serves breakfast and tempting light lunches.

If you need a respite from the excesses of country ham and Kentucky Hot Brown sandwiches, stop by **Everybody's Natural Foods & Deli**, 503 Euclid, (606) 255-4162, near the UK campus. The **Kentucky Inn**, also near campus, (606) 254-1177, is well-known for its country cooking buffet. **Rogers Restaurant**, located at 808 S. Broadway, whose typed menu changes daily, is Lexington's oldest restaurant (dating from 1923) and is marked by a classic neon sign out front. They serve plain, homemade food for lunch and dinner, with a neighborhood bar at the back, (606) 254-1077. **DeSha's**, located downtown in Victorian Square at Main and Broadway, is a Lexington favorite for Kentucky specialties and after-work socializing and is open seven days a week, (606) 259-3771.

Other downtown choices include the plain-looking but authentic **Tonio's Super Burritos**, at 102 S. Vine Street, (606) 254-3722, and **Melodeon**, 200 W. Main, which serves a late-night menu, (606) 253-3371. The **Columbia Steakhouse**, 201 N. Limestone, (606) 253-3135,

DOWNTOWN LEXINGTON

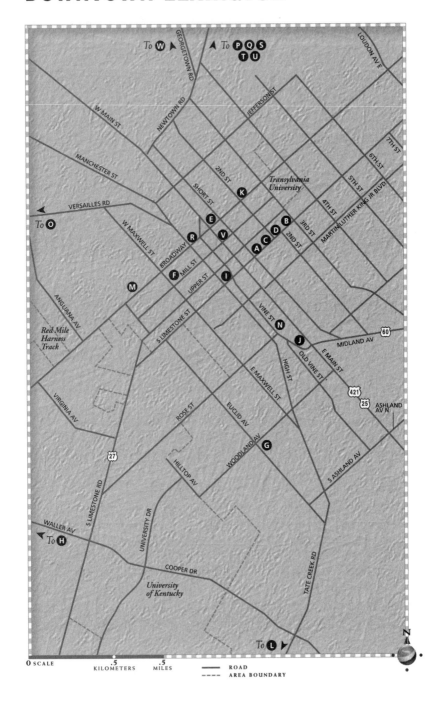

To W ▲   ▲ To P Q S
                    T U

GEORGETOWN RD
LOUDON AV E

W MAIN ST
NEWTOWN RD
JEFFERSON ST

MANCHESTER ST
2ND ST
7TH ST

SHORT ST
6TH ST
5TH ST

Transylvania
University
K

VERSAILLES RD
4TH ST
MARTIN LUTHER KING JR BLVD

To O
W MAXWELL ST
E
V
R
A C D
B
3RD ST
2ND ST

BROADWAY
F MILL ST
UPPER ST
I

M
S LIMESTONE ST

ANGLIANA AV

Red Mile
Harness
Track
VINE ST
N
J
MIDLAND AV
60
OLD VINE ST
E MAIN ST

E MAXWELL ST
HIGH ST
421
25 ASHLAND
AV N

VIRGINIA AV
ROSE ST
EUCLID AV
27

WOODLAND AV
G
S ASHLAND AV

HILLTOP AV
S LIMESTONE RD
UNIVERSITY DR
TATE CREEK RD

WALLER AV
To H
COOPER DR

University
of Kentucky

To L ▶

N

O SCALE   .5   .5
         KILOMETERS   MILES   ——— ROAD
                                   ---- AREA BOUNDARY

Food

Ⓐ A la Lucie

Ⓑ The Atomic Café

Ⓒ Coffee at the Gratz

Ⓓ Columbia Steakhouse

Ⓔ DeSha's

Ⓕ Dudley's

Ⓖ Everybody's Natural
   Foods & Deli

Ⓗ Kentucky Inn

Ⓘ Linda's Sandwich Shop

Ⓙ Magee's Bakery

Ⓚ Melodeon

Ⓛ Merrick Inn

Ⓜ Rogers Restaurant

Ⓝ Tonio's Super Burritos

Lodging

Ⓞ El Dorado Motor Inn

Ⓟ Griffin Gate Resort

Ⓒ Gratz Park Hotel

Ⓠ Holiday Inn North

Ⓡ Hyatt Regency

Ⓗ Kentucky Inn

Ⓢ Marriott Courtyard

Ⓣ Marriott Residence Inn

Ⓤ Quality Inn Northwest

Ⓥ Radisson

Camping

Ⓦ Kentucky Horse Park

Note: Items with the same letter are located in the same place.

provides room service for the Gratz Park Inn. **Dudley's**, which is in a restored schoolhouse at 380 South Mill, (606) 255-1010, is thought by some Lexingtonians to be one of the best restaurants in town. The **Atomic Café**, 265 N. Limestone, (606) 254-1969, serves Caribbean specialties and has outdoor seating and live music.

Other candidates for Lexington's finest cuisine are the charming and romantic French restaurant **A la Lucie**, 159 N. Limestone, (606) 252-5277, and the fine old **Merrick Inn**, 3380 Tate's Creek Road, (606) 269-5417. Merrick Inn is closed Sunday except during Keeneland's spring and fall race meetings, when they open Sunday evenings for supper after the races.

LODGING

The **Gratz Park Hotel**, 120 W. Second, (800) 227-4362, is a quiet, elegant hotel that is nearly hidden in a historic neighborhood. Rooms start at $120, with AAA and AARP discount rooms at $90 when the hotel isn't heavily booked.

Lexington has two large downtown hotels, the **Hyatt Regency** and the **Radisson**. Near UK is the older **Kentucky Inn**, (606) 254-1177, and out near Keeneland is the nice-looking **El Dorado Motor Inn**, (606) 255-9451, a classic of its type. There is a group of some of the more upscale national chain hotels on Newtown Road at New Circle, including Marriott's deluxe **Griffin Gate Resort**, **Marriott Courtyard**, **Marriott Residence Inn**, **Holiday Inn North**, and **Quality Inn Northwest**.

CAMPING

The **Kentucky Horse Park** offers year-round camping at $11.50–$15 per night, (606) 233-4303, ext. 257.

NIGHTLIFE

The limestone-filtered water that's good for making bourbon whiskey is also a fine beginning for brewing beer. Two new breweries have opened recently in Lexington, each with their own local brews. **Lexington City Brewery**, 1050 S. Broadway, (606) 259-BREW, has a fine Burley Red and a lager named after a legendary Lexington dog, Smiley Pete, whose story can be read on a historic marker downtown. Their friendly restaurant serves an extensive menu and makes a great place to watch UK basketball, since tickets to Rupp Arena are scarce. **Lexington Brewing Company**, 401 Cross, (606) 252-6004, makes Limestone Ale and offers brewery tours by appointment.

Two of Lexington's favorite downtown music clubs are **Cheapside Bar & Grill**, 131 Cheapside, (606) 254-0046, which has music almost every night and is also a good place for lunch, and **Blues on Broadway**, 142 N. Broadway, (606) 243-0379.

For concert events, check out both the **Kentucky Theater**, a 1920s movie theater that also shows foreign and classic films, 214 E. Main, (606) 231-6887, and the **Lexington Opera House**, dating from the 1880s, that is also home to the **Lexington Ballet**, (606) 257-4929. Lexington's primary source of cultural programming is the **Singletary Center for the Arts**, at UK, (606) 257-4929, which features major performing arts, music, and theater events throughout the year.

12

CUMBERLAND GAP, WILDERNESS ROAD, AND BEREA

In 1775, Daniel Boone and a party of 30 men blazed a trail through the Cumberland Gap. Boone was following in the footsteps of those who came before—Thomas Walker in 1750, who had given it a name; the scouts, hunting parties, and war parties of Indian tribes, who regarded the area as common ground belonging to none; and, as always, the animals which had first found the passage through the high hilly country.

Today visitors driving through the Cumberland Gap on the four-lane Hwy 25 will notice the destruction coal mining and road building have forced upon the landscape, and see a number of small Appalachian cities and towns tucked into pockets of poor soil or wedged up against unforgiving rock and rushing river. A stop in the town of Berea will help fill in the history of Appalachian Kentucky. The history of Berea College shows how the preservation of the craft tradition has worked in the service of higher education for mountain youth. Berea is also a living example of the first experiment in interracial living in the pre-Civil War South. Just north of Berea is White Hall, home of abolitionist politician Cassius Marcellus Clay, one of the founders of Berea College and a friend of Abraham Lincoln's. The destinies of the earliest citizens of Kentucky and the strong-willed and proud mountain peoples who have stayed in this sparsely populated Appalachian region despite severe economic disadvantages, remain inextricably linked. ◼

A PERFECT DAY IN CUMBERLAND GAP AND BEREA

For the best glimpse of the deep woods and rugged terrain encountered by settlers moving through the area in the early 1800s, spend a night in the Cumberland Gap National Park. Be sure to reach the Pinnacle, from which point you can see three states. In the town of Cumberland Gap, on the eastern side of the mountain, enjoy an excellent lunch of chicken and dumplings or a Dijon tenderloin sandwich in a historic setting at the up–scale Ye Olde Coffee and Tea Shoppe. Drive north along Hwy 25 to Berea, stopping at Wilderness Road sites at your leisure. Spend the late afternoon touring the campus, browsing the college bookstore for books by Appalachian authors, and visiting the many craft shops of Berea College. Then dine on regional specialties in Berea's famous Boone Tavern Dining Room before turning in upstairs for a sleep that will take you back in time.

DANIEL BOONE AND THE WILDERNESS ROAD

Daniel Boone actually explored the Cumberland Gap area around 1769, but it was the signing of the Treaty of Sycamore Shoals six years later between the Cherokee and the Transylvania Land Company that gave white settlers Cherokee permission to inhabit the entire watershed of the Cumberland River as well as the southern watershed of the Kentucky River. Under the auspices of Transylvania Land Company owner Richard Henderson, Boone established Fort Boonesborough on the Kentucky River near what is now Richmond, and ultimately moved his family there.

In the decades that followed, many settlers from the areas that are now Virginia, Tennessee, and North Carolina walked and rode along Boone's route. Some wanted to make their way toward the more populated Fort Harrod, which in 1774 had been established as the first permanent English settlement west of the Alleghenies. The designated Wilderness Road began to diverge from Boone's Trace, near where London, Kentucky, is today. It can still be followed along what is now Hwy 150 from Mt. Vernon to Harrodsburg, where visitors can see the reconstructed Fort Harrod and watch the outdoor dramas *The Legend of Daniel Boone* and *Shadows in the Forest* (the same history told from the Shawnee perspective) during the summer months. Call (800) 852-6663 for more information. Fort Harrod (handicapped accessible) is closed December through mid-March, (606) 734-3314.

CUMBERLAND GAP

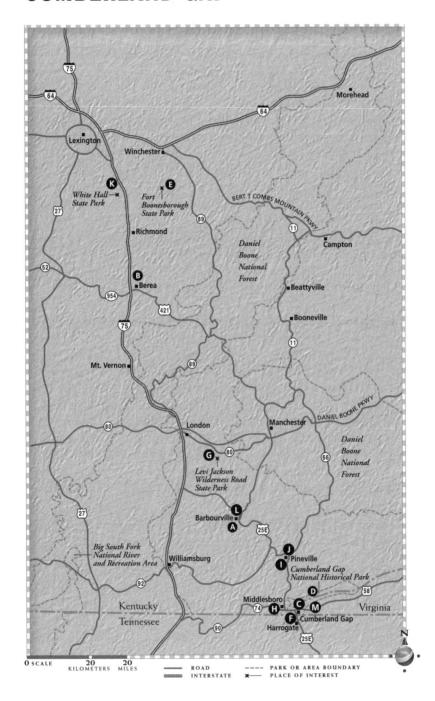

75

64

Morehead

64

Lexington

Winchester

K White Hall State Park

E Fort Boonesborough State Park

27

BERT T COMBS MOUNTAIN PKWY

89

Richmond

11

Campton

Daniel Boone National Forest

52

B Berea

Beattyville

954

421

Booneville

75

11

Mt. Vernon

89

DANIEL BOONE PKWY

London

Manchester

Daniel Boone National Forest

80

80

66

G Levi Jackson Wilderness Road State Park

27

Barbourville

L

A

25E

J Pineville

Big South Fork National River and Recreation Area

Williamsburg

I Cumberland Gap National Historical Park

92

D

58

Middlesboro

Kentucky

74

H

C

M

Virginia

Tennessee

F Cumberland Gap

90

Harrogate

25E

N

0 SCALE   20   20
KILOMETERS   MILES

ROAD

PARK OR AREA BOUNDARY

INTERSTATE

PLACE OF INTEREST

Sights

Ⓐ Barbourville/Dr. Thomas Walker State Historic Site

Ⓑ Berea

Ⓒ Cumberland Gap

Ⓓ Cumberland Gap National Park/Pinnacle Overlook

Ⓔ Fort Boonesborough

Ⓕ Harrogate/Lincoln Museum

Ⓓ Hensley Settlement

Ⓖ Levi Jackson Wilderness Road State Park

Ⓗ Middlesboro

Ⓘ Pine Mountain Lake State Resort Park

Ⓙ Pineville

Ⓗ Ridgerunner B & B

Ⓚ White Hall/Clermont

Ⓒ Ye Olde Tea and Coffee Shoppe

Food

Ⓕ Reed's

Ⓛ Vintage House

Ⓒ Webb's Kitchen

Ⓒ Ye Olde Tea and Coffee Shop

Lodging

Ⓗ Holiday Inn

Ⓘ Pine Mountain Lake State Resort Park

Ⓗ Ridgerunner B&B

Ⓒ Ye Olde Tea and Coffee Shoppe (hotel)

Camping

Ⓓ Cumberland Gap National Park

Ⓔ Fort Boonesborough State Park

Ⓖ Levi Jackson Wilderness Road State Park

Ⓜ Wilderness Road Campground

Note: Items with the same letter are located in the same area.

SIGHTSEEING HIGHLIGHTS

★★★ **Berea**—This small city, located on Hwy 25 or just off I-75 at Exits 76 and 77, is 37 miles north of London and 35 miles south of Lexington. Berea has become known as the "folk arts and crafts capital of Kentucky" and is home to the small, private liberal arts college of the same name. The college square in the center of town is ringed with craft shops, as is Old Town Berea, located near the old train depot on N. Broadway. There are also a number of antique shops along Hwy 25 South.

Berea College offers tours of its campus, as well as its **Appalachian Museum** and its **Log House Craft Shop** and student workshops. Berea was not only the first integrated school in the South, but also the first to offer work-study, tuition-free education to the best and brightest Appalachian youth. Students at Berea learn to produce the Berea-style woodcraft, ironware, weaving, and pottery that is sold to support the school. A spirit of enlightened enterprise pervades this serene mountain town; just walking onto the campus is inspiring. Be sure to seek out the Fine Art Department's **Doris Ullman Galleries**, located in the Rogers-Traylor Art Building, for outstanding exhibits of contemporary regional art. The **Boone Tavern Hotel** on the college square, founded in 1909, offers comfortable rooms furnished with Berea-made furniture, and a waitstaff of Berea students serve breakfast, lunch, and dinner in the Boone Tavern Dining Room.

★★★ **Cumberland Gap, Harrogate, and Middlesboro**—All three towns were founded in the late 1800s by Alexander Arthur and the American Association, British venture capitalists in the railroad, coal, and steel industries who were financed by the Bank of England. The story of their bold plans and ultimate failure adds a fascinating second chapter to the history of the region. A walking tour of Cumberland Gap is available by calling the City Recorder, Judy Barton. Phone: (423) 869-3860.

★★★ **Cumberland Gap National Park**—The **Pinnacle Overlook** onto the Gap itself can be reached by a short walk up a paved path behind the visitor's center. The Gap has a fascinating Civil War history—it changed hands four times during the war, as it was a major conduit for supplies and soldiers moving in both directions. This fact is delineated in historic markers and the artifacts that remain. The 20,000-acre Cumberland Gap National Park, which spans Virginia, Kentucky, and Tennessee, offers a variety of ranger-led activities as well as hiking trails and campgrounds where you are unlikely to encounter many other visitors, even in the busiest of summer seasons. There is a nice visitor's center with interpretive historical exhibits on the Kentucky side of the Gap. The **Hensley Settlement** can be reached hiking into the park about 11 miles. It is a preserved mountain community of three farmsteads originally built around 1905, where two Park Service farmer-demonstrators maintain the buildings and fields using old farming methods. Phone: (606) 248-2817.

★★ **Fort Boonesborough**—Now a state park, this is the site of Fort Boone. It was established by Daniel Boone on April 1, 1775, as several log huts near a salt lick by the Kentucky River. After the arrival of Richard Henderson and his Transylvania Colony, the fort was moved and built into four blockhouses and 26 log cabins. The fort has been reconstructed, and an excellent walking trail guide prepared by the Kentucky Historical Society will assist visitors in retracing the paths of major events in the history of this key pioneer outpost. A "forage trail" brochure calls attention to the ways in which the first white settlers made use of nature's bounty for survival. Address: 6 miles northeast of White Hall on Hwy 627. Phone: (606) 527-3131.

★★ **Newlee Iron Furnace**—Dating from the 1820s, this primitive furnace in Berea—a limestone rock chimney for melting iron ore mined in the mountain above, served by a waterwheel and bellows arrangement—inspired the speculative development of the American Association in the late 1880s. Nearby is the hand-laid limestone railroad tunnel (built in 1880) through the Gap that signaled the beginning of industrialization for the region.

★★ **White Hall**—White Hall is just off I-75 at Exit 95. This imposing 3½-story brick house sits alone on vast acreage. It was the home of Cassius Marcellus Clay, a staunch abolitionist, friend of Abraham Lincoln's, and Ambassador to Russia through most of the 1860s. Clay's father, Green Clay, was one of the wealthiest men in Kentucky when he built the elegant **Clermont** in 1797. An early surveyor of the Kentucky territory for the State of Virginia, Green Clay bought a large tract of land and founded a ferry and a distillery nearby. White Hall (circa 1860), which is actually built adjoining Clermont, had the first indoor plumbing in the state. All of the bricks for both homes were manufactured on the property. Furnished with some original pieces and period furnishings throughout, the top floor has been made into a small museum containing fascinating family documents, photographs, and memorabilia. Admission is $4 per adult, $2.50 per child. Open April 1– October 31, closed Monday. Phone: (606) 623-9178.

★★ **Wilderness Road Tours**—Former coal mine operator Tom Shattuck, a resident of Middlesboro and an amateur historian of Daniel Boone and the Wilderness Road, leads tours of the area. His comfortable van runs twice daily from Middlesboro and Pineville, covering the Gap, the Wilderness Road, Daniel Boone's Trace, Civil War Breastworks, and the history of Cumberland Gap and the original Middlesboro. Tom is not only a knowledgeable guide and an outdoorsman, he also knows a lot about the recent history of the area, and he is good company. The fee is $12 per adult, $5 per child. Discounted rates are available for groups of more than five people. Phone: (606) 248-2626.

★★ **Ye Olde Tea and Coffee Shoppe**—This restaurant was created in 1991 by combining three buildings that originally housed the bank, the post office and general merchandise store, and the hardware store, all dating from 1889. Address: 528 Colwyn Street, Cumberland Gap. Phone: (800) 899-4844.

Dr. Thomas Walker State Historic Site—Barbourville is home to this historic site, which consists of little more than a picnic area and is located approximately 11 miles south of the city in a protected valley, (606) 546-4400. Walker, who found the Gap in 1750 on a surveying trip, named it after the Duke of Cumberland. A physician, he was the personal doctor and trusted friend of Peter Jefferson, the father of Thomas Jefferson, in Charlottesville, Virginia. Upon Peter's death, 12-year-old Thomas became Walker's godson, and the young Jefferson is thought to have been much influenced by Walker's mentorship. On the town square in Barbourville is the newly opened Vintage House restaurant in the town's oldest building.

Harrogate—This town once housed the American Association's 700-room Four Seasons resort hotel. It is now home to Lincoln Memorial University, whose **Lincoln Museum** has a fine collection of memorabilia relating to Abraham Lincoln. The university was founded by Lincoln's friend General O.O. Howard. Hours: Open 9 a.m.–4 p.m. Phone: (606) 869-6235.

Levi Jackson Wilderness Road State Park—Located just south of London, this park commemorates a site where both the **Wilderness Road** and **Boone's Trace** are known to have passed. Inside the park are a working gristmill, a pioneer cemetery, and a museum interpreting mountain life. Closed in winter. Phone: (606) 878-8000.

Middlesboro—The American Association had its greatest influence on Middlesboro, a town planned to reach a population of 100,000, with its grand Cumberland Avenue laid out 100 feet wide. Founder Alexander Arthur, who dreamed of creating the Pittsburgh of the South, built beautiful downtown Victorian gothic and Romanesque buildings and lovely homes in a hilly neighborhood now called Arthur Heights. The **Ridgerunner B & B**, (602)248-4299, is in one of these original homes. The nearby 1889 **Middlesboro Golf Club**, nine holes, is of British design and is one of the oldest continuously played courses in the country. Unfortunately, its original clubhouse is no longer standing. The club is private, but visitors are allowed.

Pineville—Located 13 miles north of Middlesboro, Pineville is situated at the second gap back from Cumberland, which is a steep water pass through the mountains. **Pine Mountain Lake State Resort Park**, founded in 1924, is Kentucky's first state park and is thought by many to be its most beautiful. It is located on a mountaintop 2 miles outside the city.

FITNESS AND RECREATION

Cumberland Gap National Park offers a variety of ranger-led activities as well as hiking trails and campgrounds. Horses are permitted on many park trails and in three of the overnight campgrounds. There is a private livery stable near Ewing, Virginia, outside of the park on Hwy 58. Bikes can be ridden on all paved roads and on some off-road trails as well. Call (606) 248-2817 for information.

    Pine Mountain Lake State Resort Park, which sponsors the 10K "At the Top" run along the crest of Pine Mountain every April, (606) 337-3066, also has a swimming pool and a nine-hole golf course. For information, call (800) 325-1712. **Levi Jackson Wilderness Road State Park**, (606) 878-8000, offers hiking trails and a swimming pool. **Fort Boonesborough State Park** has designated hiking trails, a swimming pool, and a miniature golf course.

FOOD

Ye Olde Tea and Coffee Shop in Cumberland Gap, which features an extensive menu and gets rave reviews from many quarters, is open for dinner and, yes, they also serve good coffee. The same folks are opening a hotel 2 blocks away in summer 1996, (800) 899-4844. Across the street in a smaller storefront building is **Webb's Kitchen**, which serves fine down-home meals. In Harrogate try **Reed's**, an unpromising looking place right on Hwy 25 across from LMU in Harrogate that serves good hearty food.

The **Vintage House** in Barbourville offers good-looking sandwiches and specials for lunch daily. They also offer a weekly changing dinner menu on Friday and Saturday evenings, for which reservations are recommended, (606) 546-5414.

In Berea the **Boone Tavern Dining Room** serves breakfast, lunch, and dinner, with a waitstaff of Berea students. No alcohol is served, but regional specialties like spoonbread and homemade yeast rolls, fried green tomatoes, black-eyed pea dip, corn pudding, and pecan crusted catfish make this a requisite stop on any itinerary. It's best to make advance reservations for meals, (800) 366-9358. Try the **Cardinal Deli**, just a few doors down for breakfast or lunch with the locals, and the **Berea Coffee and Tea Company** next door for a morning or afternoon pick-me-up.

LODGING

There is a **Holiday Inn** right off Hwy 25 at Cumberland Gap, U.S. Hwy 25, (423) 869-3631 or (800) HOLIDAY, which mars the incredible view but provides a convenient place to overnight. Or check in town at **Ye Olde Tea & Coffee Shop** to see if their new hotel is ready. The **Ridgerunner B&B** in Middlesboro, (606) 248-4299, comes highly recommended by Tom Shattuck, as does **Pine Mountain Lake State Resort Park**, which offers rustic cottages as well as a 30-room lodge. For reservations, call (800) 325-1712.

The **Boone Tavern** in Berea has 59 guest rooms at reasonable rates ($63 for a double room), (800) 598-5263. If you happen to reach Berea when the tavern is full, try one of the B&Bs in town: **Shady Lane**, (606) 986-9851, or **Morning Glory**, (606) 986-8661. Stop by the welcome center in Old Town Berea for information on these, or call (800) 598-5263. Otherwise, the **Holiday Motel** is a clean, locally

BEREA

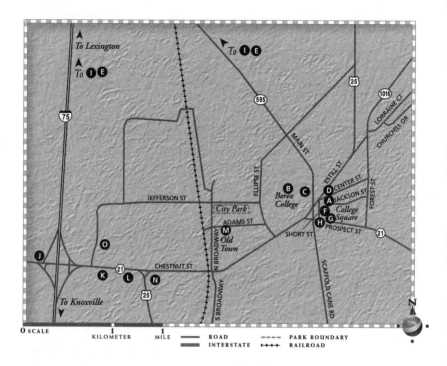

Sights

- **Ⓐ** Appalachian Museum
- **Ⓑ** Berea College
- **Ⓒ** Doris Ullman Galleries
- **Ⓓ** Log House Craft Shop
- **Ⓔ** Fort Boonesborough

Food

- **Ⓕ** Berea Coffee and Tea Company
- **Ⓖ** Boone Tavern Dining Room
- **Ⓕ** Cardinal Deli

Lodging

- **Ⓗ** Boone Tavern Hotel
- **Ⓘ** Days Inn
- **Ⓙ** Econolodge
- **Ⓚ** Holiday Motel
- **Ⓛ** Howard Johnson's
- **Ⓜ** Morning Glory
- **Ⓝ** Shady Lane
- **Ⓞ** Super 8 Motel

Note: Items with the same letter are located in the same area.

owned option, (606) 986-3771, and there are several national chain motels located just off I-75 including **Howard Johnson's, Days Inn, Super 8 Motel**, and **Econolodge.**

CAMPING

Fort Boonesborough State Park has a large camping area with hookups and primitive camping sites near the Kentucky River. Camping areas may not be reserved in advance, (606) 527-3131.

Cumberland Gap National Park has several campgrounds with no hookups, but comfort stations with hot showers. One has a simple cabin with six bunks and a fireplace. The **Wilderness Road Campground**, on Virginia Hwy 58, located 2 miles from the Gap, is open year-round for tents and trailers. Except for group camping, reservations are not accepted, (606) 248-2817. **Levi Jackson Wilderness Road State Park** offers year-round camping with hookups, (606) 878-8000.

SPECIAL EVENTS

One of the best ways to get to know this region is to participate in the celebration of Appalachian traditional culture. Any one of these events would be worth planning a trip around. Middlesboro's **Cumberland Mountain Fall Festival**, in October, features the **Official State Banjo Contest**, (606) 248-1075. Barbourville has an annual **Daniel Boone Festival**, in October, that has been ongoing for more than 45 years, (606) 546-6062. Pine Mountain State Resort Park sponsors a dulcimer convention in September, (606) 337-3066, and a **Mountain Laurel Festival** in May that has been in existence since 1931. Levi Jackson Wilderness Road State Park has a **Mountain Folk Festival** weekend in September that features contra dancing, (606) 986-9341. London sponsors the **Camp Wildcat** reenactment of the first Union victory of the Civil War in 1861. The visitor's center can give more information, (800) 348-0095.

Berea hosts the **Kentucky Guild of Artists and Craftsmen's Spring and Fall Fairs** in May and October, (606) 986-3192, along with the **Big Hill Mountain Bluegrass Festival** in August, (606) 986-2540, and the **Celebration of Traditional Music** in October, (606) 986-9341.

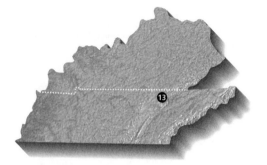

13
RUGBY AND
THE BIG SOUTH FORK

The Big South Fork, created by the U.S. Army Corps of Engineers from former mining and timbering lands beginning in the 1970s and turned over to the Park Service in 1990, is one of the best-kept secrets in Tennessee among white-water paddlers and back-country campers. Rugby, Tennessee, a Victorian-era utopian community, is located in a rural area on the northern Cumberland Plateau of Tennessee about 25 miles south of the Kentucky border. Combining the two makes for an unusual and delightful vacation destination.

The Big South Fork, a national recreation area, is between Rugby and the Kentucky border. Its 110,000 acres of rugged, rocky gorge surround a fork of the Cumberland River flowing down from Kentucky and offer spectacular scenic views, challenging water recreation, miles of hiking and backpacking trails, and unrestricted back-country camping—providing the experience that many wish was still possible in the now heavily touristed Great Smoky Mountains National Park. The area is bounded on the west by Pickett State Park, one of Tennessee's oldest, and on the south by Rugby, a charming village filled with Victorian architecture. A welcome respite from the rigors of nature, the Historic Rugby Preservation Association offers period lodging and dining in what feels for all the world like the middle of nowhere. ◪

THE BIG SOUTH FORK

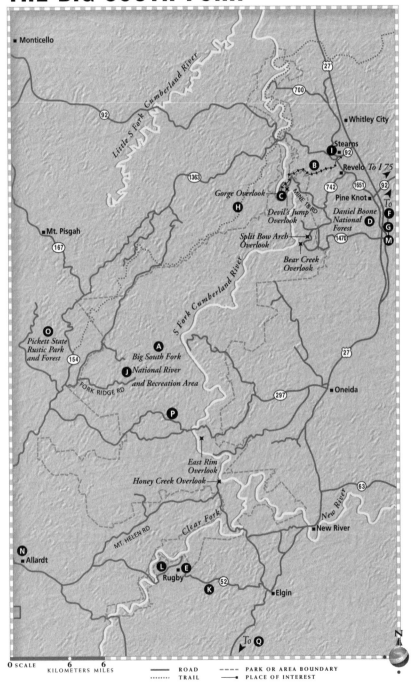

Monticello

Little S Fork Cumberland River

92

27

700

Whitley City

Stearns
92
I
B
Revelo *To I 75*
1363
742
1651
92
To
Gorge Overlook **C**
MINE 18 RD
Pine Knot
F
H
Devil's Jump
Overlook
Daniel Boone
National
Forest
D
G
M
Mt. Pisgah
Split Bow Arch
Overlook
1470
167

Bear Creek
Overlook

S Fork Cumberland River

O
Pickett State
Rustic Park
and Forest
154
A
27
J
Big South Fork
National River
and Recreation Area
FORK RIDGE RD
297
Oneida

P

East Rim
Overlook
Honey Creek Overlook
63

New River
MT. HELEN RD
Clear Fork
New River

N
Allardt
L
E
Rugby
K
52
Elgin

To **Q**

N

O SCALE
KILOMETERS MILES
6   6

ROAD — — — PARK OR AREA BOUNDARY
.... TRAIL ⊢ PLACE OF INTEREST

Sights

A Big South Fork National Recreation Area

B Big South Fork Scenic Railway

C Blue Heron Outdoor Historical Museum

D Daniel Boone National Forest

E Historic Rugby

F Natural Bridge State Park

G Red River Gorge

H Sheltowee Trace National Recreation Trail

I Stearns Museum

Food

E Cumberland Safari Club Barbecue

E Harrow Road Café

Lodging

E 1880 Pioneer Cottage

J Charit Creek Lodge

K Clear Fork Farm B&B

L Grey Gables Bed & Breakfast Inn

M Hemlock Lodge and Cottages

F Natural Bridge State Park

E Newbury House B&B

N Old Allardt Schoolhouse

E Percy Cottage

O Pickett State Park

Camping

P Bandy Creek Campground and Stables

A Big South Fork

Q Frozen Head State Natural Area

F Natural Bridge State Park

O Pickett State Park

Note: Items with the same letter are located in the same town or area.

A PERFECT DAY IN BIG SOUTH FORK COUNTRY

After breakfast, pack a picnic and put on appropriate gear for a daylong fresh air outing. In the morning, tour the remains of mining operations by boarding the Big South Fork Scenic Railway at Stearns, Kentucky. It will take you along the routes of the coal trains that used to service the mine, to the Blue Heron Outdoor Historical Museum. Enter Big South Fork at the Bandy Creek headquarters and spend the day hiking, floating the river in a canoe, or joining a white-water rafting expedition for the afternoon. After a full day outdoors, drive to Rugby for dinner at the Harrow Road Café and a quiet overnight at one of the Historic Rugby lodgings. Spend the next morning walking in this surprisingly civilized enclave as if it were your own neighborhood back in 1885.

SIGHTSEEING HIGHLIGHTS

✫✫✫ **Big South Fork National Recreation Area**—Named after the southern fork of the Cumberland River, Big South Fork connects with Kentucky's 670,000-acre **Daniel Boone National Forest**, cutting a swath of protected timber across the eastern third of both states. The **Sheltowee Trace National Recreation Trail** (a sort of mini-Appalachian Trail, 257 miles in length) runs through the length of Daniel Boone, across the top of Big South Fork, and ends at Tennessee's Pickett State Park. Sheltowee, which means turtle, is the Shawnee name given to Boone by Chief Blackfish as he adopted the captive Boone into the tribe. There is also a stretch of hiking trail named for and mapped by John Muir.

At the northern end of Daniel Boone National Forest, about 50 miles east of Lexington, you'll find the spectacular **Red River Gorge** and **Natural Bridge State Park**, where you can see more than 80 natural sandstone arches. For information on the Daniel Boone National Forest, contact the nearest ranger district. Listed south to north, they are: Stearns, (606) 376-5323; Somerset, (606) 679-2018; London, (606) 864-4163; Redbird, (606) 598-2192; Berea, (606) 986-8434; Stanton, (606) 663-2852 (Red River Gorge is located in Stanton); and Morehead, (606) 784-5624.

✫✫✫ **Historic Rugby**—Founded in 1880 by English social reformer Thomas Hughes as a place where the second sons of the British landed gentry could "work like peasants and live like gentlemen," Rugby was an idealist's dream that failed within ten years. At its height in 1885, the colony, sponsored as a commercial venture by the Board of Aid to Land Ownership, owned 75,000 acres of land and had as many as 450 members who built at least 75 structures. English, Scottish, and American colonists worked together, lived side-by-side, and enjoyed a somewhat esoteric lifestyle. They dressed for tea everyday at 4 p.m. and spent most of their free time reading or playing at croquet, tennis, lawn bowling, and other pursuits of the British leisure class—it's no wonder Rugby's agriculture and home-grown industry efforts failed. Walking tours are available year round, except in January, when the school closes. Church services are still held every Sunday in the 1887 Episcopal church, and the library remains intact as one of the finest collections of Victoriana in the United States. Admission is $4 per adult, $2 per student. Phone: (423) 628-2441.

★★ **Blue Heron Outdoor Historical Museum**—A very effectively interpreted coal mining and logging camp open April–October. Phone: (615) 879-3625. It can be reached via Hwy 92 from Stearns or by a ride on the **Big South Fork Scenic Railway**. Phone: (800) 462-5664 or (606) 376-5330.

★★ **Stearns Museum**—This museum offers a look at the history of the Stearns Coal and Lumber Company as it existed from 1902–1976. Admission is $2 per person. Open April–October. Address: Off Hwy 27 at Stearns, Kentucky. Phone: (606) 376-5730.

FITNESS AND RECREATION

Big South Fork National Recreation Area, located between Highway 27 and Highway 127 at the border of Tennessee and Kentucky, offers back-country hiking, camping, biking, horse trail riding, and all forms of river sports. For information and a map of the area, write: National Park Service, Big South Fork, P.O. Drawer 630, Oneida, TN 37841. Stop by Bandy Creek Visitors Center on Route 297 for information about outfitters, horseback riding stables, and other activities, (615) 879-3625.

The **Daniel Boone National Forest** connects with the Big South Fork near Stearns, Kentucky. Not only does the forest contain all manner of scenic trails, hiking, and river recreation opportunities, but the **Red River Gorge**, in the northern part of the park, is a well-known rock-climbing area. **Sheltowee Trace Outfitters** serves the Stearns area in the south with guided canoe and raft expeditions ($20–$65 per person) from March–October. Call them at (800) 541-RAFT. While you are nearby, stop by the Daniel Boone National Forest's southernmost visitor's center, located in Whitley City, Kentucky, on Hwy 27, (606) 376-5323, so you can plan your trip to the rest of the forest.

Pickett State Park, located adjacent to Big South Fork off Hwy 154 to the west, is known for its diversity of botanical growth (second only to that found in the Smokies), its rugged rock formations and natural bridges, and its wealth of hiking trails. Pickett also has some of the nicest rustic stone cabins of any of Tennessee's state parks.

At **Frozen Head State Natural Area,** about 40 miles from Rugby, in the Cumberland Mountains, you can hike in mountainous terrain that contains 14 peaks. Its namesake snow-covered mountain stands at 3,324 feet. This area was an Indian hunting ground, and there is evidence of a Woodland Indian trail over the mountains from the Clinch River Valley to the east down into the Cumberland River Valley. Frozen Head, with no less that 12 trails built by the Civilian Conservation Corps in the 1930s, will provide a nice day of rugged hiking and spectacular views across the Cumberland Plateau. The park entrance is at Wartburg, Tennessee; call for information, (423) 346-3318.

From the Wartburg visitor's center, you can get directions to the **Obed Wild and Scenic River,** a National Park Service site that is co-managed by the Tennessee Wildlife Resources Agency. The Obed lives up to its name, offering impressive limestone gorges and clear rushing streams. Hiking, fishing, rafting, and canoeing (as well as swimming in a few quiet spots) are all available here in relative isolation. River put-ins and difficulty ratings are marked so that canoe expeditions can be planned for maximum enjoyment. This is another of Tennessee's virtually pristine natural treasures. The Obed encompasses the **Catoosa Wildlife Management Area,** which is a designated site for managed game hunting in the spring and fall. Call (423) 346-6294 for information.

FOOD

The **Harrow Road Café,** operated by Historic Rugby, serves regional specialties with an old-fashioned air, such as spoon rolls, shepherd's pie, fried catfish, ham and biscuits, and bread pudding. Breakfast, lunch, and dinner are offered at reasonable prices, (423) 628-2441.

Cumberland Safari Club Barbecue, Hwy 52E in Rugby, is open for lunch and dinner every day but Monday. In addition to pork and chicken pit barbecue, they also smoke ribs and serve Guiness Stout. You'll probably want to order a carry-out picnic for the next day, (423) 627-4444.

LODGING

Charit Creek Lodge is situated within Big South Fork. This establishment, to which there is no road access, is located approximately 1.8 miles in by the shortest route. It stands at the site of a cabin built in 1817 in a pasture framed by bluffs. Both lodge accommodations and private cabins are available, with rates including dinner and breakfast. A horse stable is also available. This lodge is under the same management as the LeConte Lodge on top of Mt. LeConte in the Great Smoky Mountains National Park. Call (423) 429-5704.

Pickett State Park offers chalets, rustic cottages, and cabins—its stone cottages with fireplaces are some of the first such public facilities built in the state and some of the best the Tennessee state parks have to offer. Rates for rustic cottages are $85 weekend, $65 weeknight. The cabins go for $60 weekend, $50 weeknight, and some of the newer cabins for $100 weekend, $80 weeknight. Call (800) 421-6683 for an information packet or (423) 879-5821 for reservations.

If you decide to travel north into the Daniel Boone National Forest, you might want to call ahead for reservations at **Natural Bridge State Park,** in Slade, Kentucky. This popular destination, located about an hour east of Lexington, is in a very isolated location. Their **Hemlock Lodge and Cottages** might be just the sort of end-of-the-trail stop you need after some time spent on heavily traveled I-75. Call (800) 325-1710 for lodging reservations.

Outside of the parks, Historic Rugby, Inc. runs three lodging facilities in historic buildings: **Newbury House B&B,** the **1880 Pioneer Cottage** (where Thomas Hughes stayed when he first came to Rugby), and **Percy Cottage.** Call them at (423) 628-2441 for rates and reservations.

If you can't book a room in Rugby, there are several other nearby B&Bs. The **Grey Gables Bed & Breakfast Inn,** Hwy 52 west of Rugby, is a contemporary rustic lodge with eight rooms and private baths, where a $90 double and $70 single includes the evening meal and breakfast. Horse boarding is available, (423) 628-5252. **Clear Fork**

Farm B&B, south of Hwy 52 and Rugby, is a brick farmhouse with three rooms and private baths that also has a horse barn. Rates are $65–$75 for a double, (423) 628-2967. To experience an ingenious historic rehabilitation, stay at the **Old Allardt Schoolhouse**, built circa 1910, which has been remodeled into a two bed and two bath lodge with a shared kitchen. There is a porch on either end, and the entrances are separate. Located on Hwy 52 west of Rugby at the intersection of Hwy 296, the Schoolhouse is open year-round, and weekly rates are available. Rates range from $55 during the week per double to $75 on weekend nights, (800) 771-8940.

CAMPING

Frozen Head State Natural Area in Tennessee offers tent camping with facilities and back-country camping. Like most Tennessee state parks, reservations are not accepted for campsites, but you can call for information, (423) 879-4013. **Pickett State Park**, also in Tennessee, offers camping and hookups, but takes no reservations, (423) 879-5821. At **Big South Fork**, back-country camping is allowed without permits year-round. **Bandy Creek Campground and Stables** has tent and RV camping, (423) 879-4013.

Unicorn/Robin Rudd

In the Daniel Boone National Forest, there are many camping areas for which information can be obtained at the closest of six ranger district offices (see "Sightseeing Highlights" for locations). **Natural Bridge State Park**, in Slade, Kentucky, has two campgrounds with primitive camping as well as full hookups. Camping is first-come, first-served. Call (606) 663-2214, or fax (606) 663-5037, for park information.

SPECIAL EVENTS

Historic Rugby, Inc. sponsors a traditional **Spring Music and Crafts Festival** in early May and their **Rugby Annual Pilgrimage** the first week of October. Either offers a fine opportunity to see Rugby come alive. Many of the privately owned homes are open for tours on festival days, and craftspeople and musicians from the surrounding areas come in to participate. Historic Rugby will respond graciously to your inquiries when you call or write to them at: (423) 638-2441 or (423) 628-2430, P.O. Box 8, Rugby, TN 37733.

Highway 127 stretches from Frankfort, Kentucky, through Danville, Jamestown, Kentucky, and Jamestown, Tennessee, before it winds down into the Sequatchie Valley of Tennessee and into Alabama. This road and Hwy 27, about 40 miles to the east, run parallel to I-75, the major north-south corridor from Atlanta to Cincinnati and beyond. Try the old road if you like to see things as they used to be. The same rugged terrain you can see from I-75 is heightened by comparison to the tiny communities that have grown up beside them.

On the Cumberland Plateau in Kentucky, around Albany and Jamestown, is the **Cumberland Lake/Wolf Creek Dam** recreation area—a prime lake resort, hunting, and vacation area for Kentuckians, where fishing cabins and bait shops can be found along dirt roads leading off Hwy 127. Driving a road like this is the closest thing you can find in Kentucky and Tennessee to the Maine backroads experience. The one unfortunate difference is billboard advertising along the way.

Highway 127 is proud of its yearly "World's Longest Yard Sale" in late summer, which runs the length of the highway and finds RV entrepreneurs renting farmer's fields with road frontage for their temporary knickknack displays. Experiencing this firsthand is actually more fun than it sounds.

Route: Headed south on Hwy 127 from Russell Springs, Kentucky, you'll pass **Bray's General Store** at Jamestown, Kentucky, and the quaint **Pinehurst Motel**, (502) 343-4143, just south of Jamestown. Craft shops and hand-lettered signs along the road advertise quilts, handmade wood and willow furniture, and bluebird houses. The **Lake Cumberland Motel** is located at Hwy 55 and Hwy 127, and **The Woods Inn**, (502)343-3969, and **Pioneer Antiques** beckon a little further down the road. Near Albany, which is home to the **Foothills Festival**, you'll pass the **Hopkins Rural School**, **Caney Gap Antiques**, and the **Branham Motel**.

As you cross into Tennessee, you may stop at **Forbus General Store** for a few photos, but save souvenir shopping for the Cumberland Mountain General Store, about 40 miles south. At Pall Mall, just north of Jamestown, the **Alvin York Gristmill**, a beautiful red clapboard structure astride a stream on limestone piers, is the center of a small park commemorating one of Tennessee's best-loved World War I heroes. At the same road curve is the **Craft Shop of the Three Forks**.

From Jamestown you can take Hwy 154 east to Big South Fork and Pickett State Park or continue south toward Allardt, to find **Allardt Haus Antiques, Indianman Wooden Indians**, and the **Old Schoolhouse B&B. East Fork Stables**—built from the characteristically brown, gold, and pink native Cumberland Mountain stone—offers cabins, camping, and stables. At Clarkrange, you'll find the original **Cumberland Mountain General Store** (there's another south of Crossville) and the turnoff (Hwy 62) for the **Muddy Pond Mennonite Community** about 5 miles west. Muddy Pond is sizable, with a number of working communal farms. Stop at the **General Store**, (615) 445-7829, for a driving map. While many of the houses sell baked and canned goods and fresh produce at the front door, don't miss the **Muddy Pond Backen Haus**, about 10 miles down the road, where you can enjoy a sweet bite in a friendly atmosphere and take wonderful cinnamon rolls and coffeecakes to go. You might even wish to call ahead, (615) 445-3875.

Continuing down Hwy 127 and crossing I-40 (east to

HIGHWAY 127

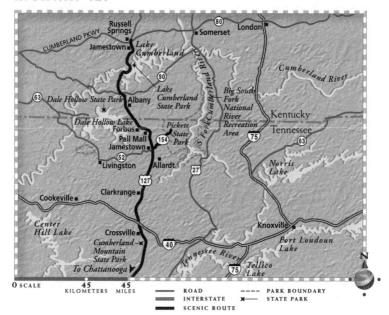

Knoxville, west to Nashville) takes you to **Crossville**. After the unsightly strip of commercial motels and restaurants that leads from the interstate to the center of town, you'll begin to notice buildings made from native stone. The old quarries are located east of town toward Crab Orchard. Continue 4 miles south on Hwy 127 to **Cumberland Homesteads**, a model New Deal project that created a community of stone homes on 30-acre plots that remain intact today. The **Homestead Museum**, (615) 456-9663, located in a cone-shaped stone water tower, contains original documents telling the story. Across the road is another **Cumberland Mountain General Store**, (615) 484-8481.

While in Crossville, call the **Cumberland County Playhouse** to see what they're staging, (615) 484-5000. This professional theater group offers a year-round schedule of plays that includes performances by national traveling troupes and original works based on regional subject matter or the works of regional writers. The clean and quiet **Thunder Hollow Resort** on Hwy 70 East is close to the Playhouse and has rooms at reasonable rates ($50 double), (615) 484-9566. They have no dining room, but will send you to **The Donut Shoppe** a few miles away for breakfast or lunch. This local favorite is the only establishment I've ever seen with posted hours of 4:30 to 3:30.

As Hwy 127 curves southward, you'll find **Cumberland Mountain State Park**, one of Tennessee's oldest and most beautiful. The native stone bridge over the lake as you enter was built by the Civilian Conservation Corps under the supervision of Alvin York in 1934. Cumberland Mountain State Park, a hidden treasure, has won awards for its park restaurant. The rustic cabins have individual screened porches and fireplaces. There are swimming and paddleboats in the summer and hiking year-round, (615) 484-6138.

About 10 miles south of Cumberland Mountain State Park, you will enter the **Sequatchie Valley**, formed from a rift in the escarpment of the Cumberland Plateau. The road drops a gradual 800 feet into one of the most scenic landscapes in the region. The valley, no wider than 5 miles at any one point, runs along with the Sequatchie River down towards Chattanooga, about 65 miles south. ◼

14
THE GREAT
SMOKY MOUNTAINS

The highest peaks in the Appalachian chain rise up in Tennessee and North Carolina to become the Great Smoky Mountains, a land of legendary beauty, deep forests, and panoramic views. The Great Smoky Mountains National Park, opened in 1934, has become one of the most visited parks in the United States. On the west side of the park is the Qualla Boundary, 56,000 acres that was formerly the Eastern Cherokee reservation, which is still governed by the Cherokee Tribal Council. The Appalachian Trail crosses the park along the ridge, dividing Tennessee and North Carolina. At Newfound Gap, viewers can look off into either state and see rows and rows of mountains, often cloud-covered, receding slowly into the distance.

The Great Smoky Mountains National Park—home to impressive botanical specimens, many native and migrating birds, and some interesting wild creatures—is an International Biosphere Reserve. Unfortunately, the roads to the park are cluttered with motels, restaurants, souvenir stands, outlet malls, water slides, miniature golf courses, and various promotional shops and theaters of country music stars—the best known being "Dollywood." However, by timing your trip carefully and entering the park through alternative routes, you can still experience the majesty of untroubled nature. Hiking, biking, wildflower walking, horseback riding, fly-fishing, listening for bird calls, and sleeping outside in the Great Smokies can be a unique adventure. ◼

GREAT SMOKY MOUNTAINS NATIONAL PARK AREA

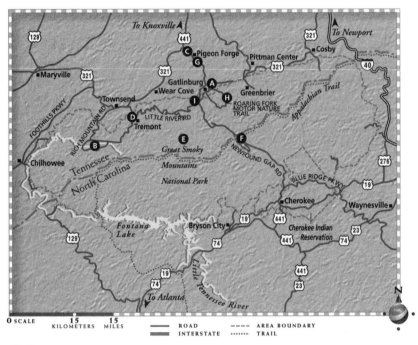

O SCALE   15 KILOMETERS   15 MILES   ROAD   AREA BOUNDARY   INTERSTATE   TRAIL

Sights

- **A** Arrowmont School of Arts and Crafts
- **B** Cades Cove Loop Road
- **C** Dollywood
- **A** The Great Smoky Arts and Crafts Community
- **D** Great Smoky Mountains Institute at Tremont
- **E** Great Smoky Mountains National Park

- **A** Great Smoky Mountains Natural History Association
- **F** Newfound Gap/Appalachian Trail
- **A** Ober Gatlinburg
- **G** Old Mill
- **G** Pigeon Forge Pottery
- **H** Roaring Fork Motor Nature Trail
- **I** Sugarlands Information Center

Note: Items with the same letter are located in the same town or area.

A PERFECT DAY IN THE GREAT SMOKY MOUNTAINS

The best strategy is to get up very early and take a thermos of coffee and a snack into the park (or even better, camp there the night before), entering at Cades Cove. My husband likes to hike in about 3 miles up Abrams Creek toward Abrams Falls and fish back to where he started, wading in the rocky rushing water looking for brown or rainbow trout. If it's off-season (early spring, late fall, or winter), it's always fun to stop in Gatlinburg and visit the gallery at Arrowmont, then lunch in town or enjoy a picnic along the Roaring Fork Motor Nature Trail. We often hike one of the many trails that afford spectacular views as a reward for an afternoon of serious uphill walking, but a leisurely lowland trail can be just as gratifying for those interested in bird spotting or wildflower identification.

TRAVEL TIPS

This area has become so heavily visited on the Tennessee side that a cautionary note is in order. Gatlinburg, the small village that had three hotels and a few clusters of resort cabins in 1934 when the park was opened, has grown into a crowded complex of hotels, motels, and tourist attractions. Its main street (Hwy 441) carries bumper-to-bumper traffic nearly year-round. Approaching the city on Highway 441, you will see a bypass that allows you to circumvent the town and head straight into the park. In the busy season (late spring, summer, and early fall), you are likely to encounter traffic jams as far back as Pigeon Forge (5 miles east) and even Sevierville (13 miles east).

Hwy 441 between Sevierville—an otherwise charming small town with an unusual five-domed courthouse—and Pigeon Forge— once a sleepy community that contained little more than an old mill on the little Pigeon River—are now lined with motels and tourist attractions and can become a bottleneck for through traffic. There are several ways to approach the situation. One is to avoid it altogether by driving in from the north through Newport or south through Townsend. Another is to choose one of two alternate routes from Sevierville (Middle Creek Road or Pittman Center Road) and avoid as much of Pigeon Forge as possible.

SIGHTSEEING HIGHLIGHTS

★★★ **Great Smoky Mountains National Park**—The main attraction, the park is one of Roosevelt's New Deal public works projects. Entering the park from Gatlinburg on Hwy 441 will take visitors past the **Sugarlands Information Center**, where trail maps and seasonal information about road and hiking conditions are available, and then through Newfound Gap into North Carolina.

Stop at **Newfound Gap** (5,045 feet), where the **Appalachian Trail** crosses just a few hundred yards from the road, and read the historical markers concerning the park's founding. From there you can descend via the **Indian Gap Trail** to **Alum Cave** (a source of saltpeter, where Indians led the impoverished Confederates hiding out in the mountains so that they could make gunpowder), or hike north along the high ridge to **Mt. LeConte**, where the only overnight food and lodging accommodations in the park can be found at LeConte Lodge.

Walking or driving in the other direction will take you to **Clingman's Dome**, the second highest peak in the park, at 6,642 feet. The road itself climbs to 6,311 feet, affording some pretty spectacular views as it heads over into North Carolina. **Roaring Fork Motor Nature Trail** enters the west side of the park from the heart of Gatlinburg and provides access to a number of hiking trail destinations including **Rainbow Falls, Grotto Falls**, and **Trillium Gap**.

You'll reach **Cades Cove** at the south end of the park by driving in through Townsend on Hwy 321. An excellent auto tour booklet can be obtained at the Cades Cove Visitor's Center. On Saturday morning during late spring and summer, the **Cades Cove Loop Road** is open only for bicycling—would that it were always so! Many trails lead out of Cades Cove, including **Abrams Falls Trail** and the **Rich Mountain Loop Trail**. On the north side of the park, there are entrances near **Cosby** and **Greenbrier** from Hwy 321. This is one of the least-frequented areas of the park, and the hiking trails that lead in from here are short, steep trails with spectacular views.

If you want to make the most of your visit to these amazing mountains, you might wish to gather information in advance from one or more of the following resources: The **Great Smoky Mountains Natural History Association**, 115 Park Headquarters Road, Gatlinburg, TN 37738, (423) 436-7318. Their annual membership fee is $15. They publish a quarterly newsletter highlighting changing attractions in the park and giving updated information on camping, fishing, horseback riding, nature programs, and volunteer opportunities for park ecosystem maintenance activities. The **Great Smoky Mountains Institute at Tremont,** a nature center sponsored by the park and the Great Smoky Mountains Natural History Association, offers environmental education programs year-round on weekends and special youth summer camps. Participants stay overnight and have all meals at the institute. For a brochure, call (423) 446-6709. **Smoky Mountain Field School**, operated in conjunction with the University of Tennessee at Knoxville, offers weekend adult workshops, hikes, and adventures led by experts in Smoky Mountain flora and fauna. You can call them at (800) 284-8885.

✴ **Gatlinburg**—Once a charming mountain town, now it is not only a popular honeymoon spot but also a veritable tourist magnet for about half the year. Gatlinburg in the off-season can be quite pleasant, but watch out for overcrowding in summer and fall. Tennessee's only ski resort is located here, and many would like to boost the winter tourist season by promoting Gatlinburg as a ski town. **Ober Gatlinburg** has a peak elevation of 3,000 feet, much lower than the slopes to be found further north and across the state line in North Carolina at Boone, Banner Elk, and Wolf Laurel.

In the very center of town is **Arrowmont School of Arts and Crafts,** founded by Pi Beta Phi fraternity (the first women's sorority) in the early part of the century in an effort to promote and preserve mountain crafts. They also built the Pi Beta Phi elementary school in 1912 for the children of mountain crafters and helped create a market for the traditional wares with their Arrowcraft Shop and mail-order catalogue. You can still visit the Arrowcraft Shop and purchase these traditional, handmade goods. Arrowmont, which has a complex of studios and dormitories in a secluded hollow right off the main road, is now an internationally known craft school with resident artists and a year-round schedule of classes. The Arrowmont Gallery, library, and bookstore are open to the public. Call or write for an exhibit schedule or a course prospectus. Address: P.O. Box 567, Gatlinburg, TN 37738. Phone: (423) 436-5860.

The **Great Smoky Arts and Crafts Community** houses over 80 artist shops and studios in an 8-mile loop that takes in Buckhorn and Glades Roads and part of Hwy 321 north. Many of the artist workshops are open year-round, and all are free to the public. Phone: (423) 671-3600, ext. 3504.

A city trolley will take you out from the city center for $1 (you can ride around downtown for 25 cents).

★ **Pigeon Forge**—Driving into Pigeon Forge can be a distressing experience as you wonder why anyone would want to visit the Smoky Mountain Police Museum, the Haunted Golf and Video Arcade, or Stars on Ice (impersonations of country music stars in an ice skating show)—or spend their time at one of nine racetrack and go-cart arcades when real-life adventure is so near at hand up in the rugged mountain landscape that forms a backdrop for the town.

If you take Middle Creek Road from Sevierville, you will pass the entrance to **Dollywood**. As you start to come into Pigeon Forge you'll see both the **Old Mill**, an 1830s gristmill still in operation, and the **Pigeon Forge Pottery**, a charming spot where the same soft matte-finish gray/brown glazes have been created since its founding more than 50 years ago. Up until about 15 years ago, these were the only tourist sites in Pigeon Forge. Both are worth a look and, other than Arrowmont's Arrowcraft Shop, they are your best bet for purchasing gifts to take home.

Dollywood, Dolly Parton's amusement park, has live music shows, upscale carnival rides, and seasonal exhibits and events. I should mention that Dolly is actually from this area and has been tremendously supportive of her hometown over the years, coming home for many years to perform annually at the high school to raise money for band uniforms. Perhaps her park reflects some of her genuine, down-home persona. Find out for yourself if you happen to be in the area between Memorial Day and Christmas. Phone: (423) 428-9488.

FITNESS AND RECREATION

The Great Smoky Mountains National Park offers boundless opportunities for hiking and walking. There are 149 official trails through the park. Pick up trail guides at the **Sugarlands**, **Cades Cove**, or **Oconaluftee** (in North Carolina) **Visitor's Centers**. Or call the park at (423) 436-1200. A comprehensive hiking trail guide can be purchased for $16.95.

Horseback riding is also popular, and five park concessions will rent you a mount for around $15/hour. Call the following for information in Tennessee: **Cades Cove**, (423) 448-6286; **McCarter's**, (423) 436-5354; and **Smoky Mountain**, (423) 436-5634. In North Carolina, call **Deep Creek**, (704) 497-7503, or **Smokemont**, (704) 497-2373. The **Wonderland Hotel**, located outside the park, also has stables. Call them to arrange your own horseback riding adventure, (423) 436-5490. Bicycles are recommended for use in the park only at Cades Cove, where the 11-mile loop trail is open in warm weather only to bicycles at least one morning a week. Generally the park roads are too heavily traveled to allow for bike traffic, and all park trails are off-limits to bikers.

Fishing, using both fly and spin rods, is a major pursuit of both visitors and locals in the area. They make it easy here—you can obtain a license at the Gatlinburg Welcome Center or from some of the local merchants, and many begin fishing the Little Pigeon River as it passes through the city. A Tennessee or North Carolina fishing license is required for fishing in the park, but you don't need a trout stamp because park naturalists are eager to keep the nonnative rainbow trout population under control. By the same token, native brook trout are off-limits.

FOOD

Judging by the number of restaurants in town, you might conclude that visitors to Gatlinburg come primarily to eat and shop at discount malls. In the ten or so years I have lived in the area, many of the charming old restaurants by the river and homey hotel dining rooms have disappeared, replaced by sure-to-be-crowded, buffet-style eateries or franchise restaurants. Contrary to what one might assume, there are few, if any, country-cooking restaurants in the area, so consider finding lodgings in a cabin with a kitchenette and stocking up on groceries in order to save yourself time, money, and frustration.

For when you do dine out, I offer a few tried-and-true suggestions: **The Peddler**, beside the river in a log cabin on River Road in downtown Gatlinburg, offers good service and fine quality steaks cut-to-order at tableside, (423) 436-5794; **Rio Grande**, a friendly Mexican restaurant on Hwy 441 in the middle of downtown Gatlinburg, serves good food at moderate prices, (423) 436-0380; and **Ruby Tuesday**, one of the first fern-bar restaurants in Tennessee and one of the first in Gatlinburg to serve liquor, is located in the same vicinity. Although its menu items are pretty standard stuff, the cozy atmosphere seems just right for Gatlinburg, and the quality of their burgers and salads has remained consistently high, (423) 436-9251. The new **Park Grill**, a log structure located at the far end of town just before you enter the park, offers gourmet dining in a rustic atmosphere. Vegetarian entrees and desserts get special marks there (about $25 per person). Phone: (423) 436-3800.

Just outside the city (accessible from the Newport side) is my skier friend's favorite restaurant for dinner, **The Greenbrier**, between Gatlinburg and Newport on Hwy 321 North, (423) 436-6318. Between Pigeon Forge and Townsend on Hwy 321 South, it is well worth making a pilgrimage to **Chef Jock's Tastebuds Café**, a restaurant in a remote location on Wear's Valley Road that is reputed to serve wonderful French cuisine, (423) 428-9781.

LODGING

Between Pigeon Forge and Townsend on Hwy 321 South, you'll find the **Wonderland Hotel**, a newly built version of a famous old hotel that used to be within the park's perimeter. The Wonderland has lodge accommodations, a family-style dining room, cabins, and a stable for your horse, (423) 436-5490. In the same vicinity (slightly off the beaten track) are cabin accommodations in the woods, all with hot tubs outside, run by Hidden Mountain Resorts, (800) 541-6837. They also have a location close to Sevierville, so ask for **Hidden Mountain West** and request their most privately located cottages.

If you take Hwy 321 south into Townsend, you will have a choice of motels, cottages, and bed and breakfast inns on what the locals claim is the "peaceful side of the Smokies." Smokies Realty can help you find a private vacation rental house or cabin, (423) 448-6036. **Rustling Pines Cabin Rental** has several cabins located very near the Cades Cove entrance to the park that are open year-round, (423) 448-6715, and **Old Smoky Mountain Cabins and Duplexes** has cabins available in a wide variety of sizes and prices, (423) 448-2388.

If you prefer a plain, modern motel, the **Highland Manor**, on a hilltop with a swimming pool, has fairly reasonable rates, and some of the rooms even have fireplaces, (423) 448-2211. Or you may decide to pamper yourself at the five-year-old **Richmont Inn**, which offers deluxe, unique rooms furnished with English and American antiques. A full breakfast is included with the stay. They are open year-round—perhaps they will give you a discount during low season, (423) 448-6751.

If you want to stay right in the city of Gatlinburg—although I would probably counsel against it—you might try one of the places along Roaring Fork Road, which ultimately leads into the park's

GREAT SMOKY MOUNTAINS NATIONAL PARK AREA

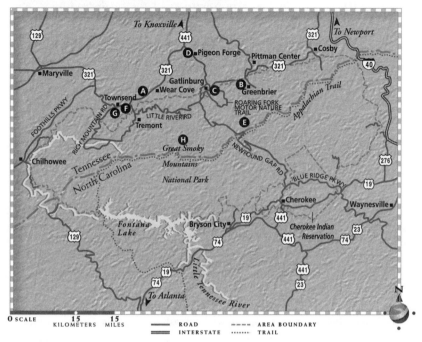

Food

Ⓐ Chef Jock's Tastebuds Café

Ⓑ The Greenbrier

Ⓒ Park Grill

Ⓒ The Peddler

Ⓒ Rio Grande

Ⓒ Ruby Tuesday

Lodging

Ⓒ Buckhorn Inn

Ⓓ Hidden Mountain West

Ⓓ Highland Manor

Ⓒ Hippensteal's Mountain View Inn

Ⓔ LeConte Lodge

Ⓑ Little Greenbrier Lodge

Ⓕ Old Smoky Mountain Cabins and Duplexes

Ⓕ Richmont Inn

Ⓖ Roaring Fork Motel and Cottages

Ⓖ Rustling Pines Cabin Rental

Ⓐ Wonderland Hotel

Camping

Ⓗ Great Smoky Mountains National Park

Note: Items with the same letter are located in the same town or area.

Roaring Fork Motor Nature Trail. This area of town is not quite as heavily traveled as the main thoroughfare or the roads leading to the ski area. **Roaring Fork Motel and Cottages**, (800) 894-4658, which has a nice stone exterior, has been around for a while and is located 4 blocks from Hwy 441.

For an outdoor adventure, book a room at **LeConte Lodge** (built in 1926, prior to the purchase of land for the park) and hike in for the night. This rustic wooden complex, accessible only on foot and the only private lodgings in the park, is still operated by the family of its builder, Jack Huff. To reach the top of LeConte, a beautiful mountain often shrouded in clouds or covered with snow, one can choose a trail leading from the Roaring Fork Motor Nature Trail in Gatlinburg, from Cosby, or from Newfound Gap. Staying in the lodge or in a tiny two-person cabin is an exhilarating experience. Visitors should be prepared for cold nights and sudden rainstorms even in the midst of a hot, dry summer. The accommodations are often booked months in advance, and LeConte Lodge is only open from late-March to mid-November, so call (423) 436-4473, or write them at P.O. Box 350, Gatlinburg, TN 37738. Although the meals are good, you might wish to carry in your own bottle of wine and perhaps a few pieces of fruit or some fresh vegetables to add to the table, as all foodstuffs are still carried up the mountain only once weekly.

Outside of Gatlinburg on Hwy 321 North is the charming old **Buckhorn Inn**, established in 1938, on 35 acres of woodlands. There are only 12 rooms at the inn; all have private baths. A full breakfast is included, and the inn is nonsmoking. Call (423) 436-4668 for rates and reservations. (If you choose to stay in Gatlinburg, it would be well worth a splurge to stay in one of these historic inns outside the city center.) **Little Greenbrier Lodge**, opened in 1939, is located very close to the park and has a beautiful view. It has 11 rooms with both private and shared baths, a no-smoking policy, and includes breakfast with overnight accommodations, (423) 429-2500 or (800) 277-8100. A bed and breakfast recently opened by one of the area's most talented painters has also attempted to preserve the ambiance of long-ago Gatlinburg. **Hippensteal's Mountain View Inn** can be reached at (800) 527-8110 or (423) 436-5761. If the inn is booked, you might try the B&B Accommodations Service of the Smoky Mountains, (800) 248-2923. Ask them to find you something near Buckhorn Road, Greenbrier, or the Glades.

CAMPING

The **Great Smoky Mountains National Park** offers both camp-grounds and back-country camping. Although all but one of the ten campgrounds can accommodate RVs, there are no hookups. The campgrounds have cold running water and flush toilets but no showers. Most sites go for $6–$8 per night, and while generally open year-round, many have been forced to close during the winter months this year because of budget limitations. Call (423) 436-1200 for information and reservations.

There are more than 100 sites and shelters for back-country camping in the park. Campers are required to have a permit (they are free and can be obtained from a ranger) and to stay at one of the designated locations. Reservations are required at 30 of the sites. Call (423) 436-0120 to reserve a camping date or to obtain a back-country map ($1) listing all sites and shelters.

15

APPENDIX

METRIC CONVERSION CHART

1 U.S. gallon = approximately 4 liters
1 liter = about 1 quart
1 Canadian gallon = approximately 4.5 liters

1 pound = approximately ½ kilogram
1 kilogram = about 2 pounds

1 foot = approximately ⅓ meter
1 meter = about 1 yard
1 yard = a little less than a meter
1 mile = approximately 1.6 kilometers
1 kilometer = about ⅔ mile

90°F = about 30°C
20°C = approximately 70°F

Planning Map: Kentucky/Tennessee

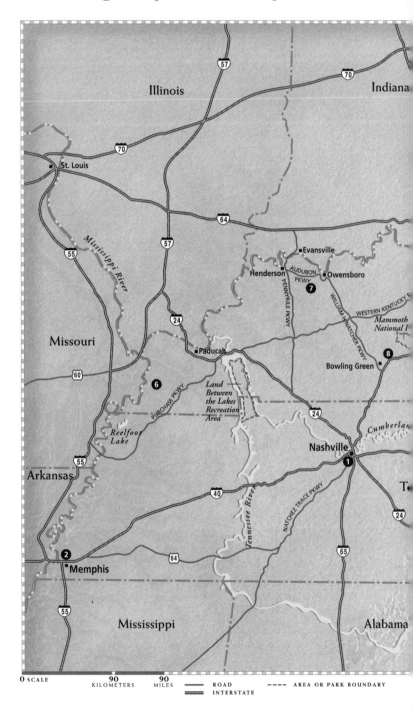

O SCALE

90 KILOMETERS   90 MILES

ROAD
INTERSTATE

- - - - AREA OR PARK BOUNDARY

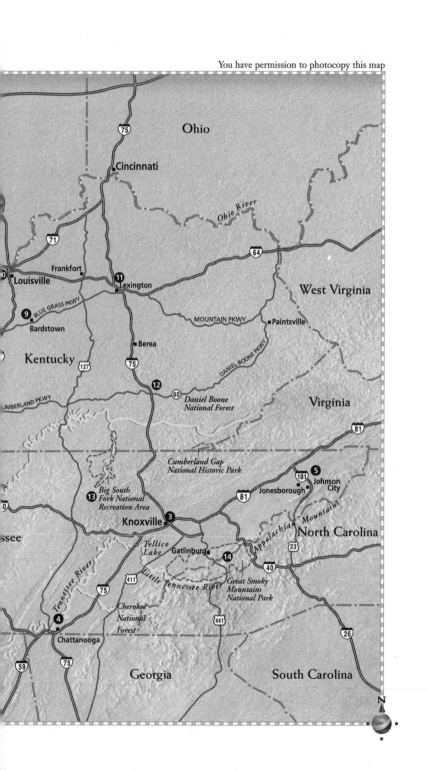

Planning Map: Kentucky/Tennessee

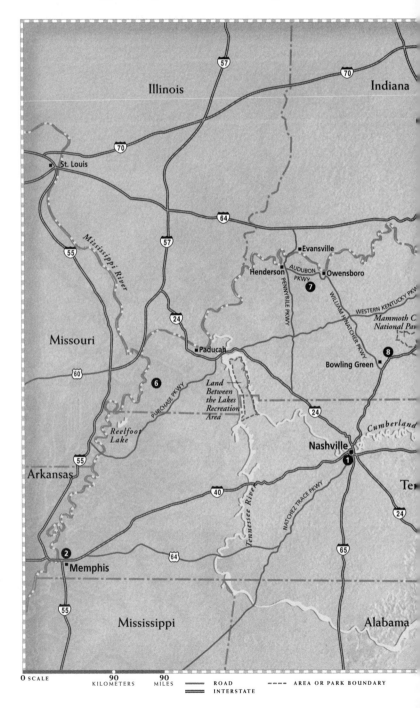

Illinois

Indiana

St. Louis

Missouri

Evansville

Henderson   AUDUBON   Owensboro
PKWY
PENNYRILE PKWY

WESTERN KENTUCKY PKWY

WILLIAM H NATCHER PKWY

Mammoth C
National Pa

Paducah

Bowling Green

PURCHASE PKWY

Land
Between
the Lakes
Recreation
Area

Cumberland

Reelfoot
Lake

Nashville

Arkansas

Te

Mississippi River

NATCHEZ TRACE PKWY

Tennessee River

Memphis

Mississippi

Alabama

0 SCALE   90   90
                 KILOMETERS MILES   ———— ROAD   ---- AREA OR PARK BOUNDARY
                                        ════ INTERSTATE

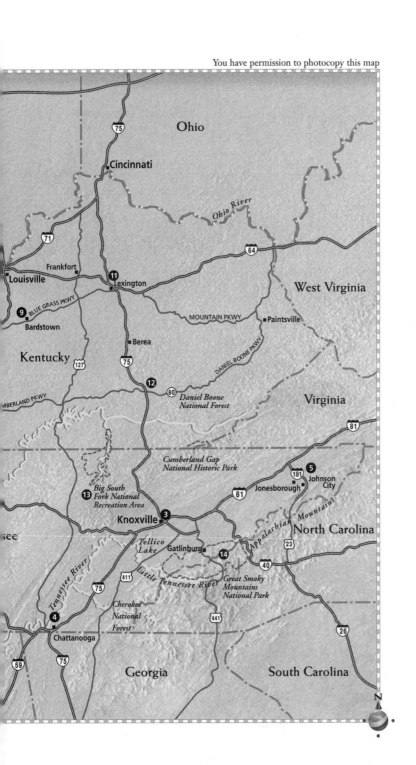

INDEX

Maps Index

Other Books from John Muir Publications

Rick Steves' Books

Asia Through the Back Door, 400 pp., $17.95

Europe 101: History and Art for the Traveler, 352 pp., $17.95

Mona Winks: Self-Guided Tours of Europe's Top Museums, 432 pp., $18.95

Rick Steves' Baltics & Russia, 144 pp., $9.95

Rick Steves' Europe, 528 pp., $17.95

Rick Steves' France, Belgium & the Netherlands, 256 pp., $13.95

Rick Steves' Germany, Austria & Switzerland, 256 pp., $13.95

Rick Steves' Great Britain, 240 pp., $13.95

Rick Steves' Italy, 224 pp., $13.95

Rick Steves' Scandinavia, 192 pp., $13.95

Rick Steves' Spain & Portugal, 208 pp., $13.95

Rick Steves' Europe Through the Back Door, 480 pp., $18.95

Rick Steves' French Phrase Book, 176 pp., $5.95

Rick Steves' German Phrase Book, 176 pp., $5.95

Rick Steves' Italian Phrase Book, 176 pp., $5.95

Rick Steves' Spanish & Portugese Phrase Book, 304 pp., $6.95

Rick Steves' French/ German/Italian Phrase Book, 320 pp., $7.95

A Natural Destination Series

Belize: A Natural Destination, 344 pp., $16.95

Costa Rica: A Natural Destination, 380 pp., $18.95

Guatemala: A Natural Destination, 360 pp., $16.95

City•Smart™ Guidebook Series

City•Smart Guidebook: Denver, 256 pp., $14.95

City•Smart Guidebook: Minneapolis/St. Paul, 224 pp., $14.95 (avail. 2/97)

City•Smart Guidebook: Portland, 232 pp., $14.95 (avail. 8/96)

Unique Travel Series

All are 112 pages and $10.95 paperback, except Georgia and Oregon.

Unique Arizona

Unique California

Unique Colorado

Unique Florida

Unique Georgia ($11.95)

Unique New England

Unique New Mexico

Unique Oregon ($9.95)

Unique Texas

Unique Washington

Travel✦Smart™ Trip Planners

All are $14.95 paperback.

American Southwest Travel ✦ Smart Trip Planner, 256 pp.

Colorado Travel ✦ Smart Trip Planner, 248 pp.

Eastern Canada Travel ✦ Smart Trip Planner, 272 pp.

Hawaii Travel ✦ Smart Trip Planner, 256 pp.

Kentucky/Tennessee Travel ✦ Smart Trip Planner, 248 pp.

Minnesota/Wisconsin Travel ✦ Smart Trip Planner, 248 pp.

New England Travel ✦ Smart Trip Planner, 256 pp.

Pacific Northwest Travel ✦ Smart Trip Planner, 240 pp.

Other Terrific Travel Titles

The 100 Best Small Art Towns in America, 256 pp., $15.95

The Big Book of Adventure Travel, 384 pp., $17.95

Indian America: A Traveler's Companion, 480 pp., $18.95

The People's Guide to Mexico, 608 pp., $19.95

Ranch Vacations: The Complete Guide to Guest and Resort, Fly-Fishing, and Cross-Country Skiing Ranches, 528 pp., $19.95

Understanding Europeans, 272 pp., $14.95

Undiscovered Islands of the Caribbean, 336 pp., $16.95

Watch It Made in the U.S.A.: A Visitor's Guide to the Companies that Make Your Favorite Products, 328 pp., $16.95

The World Awaits, 280 pp., $16.95

The Birder's Guide to Bed and Breakfasts: U.S. and Canada, 416 pp., $17.95

Automotive Titles

The Greaseless Guide to Car Care, 272 pp., $19.95

How to Keep Your Subaru Alive, 480 pp., $21.95

How to Keep Your Toyota Pickup Alive, 392 pp., $21.95

How to Keep Your VW Alive, 464 pp., $25

Ordering Information

Please check your local bookstore for our books, or call **1-800-888-7504** to order direct and to receive a complete catalog. A shipping charge will be added to your order total.

Send all inquiries to:
John Muir Publications
P.O. Box 613
Santa Fe, NM 87504